AN
INTEGRATED
ANALYSIS
FOR
MANAGERIAL
FINANCE

M. CHAPMAN FINDLAY III

Assistant Professor of Finance
University of Houston

EDWARD E. WILLIAMS

Assistant Professor of Economics
Rutgers University,
The State University of New Jersey

PRENTICE-HALL, INC.
Englewood Cliffs, New Jersey

If names of persons or companies in this book
bear any similarity to those of actual persons
or companies, the similarity is purely fortuitous.

PREFACE

This book was written to accommodate the demand for a short, concise discussion of the major problem areas in financial management. The approach adopted presents compact expositions of the most up-to-date elementary quantitative techniques in finance. Within these explanations are solved problems of the type that confront financial decision-makers. Several unsolved problems follow the explications and illustrative examples. Comprehensive problems designed to challenge the imagination of readers are presented at the end of most chapters.

Anyone concerned with the financial problems of the business firm will find *An Integrated Analysis for Managerial Finance* useful. Businessmen who wish to have a simplified explanation with examples of modern developments in corporation finance will appreciate the conciseness of the volume. Professors may employ the book in a number of capacities. The more institutional texts in corporate finance are very adequately supplemented by the quantitative tools analyzed in the book. Professors who stress theoretical material will find that the book is sufficiently terse to permit its use with a book of readings or a specialized paperback without overburdening students. The volume may also be employed to explicate with more detailed examples the discussion of some of the most recent quantitative managerial texts. A number of decision areas that are still treated descriptively in these texts are quantified in this book. Professors who teach a case-oriented course and who desire a more complete discussion of the specifics of quantification will find that the volume suits their needs. In fact, the book is structured so that it may provide the organizational basis around which cases and readings may be assigned. The detailed cross-reference matrices to the major texts in finance will be of particular use to these professors. Of course, all readers will benefit from the nearly two-hundred unsolved problems which allow the student to test his mastery of the material. A manual of comprehensive solutions to these problems will be provided to adopters of the book.

The authors are indebted to a number of people for their suggestions, advice, and technical assistance in the preparation of the manuscript. In particular, Professors John Brosky (University of Houston), N.J. Gonedes (University of Chicago), James Longstreet (University of South Florida), Bruce Morgan (University of Pennsylvania), and Donald Vaughn (Louisiana State University) provided valuable suggestions at various stages of the development of the manuscript. The idea for the volume had its genesis when the authors prepared the problems and solutions to James C. Van Horne's *Financial Management and Policy* (Prentice-Hall, Inc., 1968), and much of Professor Van Horne's pioneering contribution is reflected in the methodology of their treatment. An extra expression of gratitude is owed to Miss Judy Johnson who dutifully typed several revisions of the manuscript. Finally, the authors thank their publishers for an expeditious and conscientious treatment of the manuscript.

M.C.F.
E.E.W.

CROSS REFERENCES:
TEXTBOOKS
READINGS BOOKS
CASEBOOKS

TEXTBOOKS

1. Archer, Stephen H. and Charles A. D'Ambrosio, *Business Finance: Theory and Management.* New York: The Macmillan Company, 1966.
2. Beranek, William, *Analysis for Financial Decisions.* Homewood, Illinois: Richard D. Irwin, Inc., 1963.
3. Bradley, Joseph F., *Administrative Financial Management,* Second Edition. New York: Holt, Rinehart and Winston, Inc., 1969.
4. Cohen, Jerome B. and Sidney M. Robbins, *The Financial Manager.* New York: Harper and Row, Publishers, 1966.
5. Flink, Solomon J. and Donald Grunewald, *Managerial Finance.* New York: John Wiley and Sons, Inc., 1969.
6. Guthmann, Harry G. and Herbert E. Dougall, *Corporate Financial Policy,* Fourth Edition. Englewood Cliffs, N. J.: Prentice-Hall, Inc., 1962.
7. Hunt, Pearson, Charles M. Williams, and Gordon Donaldson, *Basic Business Finance: Text and Cases,* Third Edition. Homewood, Illinois: Richard D. Irwin, Inc., 1966.
8. Johnson, Robert W., *Financial Management,* Third Edition. Boston: Allyn and Bacon, Inc., 1966.
9. Kent, Raymond P., *Corporate Financial Management,* Third Edition. Homewood, Illinois: Richard D. Irwin, Inc., 1969.
10. Lindsay, J. Robert and Arnold W. Sametz, *Financial Management: An Analytical Approach,* Rev. Ed. Homewood, Illinois: Richard D. Irwin, Inc., 1967.
11. Mock, Edward J. et al., *Basic Financial Management: Text, Problems and Cases.* Scranton, Pennsylvania: International Textbook Company, 1968.
12. Van Horne, James C., *Financial Management and Policy.* Englewood Cliffs, New Jersey: Prentice-Hall, Inc., 1968.
13. Weston, J. Fred and Eugene F. Brigham, *Essentials of Managerial Finance.* New York: Holt, Rinehart and Winston, Inc., 1968.
14. Weston, J. Fred and Eugene F. Brigham, *Managerial Finance,* Third Edition. New York: Holt, Rinehart and Winston, Inc., 1969.

CROSS REFERENCE MATRIX (BY CHAPTERS)

TEXTBOOKS

Findlay and Williams Ch.	1 A+D'A	2 Ber	3 Bra	4 C+R	5 F+G	6 G+D	7 H,W,D,	8 J	9 K	10 L+S	11 M,S,S,S	12 VH	13 W+B(E)	14 W+B(M)
1	11	5	6	—	—	—	20	8	—	—	—	3	6	6
2	5, 10	6	5	29	—	—	—	3	—	—	—	2	9	10
3	21, 22	9	4	5	14	6	19	10	5, 6	2	5	26	4, 8	9, 4
4	9	—	1	4, 17, 23, 27, 3, 19-21	21	2, 3, 28	2	2	2	5	2	—	2	2
5	16	3-6	5, 7	9	9	7, 19	6, 20, 22	8	10, 13	10-14	8, 9	24	7	7, 8
6	15	10	11, 12	9, 14	5-7	—	3, 4	6, 7	8, 9	4, 5, 7	7	17, 18	11	13, 14
7	15	11	3, 9, 10	8	2, 8	5	5, 8	5, 9	7, 11, 12	1, 8, 9	5, 6	16, 25	5, 11	5, 13, 14
8	21, 22	—	2	6, 10	2, 3	4, 6	7	4	—	3	4	24, 25	3, 4	3, 4
9	18	—	9-12	12, 13	4, 5	22, 23, 24	9-13	12-14, 19	32, 33, 34	6, 9	17	19, 20	12	15
10	18	—	13, 14	13	11		11, 23	15		—	15, 16	12, 21	13	16
11	8, 18	8	14, 18, 20, 22	15, 16, 18, 25, 26	13, 19, 14, 16, 18	10-12, 17, 18, 30, 31	15-17, 24, 26, 30	16-18	27-31	18, 22, 27, 28	13, 14, 21, 22	10, 11	14, 17, 22	17, 19, 22
12	18, 19, 20	8	17, 18, 20	16, 25	14, 15	9, 12	17, 25	20	20, 23, 24, 29	23, 24	12	13, 14	16, 20	19, 20
13	18	8	16, 20, 22	16, 25, 28	15	3, 8, 19-21	17, 26, 27	21, 22	17-22	16, 25, 26	12, 20	13	15, 19	10, 18
14	17	8	15	17	18	26	14	22	25, 26	17	18	8, 9	18	12
15	13	9	8, 19	22	10	7	21	11	14	19	10	6	10	11
16	13	9	18, 22	18	17	13	18, 19	10	15, 16	18-21	10, 11	7	8	9
17	4, 6, 7, 11, 12	7, 12	23	7	10	—	—	—	—	15	10	—	23	1, 8, 23
18	17	3-6, 14	21	7, 24	20	25, 27, 28	29	23, 24	—	—	19	5, 22, 23	21, 24	8, 21, 24

READINGS BOOKS

1. Archer, Stephen H. and Charles A. D'Ambrosio, *The Theory of Business Finance: A Book of Readings.* New York: The Macmillan Company, 1967.
2. Ball, Richard E. and Z. Lew Melnyk, *Theory of Managerial Finance: Selected Readings.* Boston: Allyn and Bacon, Inc., 1967.
3. Brigham, Eugene F. and R. Bruce Ricks, *Readings in Essentials of Managerial Finance.* New York: Holt, Rinehart and Winston, Inc., 1968.
4. Fredrikson, E. Bruce, *Frontiers of Investment Analysis.* Scranton, Pennsylvania: International Textbook Company, 1965.
5. Mock, Edward J., *Financial Decision-Making.* Scranton, Pennsylvania: International Textbook Company, 1967.
6. Mock, Edward J., *Readings in Financial Management.* Scranton, Pennsylvania: International Textbook Company, 1964.
7. Van Horne, James, *Foundations for Financial Management: A Book of Readings.* Homewood, Illinois: Richard D. Irwin, Inc., 1966.
8. Weston, J. Fred and Donald H. Woods, *Theory of Business Finance: Advanced Readings.* Belmont, California: Wadsworth Publishing Company, 1967.
9. Wolf, Harold A. and Lee Richardson, *Readings in Finance.* New York: Appleton-Century-Crofts, 1966.

CROSS REFERENCE MATRIX
READINGS BOOKS

Findlay and Williams Chapter	1 A+D'A	2 B+M	3 B+R	4 F	5 M(F)	6 M(R)	7 VH	8 W+W	9 W+R
1	2, 3	–	–	1, 21	3, 5	–	–	–	–
2	–	20	–	–	9-11, 35	3, 4	2	–	6
3	–	–	–	–	–	–	–	–	–
4	2-4, 22, 24, 25, 30	1-11	2	28	25-29, 32, 33	16-21	17, 18, 20	4, 6-10	4, 5
5	–	–	6	2, 3, 13	21-24	13-15	5, 6	–	16
6	–	–	12	–	16-20	7, 9-12	3, 4	–	13-15
7	36, 37, 39	–	13	–	12-15	–	1	30, 31	–
8	–	–	3	14	43-48	27-32	7, 8	–	–
9	–	–	–	–	53-55	33, 38	9-11	26	18, 21
10	–	22, 23	14-16	4-7, 26, 27	56, 57, 60	36, 37, 40	12, 15, 16	12	17
11	–	21, 31	21, 25	–	58	39	13, 14	13	2
12	–	–	20, 24	–	51, 59	–	22, 26	11	19, 20
13	1, 2	16, 24, 25, 29, 32	9, 17-19, 23	8, 15-19, 29-34	–	–	–	14, 20	8, 10, 12
14	18-24	26-28, 30	22	20, 35	49-52	35	28-31	18, 21-23	7, 11
15	–	14, 15, 18	10, 11	–	36-38, 42	23	23-27	16, 19	1, 9
16	5-17	12, 13, 19	8	–	34, 39, 40	22, 24, 25	–	17	–
17	4, 15, 23-29, 33, 38, 40-43	17	28	22-25	31	–	–	2, 24, 25, 27-29	–
18	27, 31-35, 41	33	5, 26, 27	9-12	6, 8, 30	2	19, 21, 32-34	3, 5	3, 22, 23

CASEBOOKS

1. Butters, J. Keith, *Case Problems in Finance,* Fifth Edition. Homewood, Illinois: Richard D. Irwin, Inc., 1969.
2. Howard, Bion B. and Sidney Lewis Jones, *Managerial Problems in Finance: Cases in Decision Making.* New York: McGraw-Hill Book Company, 1964.
3. Hunt, Pearson and Victor L. Andrews, *Financial Management: Cases and Readings.* Homewood, Illinois: Richard D. Irwin, Inc., 1968.
4. Hunt, Pearson, Charles M. Williams, and Gordon Donaldson, *Basic Business Finance: Text and Cases,* Third Edition. Homewood, Illinois: Richard D. Irwin, Inc., 1966.
5. Mock, Edward J. et al., *Basic Financial Management: Text, Problems and Cases.* Scranton, Pennsylvania: International Textbook Company, 1968.
6. Norgaard, Richard L. and Donald E. Vaughn, *Cases in Financial Decision Making.* Englewood Cliffs, New Jersey: Prentice-Hall, Inc., 1967.
7. Walker, Ernest W. et al., *Case Problems in Financial Management.* New York: Appleton-Century-Crofts, 1968.

CROSS REFERENCE MATRIX (BY SECTION OR CASE NUMBER)

CASEBOOKS

Findlay and Williams	1 Butters	2 H+J	3 H+A	4 H,W,D	5 M,S,S,S	6 N+V	7 W et al.
Chapter 1	—	—	—	—	—	—	—
2	—	—	—	—	—	—	—
3	—	—	—	—	7-10	4	18, 19, 23, 24 3-5, 49-52
4							13, 33-41
5	40-44	13	1	29-31	11-15, 39	15-18	45-48
6	2-4, 16-20	5	5	1-5	20, 21	7, 8, 11, 12	14, 15, 20, 21
7	6-11, 15	3, 4, 7	4	13-16	3, 4, 6	6, 10, 13, 14	11, 12, 16, 17
8	5			6-12	1, 2, 5, 6	1, 9	
9	12, 13	8, 9, 11, 12	4, 5	17-21	24-26	21, 22, 26	56-61
10	14, 33-35	14-16, 26	—	22, 23, 32, 33	22, 23, 27, 33, 34	23-25	62-65
11	49-51, 53, 54	10, 25, 32, 41, 46, 47	7.1, 8 10	34, 45, 46	—	32, 42	66-79, 93-96
12		22, 23	—	35, 37	28	—	69, 72
13	21-25, 52-56	43-45	6, 7.3	38	31	28-30, 41	74-78, 90
14	23, 30-32	34, 35	7.2	24, 25	35-37	40	53-55
15	26, 29, 33	—	—	26, 28	17-19	19	25-30, 84, 85
16	27	27	7.1	36	29, 30, 32	27, 31, 33	31, 32, 73
17	—	17-19	2		16	—	
18	45-48	28, 29, 36-38	2, 6, 9	42, 44	40, 41	34-38, 45-47	79-83, 88, 91

CONTENTS

APPENDICES

LIST OF FIGURES

INTRODUCTION

As a discipline acquires sophistication in its attempt to explain phenomena, its theoretical structure becomes more complicated. This added complexity forces quantitative analysis to assume a more significant role than purely descriptive explication. In recent years, quantitative approaches to finance have been gradually replacing the older institutional discussions. The new approaches emphasize economic theory and managerial decision-making rather than taxonomic categorization.

Although this book is essentially concerned with financial decisions, there is an explicit theory of finance which underlies the presentation. It is important for the student to appreciate the elements of this theory in order to understand the problem solving approach to financial management. Thus, some introductory remarks are provided to establish a rationale for the solutions to the practical problems faced by financial managers.

The financial theory of the firm adopted in this book is merely an extension of the theory of intermediation commonly found in texts dealing with financial institutions. A financial intermediary is viewed as an organization which creates its own liabilities and sells these claims to some surplus spending unit (often in the household sector). These liabilities become indirect financial assets to the purchaser and constitute a source of funds to the issuer. The funds secured by the intermediary through the creation of liabilities are used to purchase direct financial assets (such as mortgages, commercial loans, etc.).[1]

The financial intermediary justifies its economic existence to the extent that the assets it purchases have a larger return than the liabilities it creates. The yield on direct financial assets (purchased by the intermediary) may be greater than the return on indirect financial assets (created by the intermediary) for three reasons. First, since intermediaries accumulate a wide variety of direct financial assets, they are able to offer purchasers of indirect financial assets a more diversified portfolio than these surplus units could attain if they purchased financial assets directly. Diversification

---

[1] See John Gurley and Edward Shaw, *Money in a Theory of Finance* (Washington, D.C.: The Brookings Institution, 1960); Gurley and Shaw, "Financial Intermediaries and the Savings-Investment Process," *Journal of Finance,* May, 1956, pp. 257-77; Basil Moore, *An Introduction to the Theory of Finance* (New York: The Free Press, 1968).

lowers the risk to the holders of the indirect financial assets. Hence, they are willing to accept a lower rate of return than they would demand without diversification. Second, economies of scale and superior knowledge of imperfect markets enable the intermediaries to purchase direct financial assets more efficiently than the typical surplus unit can. Surplus units, particularly those in the household sector, generally would be unable to service or evaluate the riskiness of direct financial assets. The third reason for the difference in yields derives from institutional arrangements through which governmental guarantees and other protective practices designed to assure the solvency and liquidity of certain intermediaries reduce the risk associated with the liabilities of these intermediaries and thus reduce the return demanded by their holders.[2]

The above analysis can be extended to cover all business corporations.[3] Nonfinancial business institutions generally invest in tangible assets and finance investment either from internal sources or from the issuance of primary securities. The corporate sector is invariably in deficit since business invests more every year than it "saves" in the form of depreciation (capital consumption) allowances and earnings retained. It is, therefore, a constant issuer of debt and stock. The nonfinancial business institution justifies its economic existence to the extent that it earns more on the tangible assets it purchases than it pays on the primary securities it issues. The considerations given for financial institutions apply equally to other businesses. Certainly economies of scale are present, for a rational individual who wishes to participate in the auto industry is far more likely to buy a share of GM stock than to attempt to produce cars in his garage. The diversification aspect is also important, because a large corporation is able to produce many products for many markets. A large business is also generally able to obtain greater market knowledge than an individual investor, because more money and more skills are available for research.

There are some arguments for corporate intermediation which do not apply equally to financial institutions. These arguments rely chiefly upon the special characteristics of tangible assets. An individual tends to prefer the liquidity of a share of stock in his portfolio to the illiquidity of the lathe or drill press which the corporation bought with the proceeds of a security issue.[4] For this reason alone, even if a higher income could be earned with the drill press, many individuals would prefer to buy the stock and let the firm buy the drill press. Another consideration is that a given tangible asset must generally be combined with other tangible assets and factors of production to produce a saleable good. The return from owning a given tangible asset will depend upon the owner's ability to purchase the other necessary factors of production and to operate these assets or to hire and manage others to do so. It should follow that the return from a tangible asset will vary greatly depending upon the owner. Finally, the

---

[2] See Edward E. Williams, *Prospects for the Savings and Loan Industry to 1975* (Austin: Texas Savings and Loan League, 1968), especially pp. 1-2, and 101-106.

[3] See Moore, *An Introduction to the Theory of Finance.*

[4] The degree of liquidity possessed by an asset is a function of (1) the ease of conversion of that asset into cash at or near the price paid for the asset, and (2) the time required to effect this conversion.

return from tangible assets is generally realized very slowly. A corporation with its lack of a propensity to consume and its infinite life, is often felt to be a more suitable purchaser than the individual for such long-lived, illiquid assets as fixed plant and equipment.

The financial problem that confronts the corporation is to determine which and how many tangible assets to buy and how much and what kind of securities to sell. In this book, we approach separately the twin problems of the firm's investment in assets and its financing of those investments. In Unit I, we examine the investment subsystem. We assume that the firm can sell a fixed package of securities in unlimited amounts at a known and constant cost. We find that, given this financing assumption, the firm should invest in all projects yielding a higher return than the cost of securing funds. In Unit II, we analyze the nature and costs of various sources of financing. Assuming a fixed volume of assets and a given return on the asset investment, we compute a cost of capital. This cost is found to be the investment cutoff point which is treated exogeneously in Unit I. In Unit III, we integrate the investment and financing subsystems into a dynamic decision-making framework.

I THE INVESTMENT SUBSYSTEM

1 FINANCIAL MATHEMATICS

At the heart of much financial theory lies the concept of interest. Since so much of what follows in this book depends upon a working knowledge of the mechanics of compound interest, it is imperative that the student master this chapter before advancing to any other material.

If a bank offers to pay 5 percent interest on a deposit left for one year, the value of the deposit will increase by 5 percent at the end of the year. Thus, $1,000 deposited on January 1, 1970 will be worth $1,050 on January 1, 1971. The 5 percent ($50) is the simple interest earned on the deposit. This relationship may be described symbolically. If D_0 is the value of the initial deposit and i is the rate of interest per period, the dollar amount earned during the period is iD_0. The value of the deposit at the end of the year (or viewed another way, the beginning of the next year) is given by:

$$D_1 = D_0 + iD_0$$
$$(\$1,050) = (\$1,000) + (5\%)(\$1,000) \tag{1.1}$$

Compound interest computations are slightly more complex, since the interest paid on a deposit during one period earns interest on itself during all future periods. It is assumed, of course, that interest payments are not withdrawn. In the example above if the entire $1,050 amount on deposit January 1, 1971 remained on deposit until January 1, 1972, the $50 interest earned during 1970 would earn interest on itself. Thus, for 1971, the interest earned would be 5 percent ($1,050.00) = $52.50. The value of the deposit as of January 1, 1972, would be $1,050.00 + $52.50 = $1,102.50. Expressed symbolically, the value of the deposit at the end of the second year is given by:

$$D_2 = D_1 + iD_1$$
$$(\$1,102.50) = (\$1,050) + (5\%)(\$1,050) \tag{1.2}$$

It is obvious that the original $1,000 will continue to grow by larger dollar amounts ($50, $52.50, etc.) during each year in which compounding takes place. It is also obvious that a more efficient means of computation is necessary. If one wished to determine the amount to which $1,000 would grow after twenty compounding periods, the process of repeating the multiplication twenty times would become tedious. Fortunately, some very simple algebraic manipulation can reduce the problem to a one-step operation. Let us return to Eq. (1.1). By factoring D_0, this equation may be written:

$$D_1 = D_0 + iD_0 = D_0 (1 + i)$$

We may substitute this into Eq. (1.2):

$$D_2 = D_1 + iD_1 = D_0 (1 + i) + i(D_0) (1 + i)$$
$$D_2 = D_0 (1 + 2i + i^2)$$
$$D_2 = D_0 (1 + i)^2$$

Thus, we may compute immediately the value of $1,000 left on deposit for two years. $D_2 = (\$1,000) (1 + .05)^2 = (\$1,000) (1.1025) = \$1,102.50$. The value of the deposit after one year is:

$$D_1 = D_0 (1 + i)^1$$

The value of the deposit after two years is:

$$D_2 = D_0 (1 + i)^2 \ .$$

We could repeat the above process for D_3 and find that the value of the deposit after three years is:

$$D_3 = D_0 (1 + i)^3$$

After n years, the value of the deposit would be:

$$D_n = D_0 (1 + i)^n \tag{1.3}$$

Returning to our question concerning how much $1,000 would have grown after twenty years:

$$D_{20} = (\$1,000) (1 + i)^{20} = (\$1,000) (2.6533) = \$2,653.30$$

Lest the student recoil in horror at the prospect of computing the twentieth power of 1.05, it should be noted that these computations have already been made in the form of compound interest tables. A set of these tables appears in Appendix A at the end of this book. In order to find the amount to which a deposit will grow over a number of compounding periods, one locates the appropriate row and column indicating the given rate of interest per period and the given number of compounding periods: the factor found at the intersection of the appropriate row and column is then multiplied by the original deposit amount to produce the amount to which the original sum would grow. In the example above, the number of compounding periods is 20 and the rate of interest per period is 5 percent. The resulting factor is 2.6533. This factor multiplied by $1,000 produces $2,653.30.[1]

SOLVED PROBLEMS

1. Smith has placed $2,750 in a savings account which pays 4 percent interest. If he leaves his money in the account for ten years, how much will he have?

SOLUTION

$$D_{10} = (\$2,750)\,(1 + .04)^{10} = (\$2,750)\,(1.4793) = \$4,068.08$$

2. Jones is considering the purchase of a savings bond. The bond costs $19. After seven years the bond is worth $25. How much interest would Jones earn (compounded annually) if he purchased this bond?

SOLUTION

$$\$25 = (\$19)\,(1 + x)^7 \text{ or}$$
$$\$25 = (\$19)\,(f_7)$$

Where f_7 is the factor for x rate of interest for seven years.

$$f_7 = \tfrac{25}{19} = 1.3158$$

---

[1] The answer would be the same had the rate been 5 percent per month, compounded monthly, and the time period twenty months. Thus, if consistency is maintained, the tables may be used for time periods of other than a year. In general, let C be the time period of compounding. Then, $D_n = D_0(1 + \tfrac{i}{c})^{nc}$.

Examining the compound interest table, we find that for $n = 7$, the factor 1.3158 corresponds approximately to a 4 percent compounded annual rate of return.

UNSOLVED PROBLEMS

1. To what amount will $10,000 grow over twenty-five years if the rate of interest is 10 percent?

2. Mr. and Mrs. King retired last year. They plan to supplement their social security pensions with the interest they earn from their savings account. They have $50,000 in their account which pays 5 percent interest. Mr. King knows a little about the wonders of compound interest. He explained to Mrs. King that their $50,000 would one day be a much larger sum. How much will the Kings have after ten years, given the above assumptions? Why?

3. A major savings bank in New York City advertises that funds deposited in one of its special accounts will double every fourteen years. What implicit assumptions are contained within this advertisement?

SECTION 1.2

Compound interest computations may also be made where D dollars are invested each period. The annuity (terminal) value after one period of a deposit of D dollars at i rate of interest is:

$$D_1 = D(1+i)^1$$

The annuity value of deposits of D dollars made at p_0 and p_1 is:

$$D_1 = D(1+i)^1 +$$
$$D_2 = D(1+i)^2$$

The value of deposits of D dollars made at periods $p_0, p_1, \ldots, p_n$ is:

$$D_1 = D(1+i)^1 +$$
$$D_2 = D(1+i)^2 +$$
$$\ldots +$$
$$D_n = D(1+i)^n$$

or,

$$V_A = \sum_{t=1}^{n} D(1 + i)^t \qquad\qquad (1.4)$$

Where: V_A is the annuity value of deposits of D dollars made for n periods.

The annuity value of a deposit of D dollars for n periods may be obtained from Appendix B, which presents the sum of the appropriate factors from Appendix A.

SOLVED PROBLEM

Brown puts $1,000 in a 4 percent savings account at the beginning of each year. At the end of three years how much will he have?

SOLUTION

$$D_3 = (\$1,000)(1 + .04)^3 = (\$1,000)(1.1249) = \$1,124.90$$
$$D_2 = (\$1,000)(1 + .04)^2 = (\$1,000)(1.0811) = 1,081.10$$
$$D_1 = (\$1,000)(1 + .04)^1 = (\$1,000)(1.0400) = \underline{1,040.00}$$
$$ \$3,246.00$$

or

$$V_A = (D)(f_3)$$
$$V_A = (1,000)(3.246) = \$3,246$$

UNSOLVED PROBLEMS

1. Mrs. Smith saves $100 each quarter. She places her savings with the First Conservative California Savings and Loan Association which compounds interest quarterly. The annual rate paid by the association is 4 percent. How much will Mrs. Smith accumulate in three years?

2. The Smithers Corporation is planning to purchase some new plant and equipment five years from now. The sum needed for the purchase is $1,200,000. The management of the firm can invest funds at an 8 percent annual return.

    (a) How much should be put aside today in order to have the needed amount in five years?

(b) How much could be set aside annually to provide the requisite sum after five years?

SECTION
1.3
Since a dollar in hand today can be invested at some positive rate of interest, that pool of funds will grow to be worth more than one dollar by next year. In other words, a dollar to be received one year from now is not worth a dollar today, but some smaller amount; that is, it would be worth the amount that should be invested at the going rate of interest in order to grow to one dollar by next year.

The concept that sums received in the future are worth less than equivalent dollar amounts received in the present is often referred to as the *time value of money.* Assume a rate of interest of 6 percent. If $1,000 were deposited today at that rate, the $1,000 would grow to $1,060 in a year. Thus, it may be said that the *present value* of $1,060 to be received one year from now is $1,000 if the rate of interest is 6 percent.

Let us return to our compound interest formula, Eq. (1.3). If a particular amount (D_0) is placed on deposit at i rate of interest in the present, it will grow to $D_1 = D_0 (1 + i)$ in 1 year, $D_2 = D_0 (1 + i)^2$ in two years, and so on.

$$D_n = D_0 (1 + i)^n$$
$$\$1,060 = \$1,000 (1.06) = \$1,060$$

Compounding formula–(1.3)

This works very well if we know the amount to be deposited in the present and wish to find the amount to which it will grow in the future. Suppose, however, that the situation is reversed: we know the amount to be received or paid in the future but wish to discover what sum should be set aside in the present at the current rate of interest so that it will grow to the desired amount at the future point in time. This can be done by solving Eq. (1.3) for the initial deposit (D_0), giving us:

$$D_0 = \frac{D_n}{(1 + i)^n}$$

$$\$1,000 = \frac{\$1,060}{1.06}$$

Present value formula–(1.5)

or

$$D_0 = D_n \frac{1}{(1 + i)^n}$$

$$\$1,000 = \$1,060 \frac{1}{1.06} = \$1,060\,(.943) = \$1,000$$

(1.5a)

The tables in Appendix A are quite suitable for determining present values by Eq. (1.5). Since most people find it easier to multiply than to divide, Eq. (1.5a) is more often used. A table of discount factors that gives the present value of $1 to be received n years hence may be found in Appendix C. As shown above, the present value of $1 to be received in one year, if the interest discount rate is 6 percent, is $0.943. We may check this by noting that 6 percent interest on $0.943 would be about $0.057, giving us a total of $1 at the end of the year. It should be stressed that each discount factor in Appendix C is nothing more than the reciprocal of the corresponding compounding factor in Appendix A.

SOLVED PROBLEMS

1. What is the present value of $1,000 to be received five years from now if the discount rate is:
   (a) 2 percent
   (b) 10 percent
   (c) 50 percent

SOLUTION

(a) $$D_0 = \frac{D_5}{(1 + i)^5} = \frac{\$1,000}{(1 + .02)^5} = \frac{1}{(1.02)^5}\,(\$1,000)$$

$1/(1.02)^5 = .906$. This may be taken directly from the table. The present value of $1 to be received five years from now with a discount rate of 2 percent is $.906.

$(.906)\,(\$1,000) = \$906$

(b) $D_0 = \dfrac{\$1,000}{(1.10)^5} = (.621)\,(\$1,000) = \$621$

(c) $D_0 = (.132)\,(\$1,000) = \$132.$

2. Assume a discount rate of 10 percent. What is the present value of:

   (a) $625 received in ten years?
   (b) $150 received in six years?

SOLUTION

(a) $D_0 = (.386)(\$625) = \$241.25$

(b) $D_0 = (.564(\$150) = \$84.60$

UNSOLVED PROBLEMS

1. Determine the following present values:
    (a) $i = 8\%, D_n = \$600, n = 20$ years, $D_o = ?.$
    (b) $i = 14\%, D_n = \$850, n = 16$ years, $D_0 = ?.$

2. Complete the following matrix:
    (a) $i = ?, D_n = \$6,000, n = 5$ years, $D_0 = \$4,482$
    (b) $i = 12\%, D_n = ?, n = 5$ years, $D_0 = \$3,402$
    (c) $i = 24\%, D_n = \$6,000, n = ?, D_0 = \$2,046$

3. Charles Bower just bought a corporate bond. The bond pays interest of $60 at the end of each year. In five years, the bond will mature and Bower will receive $1,000 in addition to his $60 interest for year five. If Bower wants to earn 8 percent interest, how much should he have paid for this bond today?

SECTION 1.4   The present value of a series of payments is merely the summation of the present values of the individual payments. Assume that 1 year from now we are to receive D_1 dollars, that two years from now we will receive D_2 dollars, that three years from now we will obtain D_3 dollars, and so forth. The present value of each future amount is given by:

$$D_0 = \frac{D_1}{(1+i)^1}$$

$$D_0 = \frac{D_2}{(1+i)^2}$$

$$D_0 = \frac{D_3}{(1+i)^3}$$

The present value of these three future sums is, consequently:

$$PV = \frac{D_1}{(1 + i)^1} + \frac{D_2}{(1 + i)^2} + \frac{D_3}{(1 + i)^3}$$

The present value of a series of payments received over t periods is simply:

$$PV = \frac{D_1}{(1 + i)^1} + \frac{D_2}{(1 + i)^2} + \ldots + \frac{D_n}{(1 + i)^n}, \text{ or} \qquad (1.6)$$

$$PV = \sum_{t=1}^{n} \frac{D_t}{(1 + i)^t}, \text{ or} \qquad (1.6a)$$

$$PV = \sum_{t=1}^{n} D_t \frac{1}{(1 + i)^t} \qquad (1.6b)$$

Let us assume an interest rate of 6 percent. Let us further assume that we shall receive $1,000 per year for the next four years. How much is this stream of payments worth presently? The answer can be found immediately in the present value tables. At 6 percent, the present value of $1 to be received one year from now is $.943. The value of $1 received two years from now is $.890, etc. The present value of the entire stream is thus:

PV = (.943) ($1,000) + (.890) ($1,000) + (.840) ($1,000) + (.792) ($1,000)
    = $3,465.

In the unique case where the flows in each year are the same ($D_1 = D_2 = D_n$), the present value computation becomes even easier. Consider the previous example. A stream of $1,000 is to be received for each of four years. The equation may be rewritten factoring the $1,000, or

PV = ($1,000) (.943 + .890 + .840 + .792) = $3,465.

The second term on the right side of the equation merely sums the annual discount factors. In this case,

.943 + .890 + .840 + .792 = 3.465

When a given sum is to be received annually for n years, it is unnecessary to perform each multiplication operation. It is not even necessary to add the discount factors. This operation is accomplished in a second set of present value factors, which can be found in Appendix D. In this table the present value of $1 received annually for n years is given. Reading directly from the table, we find that at $i = 6$ percent, the present value of $1 received annually for four years is 3.465. Thus, (3.465) ($1,000) = $3,465 as above.

SOLVED PROBLEMS

1. What is the present value of $1,000 to be received annually for each of five years if the discount rate is
(a) 2 percent
(b) 10 percent
(c) 50 percent

SOLUTION

(a) $PV = (4.713) (\$1,000) = \$4,713$
(b) $PV = (3.791) (\$1,000) = \$3,791$
(c) $PV = (1.737) (\$1,000) = \$1,737$

2. The Jarvis Company can invest funds at 10%. The proposed purchase of a piece of equipment will result in the following increased inflow to the company over the next six years:

Year	
1	$ 750
2	800
3	850
4	900
5	950
6	1000

How much is this equipment presently worth to the firm?

SOLUTION

Cash Flow	Discount Factor		
$ 750	.909	=	$ 681.75
800	.826	=	660.80
850	.751	=	638.35
900	.683	=	614.70
950	.621	=	589.95
1,000	.564	=	564.00
			$3,749.55

3. The Kingston Company has an opportunity investment rate of 8 percent. The firm expects to earn the following for the next six years:

Year		Year	
1	$20,000	4	$10,000
2	20,000	5	10,000
3	20,000	6	10,000

What is the present value of the Kingston Company?

SOLUTION

This problem may be solved in a fashion similar to number 2 above by using the tables in Appendix C. Students who wish to reduce the number of required computations may use the tables in Appendix D. Several approaches are possible. Since there is a constant $10,000 figure for all six periods, it is possible to take the present value of $10,000 for each of the six periods. To this would be added the present value of the additional $10,000 payments received during periods 1-3.

$$(\$10,000)\,(4.623) + (\$10,000)\,(2.577) = \$72,000$$

A second approach would take the present value of $20,000 to be received for three periods. To this would be added the present value of $10,000 to be received for three periods after the lapse of three periods. The first part of the computation follows directly:

$$(\$20,000)\,(2.577) = \$51,540$$

The second part of the computation is only slightly more difficult. Since the sums received during years 4-6 are not received during years 1-3, the factor for these years should not be included. The present value of $1 to be received annually for years 1-6 is given by factor 4.623. The present value of $1 to be received annually for years 1-3 is given by 2.577. Thus, the present value of $1 to be received annually for years 4-6 is given by 4.623 − 2.577 = 2.046. The present value of the $10,000 sum received during years 4-6 is:

$$(\$10,000)\,(2.046) = \$20,460$$

The total present value is $51,540 + $20,460 = $72,000.

UNSOLVED PROBLEMS

1. Determine the following present values:

    (a) $i = 8\%, D_1 = D_2 = D_3 = D_4 = \$1,200$ $PV = \underline{?}$

    (b) $i = 12\%, D_1 = D_2 = \ldots = D_6 = \$1,600$ $PV = \underline{?}$

2. Complete the following matrix:

    (a) $i = \underline{?}, D_1 = D_2 = \ldots = D_8 = \$1,000$ $PV = \$6,733$

    (b) $i = 10\%, D_1 = D_2 = \ldots = D_8 = \underline{?}$ $PV = \$5,335$

    (c) $i = 20\%, D_1 = D_2 = \ldots = D_? = \$1,000$ $PV = \$3,837$

3. What is the present value of \$2,500 to be received annually for four years, if $i = 6$ percent and the first payment will not be received until five years from now?

4. James McBride has just completed an M.B.A. at Harvard. After sifting through a number of job offers, McBride reduced the number of acceptable offers to two. The first offer guaranteed him \$15,000 as a starting salary plus \$1,000 annual raises for five years. The second offer guaranteed him \$10,000 as a starting salary plus \$3,000 annual raises for five years.

    (a) Assume that McBride plans to work on his first job only five years. Assume further that McBride will be able to invest all his earnings (i.e., ignore taxes and personal consumption). If McBride can earn 15 percent on his money, which offer is the better one? (Assume that maximizing wealth is McBride's only objective, that pleasant surroundings, an interesting job, etc. are not important to him).

    (b) Assume that the second offer also included a \$10,000 bonus at the end of the fifth year. Would this added factor change the decision?

    (c) Given the added assumption in b, would altering the first assumption so that McBride could earn only 6 percent on his investment affect the decision?

5. (a) Assume that the Jarvis Company (see solved problem number 2 on pg. 15) is able to purchase the equipment for \$4,000. Ignoring taxes, should the project be undertaken? If so, why?

    (b) Would your decision be altered if Jarvis could only invest funds at 6 percent?

    (c) Suppose that Jarvis can invest funds at 10 percent but that the manufacturer of the equipment would allow Jarvis to pay \$1,000 down (in year 0) and \$1,000 in each of years 1-3. What is your decision now?

6. A prominent Texas congressman once remarked, "A dollar today is worth more than a dollar in the future for one reason: inflation. The fact is that

$1.00 today will only buy what $.34 would have bought forty years ago." Comment on this observation.

2 INTRODUCTION TO CONCEPTS OF VALUE AND RISK

SECTION 2.1   To the economist objects are valuable only if they are scarce and provide utility. Scarcity is an important criterion of value, since free goods have no value. Air, for example, is quite useful, but because there is an abundance of air, it is worthless. Similarly, there is a scarcity of alchemists; but since the utility of their services is questionable, these services have little if any value.

Although defining value is a relatively simple matter, determining value is much more difficult. In a market economy, there is a tendency to value goods and services at their market prices. Nevertheless, because of differences in tastes, the "value" to one individual (i.e., the utility) of a certain commodity may be less than or greater than the "value" of the identical commodity to someone else. Indeed, the very rationale for sales transactions is the fact that a particular commodity has greater utility for one individual than for another. The price offered to the seller is greater than the value he places on the commodity being sold. Thus, he sells. The price paid by the buyer is less than the value he places on the commodity. Thus, he buys.

Economists have wrestled with questions of valuation for years, and the theoretical pronouncements on the subject are voluminous. In this book we are not concerned with the esoteric properties of value. We shall be content with examining the techniques and methodologies of valuation available to the financial manager.

Not surprisingly, accountants have played a major role in providing measures of value to financial managers. Accountants have argued vociferously that assets were worth their historical (book) costs less depreciation. Thus, if a piece of equipment were purchased in 1950 at a price of $100,000 with a life expectancy of twenty years (assuming no salvage), the "value" of that equipment in 1970 would be zero. Of course, the major drawback of this valuation procedure is the difficulty in determining real (as opposed to bookkeeping) depreciation. In the above case, if after twenty years had passed it appeared that the asset could be useful for ten more years, the actual life expectancy of the equipment would have been incorrectly estimated and depreciation charges against the asset would have been too large

In order to reflect the possibility of incorrect depreciation charges and to give recognition to the fact that the general level of prices has risen considerably since the end of World War II, the accounting community is moving toward the adjustment of the book value of assets by some appropriate inflater (deflator). This approach to valuing assets has struck many economists as being conceptually unsound. Many academic accountants have also objected to the proposed methodology. Some have gone so far as to propose that an asset be valued at its replacement cost or the price at which the asset could be sold. Others have recommended that assets be appraised regularly to determine value.

Economists who deal in the "real world" (frequently called managerial economists) have long contended that a consumer good was "worth" the expected utility provided by consuming the good, while a capital good (used to produce consumer goods or other capital goods) should be valued in terms of the income-generating capacity of that good. Thus, to the economist, the value of an asset is the discounted present value of the earnings stream generated by that asset. To determine value, the economist employs the discounting process outlined in the previous chapter.

In order to detail the procedure of valuing assets on the basis of discounted present values, we must be more specific about the nature of cash flows. In this discussion, it will be assumed that the student has a rudimentary familiarity with accounting terminology and procedure.

Let us assume that a piece of plant and equipment will generate the following additional sales for a firm during the life expectancy of the asset: year 1, $13,000; year 2, $10,000; year 3, $7,000. Let us further assume that cash outflows required to sustain these sales levels (for raw materials, salaries, etc.) are $5,000, $4,000, and $3,000, respectively. The net cash flows before depreciation and taxes are:

Year	Δ Sales	Operating Cash Outlays	Net Cash Before Depreciation and Taxes
1	$13,000	$5,000	$8,000
2	10,000	4,000	6,000
3	7,000	3,000	4,000

Now, in valuing this asset we are interested in the *net cash* which the asset will generate. In order to get net cash, there is one more cash outflow which must be considered—income taxes. Since depreciation charges are only bookkeeping allocations of past capital expenditures and do not involve cash outflows in the current period, accounting depreciation should not be deducted from the cash flow. Nevertheless, in figuring income taxes, accounting depreciation is a deductible expense. Thus, in order to determine income taxes, it is necessary to know the accounting depreciation charge. Let us assume an annual depreciation charge of $3,000. Let us further assume that the firm pays 40 percent of its net income in income taxes. The net income (but not the net cash flow) earned by the piece of plant and equipment is:

Year	Net Before Depreciation and Taxes	Depreciation	Net Income Before Taxes	Taxes	Net Income
1	$8,000	$3,000	$5,000	$2,000	$3,000
2	6,000	3,000	3,000	1,200	1,800
3	4,000	3,000	1,000	400	600

To compute net cash flow, income taxes are subtracted from net cash before depreciation and taxes:

Year	Net Before Depreciation and Taxes	Taxes	Net Cash Flow
1	$8,000	$2,000	$6,000
2	6,000	1,200	4,800
3	4,000	400	3,600

The alert student will notice that the net cash flow figure may also be obtained by adding the depreciation charge (a non-cash, bookkeeping charge) to net income:

Year	Net Income	Depreciation	Net Cash Flow
1	$3,000	$3,000	$6,000
2	1,800	3,000	4,800
3	600	3,000	3,600

If cash can be invested elsewhere to earn 10 percent (opportunity use) by the firm, the value of this piece of plant and equipment is:

Year	Net Cash Flow	Discount Factor		
1	$6,000	.909	=	$ 5,454.00
2	4,800	.826	=	3,964.80
3	3,600	.751	=	2,703.60
				$12,122.40

Thus, the present value (worth) of a stream of cash $D_1 = \$6,000$; $D_2 = \$4,800$; $D_3 = \$3,600$ is $12,122.40 if the discount rate is 10 percent.

SOLVED PROBLEM

The Sherbourne Corporation purchased a machine in 1960 for $1,200,000. The expected life of the machine is twenty years. The machine is being depreciated on a straight-line basis and will have a salvage value of $200,000 in 1980. The machine generates $250,000 per year in net cash benefits before depreciation and taxes. The firm has an opportunity investment rate of 15 percent and pays 30 percent of its net income in taxes.

1. What is the book value of this asset in 1970?

SOLUTION

$1,200,000 − (10)($50,000) = $700,000

2. What is the present value of this asset in 1970?

SOLUTION

Year	Net Before Depreciation and Taxes	Depreciation	Net Income Before Taxes	Taxes	Net Income	Cash Flow
1971-79	$250,000	$50,000	$200,000	$60,000	$140,000	$190,000

In 1980, the cash flow will be $190,000 plus $200,000 salvage, or $390,000. Thus, the present value of the asset in 1970 is:

($190,000) (4.772) + ($390,000) (.247) = $1,003,010.[1]

UNSOLVED PROBLEMS

1. An asset will generate a net cash flow of $200,000 for ten years. With a discount rate of 6 percent, what is the present value of this asset?

2. The Ajax Corporation is considering the purchase of a machine for $20,000. The machine has an expected life of six years and a salvage value of $2,000. Determine the net cash benefits generated by the machine if the expected benefits before depreciation (straight-line) and taxes (50 percent)

---

[1] It should be pointed out that a very inferior variant of the present value approach (known as capitalization) is in wide use. This process involves dividing some net income by an interest rate. In the above example, the $140,000 net income capitalized at 15 percent would give a value to the asset of 140,000/.15 = $933,000; this merely states that $140,000 represents a 15 percent return on $933,000. To be theoretically accurate, this method requires that the asset generate constant income flows and possess an infinite life or some contrived equivalent. Use of the capitalization method when these conditions do not hold can result in some very bad valuations.

are:

Year	
1	$5,000
2	4,000
3	4,000
4	3,000
5	3,000
6	3,000

3. If the Ajax Corporation (above) has an opportunity rate of investment of 10 percent, should it purchase the machine? Why or why not?

4.
THE BENDOX CORPORATION
BALANCE SHEET AS OF JANUARY 1, 1971

Assets			Equities	
Current Assets		$250,000	Current Liabilities	$100,000
Fixed Assets	$1,000,000		Long-term debt	150,000
Less: Accum. Dep.	500,000	500,000	Common Stock	500,000
		$750,000		$750,000

The Bendox Corporation managers are trying to determine the firm's value. It has been estimated that the present asset investment in the firm will produce income for ten years without replacement. Sales anticipated over this period are:

Years	Sales Forecast
1971-1974	$130,000
1975-1978	100,000
1979-1980	80,000

The firm expects that operating cash outlays will equal $10,000 per year plus 20 percent of sales. Annual depreciation charges are $50,000. The firm pays 25 percent of its net income in taxes.

(a) What is the book value of the Bendox Corporation?

(b) Assume that the Bendox Corporation plans to go out of business after ten years, selling all assets at that time and paying off all liabilities. What is the present value of the firm? Bendox has an opportunity investment return of 10 percent.

(c) Bendox could sell its current assets for book value and its fixed assets for 80 percent of current book value. What is the liquidating market value of the firm? Would you recommend that the firm liquidate?

(d) Replacing the firm's assets would require the purchase of $600,000 worth of fixed assets, while the firm's current assets could be replaced at book value. What is the replacement value of the firm's assets? Given the future earnings estimates for the firm, if a fire consumed all of the firm's fixed assets would you recommend replacing the assets?

SECTION
2.2

In our previous discussion of value, there was an implicit assumption that all future events were known with certainty. In the real world, however, it is rare for a state of certainty to prevail, particularly for the distant future. Clearly, some events are less uncertain than others. In determining the value of a treasury bond, for example, the timing and amounts of future payments are known almost with certainty. But there is still risk associated with owning a treasury bond, particularly one with a long maturity, since changes in the prevailing level of interest rates can affect the price (value) of the bond.[2] In determing the value of a piece of plant and equipment, there may be considerable uncertainty over the timing and the amounts of future payments. In general, it may be postulated that an asset will be worth less as the uncertainty associated with the payment stream generated by that asset increases.

Statisticians frequently delineate among three states of future events: an outcome may be known with certainty, an outcome may be subject to risk, or an outcome may be entirely uncertain. Although there is a philosophical school which holds that no future event can be known with certainty, it is reasonably safe to presume that the sun will rise (although not necessarily shine) tomorrow. Thus, given two possible outcomes (the sun will rise, the sun will not rise), the probability that the sun will rise approaches certainty. The second state of future events is that of risk, in which there is more than one possible outcome but all outcomes and their likelihood of occurrence are known. An expression of relative likelihood generally takes the form of a probability distribution, which may be determined objectively (*a priori*) or subjectively. The third state of future events is that of uncertainty. Under a state of uncertainty neither all possible outcomes nor their relative likelihoods of occurrence are known. This state is completely unsatisfactory to decision making. Therefore, most events must be cast into a state of risk through the construction of subjective probability distributions by those who must deal with the future events.

Let us assume that we are attempting to value an asset which will generate a risky payment stream and that our planning division, by examining past sales performance and estimating future sales potential,

---

[2]The relationship between security prices and interest rates is discussed in Chap. 11.

has prepared the following expression of relative likelihood (probability distribution) about net cash flows to be generated by the asset:

Outcome	Probability
$80,000	.3
50,000	.5
30,000	.2

Since the distribution is exhaustive (i.e., there are only three possible outcomes) the probabilities of the future events sum to unity (.3 + .5 + .2 = 1.0). Now, we raise the question: What value should be used as the expected future cash flow, or, what is the central tendency value of the distribution? There are three common statistical possibilities. The *mode* value is the outcome with the greatest probability of occurrence. In the illustration above, the value with the greatest probability of occurrence (.5) is $50,000. The *median* is the value which divides the distribution into two equal parts. The median above is $50,000. The most useful measure of central tendency is the *mean* or average value. The mean value (also called the expected value) is found by multiplying the probabilities by the outcomes and summing the result:

$$
\begin{aligned}
(\$80{,}000) \times (.3) &= \$24{,}000 \\
(50{,}000) \times (.5) &= 25{,}000 \\
(30{,}000) \times (.2) &= \underline{6{,}000} \\
&\ \ \$55{,}000
\end{aligned}
$$

The symbol μ is frequently employed to signify the mean value.

SOLVED PROBLEM

The National Bus Company is considering the purchase of a new General Motors Diesel Special. The planning division of National Bus has estimated the following probability distribution for net cash flows generated by the Special:

Outcome	Probability
$100,000	.1
90,000	.2
60,000	.2
20,000	.4
−20,000	.1

What are the mode, median, and mean values of this distribution?

SOLUTION

Mode = $20,000   Median = $40,000, the midpoint between
                                                   $20,000 and $60,000

Mean = ($100,000) × (.1) = $10,000
         (90,000) × (.2) =   18,000
         (60,000) × (.2) =   12,000
         (20,000) × (.4) =   8,000
       (−20,000) × (.1) =   −2,000

$$\mu = \$46,000$$

UNSOLVED PROBLEMS:

1. Determine the mean, mode, and median for the following distributions.

(a)
Outcome	Probability
10	.3
8	.4
6	.2
2	.1

(b)
Outcome	Probability
$50,000	.1
40,000	.2
30,000	.4
20,000	.2
10,000	.1

(c)
Outcome	Probability
$ 115	.05
100	.14
80	.19
50	.26
20	.17
0	.10
−20	.06
−50	.03

2. Sam Small has been contemplating the purchase of common stock in the Apex Manufacturing Company. Apex now pays an annual dividend of $1 per share, and Small expects the dividends to increase according to the following probability distribution:

Years	Dividend	Probability
1-3	$1.25	.2
	1.00	.6
	.75	.2
4-8	$1.50	.3
	1.25	.6
	1.00	.1
9-10	$2.00	.1
	1.75	.2
	1.50	.3
	1.25	.3
	1.00	.1

Sam plans to hold his stock for ten years. After ten years he believes the stock's price will be:

Price	Probability
$100	.2
90	.3
80	.2
70	.2
60	.1

(a) If Sam has an opportunity investment rate of 8 percent, how much is a share of Apex worth to him?

(b) If Apex were selling at $70 per share, what expected return would Sam earn if he purchased the stock?

SECTION 2.3   We indicated previously that there is an inverse relationship between the value of an asset and the risk associated with the payment stream generated by that asset. From our measures of central tendency, it is possible for us to develop a measure of risk.

The most frequently employed measure of dispersion around the cental tendency of a distribution is the standard deviation (σ). The standard deviation is defined as:

$$\sigma = \sqrt{\sum_{t=1}^{n} (o_t - \mu)^2 \, p_t} \tag{2.1}$$

The operations implied by the rather imposing looking equation are actually very simple. Let us return to the distribution discussed above:

Outcome	Probability
$80,000	.3
50,000	.5
30,000	.2

The mean value of this distribution was $55,000. The standard deviation is calculated by subtracting the mean value from each outcome, squaring the result, multiplying the squared figure by the probability, summing the products, and taking the square root of the sum, or[3]

$O_t - \mu$	$(O_t - \mu)^2$	p_t
$80,000 - $55,000 = $25,000;	($25,000)^2 = ($625,000,000); × (.3) =	$187,500,000
50,000 - 55,000 = -5,000;	(-5,000)^2 = (25,000,000); × (.5) =	12,500,000
30,000 - 55,000 = -25,000;	(-25,000)^2 = (625,000,000); × (.2) =	125,000,000
		$325,000,000

$$\sigma = \sqrt{\$325,000,000} = \$18,028$$

Clearly, the larger the standard deviation, the greater the risk associated with the distribution.

SOLVED PROBLEM

The Omega Company has estimated the following probability distribution for next year's sales (figures in thousands):

Outcome	Probability
$250	.3
200	.4
170	.2
110	.1

1. What are the mode, median, and mean values of the distribution:

---

[3]Throughout this book, we assume that all distributions are continuous and normal. We will often describe such distributions, however, in terms of a discrete number of outcomes (as with the three outcomes in the present example). This practice may be rationalized on the basis that management cannot deal with an infinite number of outcomes and will tend to visualize each project in terms of certain good and bad possible results. See G.L.S. Shackle, *Uncertainty in Economics* (New York: Cambridge University Press, 1955).

SOLUTION

Mode = $200,000   Median = $200,000

Mean =   (250) × (.3) =   75
                        (200) × (.4) =   80
                        (170) × (.2) =   34
                        (110) × (.1) =   11
                                        ———
                                        200

$$\mu = \$200,000$$

2. What is the standard deviation for Omega's sales?

SOLUTION

250 − 200 =   50; $(50)^2$ = (2500); × (.3) = 750
200 − 200 =   0; $(0)^2$ =   (0); × (.4) =   0
170 − 200 = −30; $(-30)^2$ = (900); × (.2) = 180
110 − 200 = −90; $(-90)^2$ = (8100); × (.1) = 810
                                               ———
                                               174

$$\sigma = \sqrt{1740} = 41.7$$

$$\sigma = \$41,700$$

UNSOLVED PROBLEMS

1. Determine the standard deviations for distributions a, b, and c in unsolved problem number 1 at the end of Sec. 2.2.

2. Reexamine problem number 2 at the end of Sec. 2.2.

(a) Determine σ for each dividend distribution and for the stock price distribution.

(b) Assume that the shares of Apex are selling at Sam's expected value. Assume further that Sam's 8 percent opportunity rate applied to a riskless investment ($\sigma = 0$). Would it make sense for Sam to buy Apex? Why or why not?

COMPREHENSIVE PROBLEM

The Samuelson Book Company has determined the following discrete probability distribution for sales generated by a contemplated capital project:

Period 1	Period 2	Period 3
$1,000 (.10)	$1,000 (.20)	$1,000 (.30)
2,000 (.20)	2,000 (.30)	2,000 (.40)
3,000 (.30)	3,000 (.40)	3,000 (.20)
4,000 (.40)	4,000 (.10)	4,000 (.10)

1. Determine the mean sales value and the standard deviation for each period.

2. Assume that operating cash outflows per period will equal 20 percent of sales. Prepare a distribution of cash flows before depreciation and taxes for the project.

3. Assume the capital project will incur a depreciation charge of $2,000 per year and that the average tax rate paid by Samuelson Book Company is 40 percent. Prepare a distribution of net cash flows for the project.

4. Assume an opportunity investment rate of 10 percent. Determine the expected present value of the project.

5. If the cash flows for a project are independent (i.e., the volume of flows in one period does not depend on the volume of flows in any other period), the following formula may be used to determine the overall riskiness of the project:[4]

$$\sigma = \sqrt{\sum_{t=1}^{n} \frac{\sigma_t^2}{(1+r)^{2t}}}$$

In this equation, r is the pure (riskless) rate of interest, and σ is a standard deviation of standard deviations. For the Samuelson Book Company project above, determine the overall σ. Let $r = 4$ percent.

---

[4] See James C. Van Horne, *Financial Management and Policy* (Englewood Cliffs, N.J.: Prentice-Hall, Inc., 1968), pp. 69-70.

3 OPERATING AND
FINANCIAL LEVERAGE

In the previous chapter, the risk characteristics of individual assets were examined. In this chapter, we shall analyze several variables which influence the riskiness of the total enterprise. The most significant of these variables is the predictability of a firm's revenues. If management knows with a high degree of confidence the level of sales for a number of years in advance, the planning process is facilitated. Furthermore, knowledge of future revenues allows management to arrange disbursements without fear of possible financial embarrassment. Although a firm's revenue pattern may be highly volatile over time, if the nature of the volatility is known with certainty, the planning process can reduce the impact of fluctuations. On the other hand, if revenues are volatile *and unpredictable,* no amount of planning can abate the consequences of volatility.

A volatile sales pattern implies a highly uncertain flow of cash into the firm. This is disadvantageous for two reasons: (1) a risky pattern of cash inflows may reduce the ability of the firm to meet its cash payment obligations,[1] and (2) a risky pattern of cash inflows will generally result in an unstable pattern of net income. In the first instance, risky cash inflows increase the possibility of insolvency; in the second, they may reduce the value of the firm. We established in the previous chapter that there was an inverse relationship between the value of an asset and the uncertainty associated with the income stream generated by that asset. *Ceteris paribus,* a firm producing an erratic net income stream will be worth less than a firm generating a steady net income stream.

Although the most important determinant of the riskiness of an enterprise is the predictability of its revenues, there are other variables which may magnify the impact of a volatile cash inflow pattern. One

---

[1] A corollary disadvantage associated with a highly uncertain flow of cash into the firm is that penalties may be imposed when cash deficiencies develop. For example, a firm may be forced to borrow on unfavorable terms or, more significantly, to liquidate assets. The result may be quite costly to the firm even though it would be able to meet its payment obligations.

such variable is the degree of operating leverage characteristic of the firm. A firm possessing a high degree of operational leverage is characterized by high operating fixed costs. Operating fixed costs include such costs as depreciation, overhead, permanent salaries, etc. The presence of high operating fixed costs may increase the possibility of insolvency, since fixed costs do not vary with output, and will increase the volatility of earning. (Non-cash charges, such as depreciation, may influence the volatility of earnings, but they will not increase the probability of the firm's running short of cash.) Let us assume a firm faced with the following set of sales possibilities:

Sales	Probability
$150,000	.3
100,000	.4
50,000	.3

Let us further assume that the firm has a variable cost ratio (variable costs/sales) of .8 and operating fixed costs of $20,000. In the best of all possible worlds, where sales are $150,000, the firm's income statement is as follows:

Sales		$150,000
Variable Costs	$120,000	
Operating Fixed Costs	20,000	140,000
Earnings		$ 10,000

If sales are only $100,000, however, the firm just breaks even:

Sales		$100,000
Variable Costs	$ 80,000	
Operating Fixed Costs	20,000	100,000
Earnings		$ -0-

In the worst of all possible worlds, where sales = $50,000:

Sales		$50,000
Variable Costs	$40,000	
Operating Fixed Costs	20,000	60,000
		($10,000)

Thus, the presence of operating fixed costs in the third instance resulted in a net loss for the firm.

Operating leverage is frequently examined in terms of break-even analysis. The break-even point is defined as that level of sales where revenues exactly equal expenses. Fixed costs play a crucial role in break-even analysis, since a firm with no fixed costs would have a break-even sales point of zero.[2] The variable cost ratio is also significant, since a firm's contribution to fixed costs (and profit beyond the break-even point) depends on how much of an extra dollar of sales must go to meet variable costs. In the above example, the variable cost ratio is .8. Thus, every additional sales dollar provides a $.20 contribution to fixed costs and profit. In the case of a fixed cost level of $20,000, sales must be $100,000 to break even. Every dollar of sales less than $100,000 means a loss of $.20. On the other hand, every dollar of sales over $100,000 means a profit of $.20. These relationships are described in the following equation:

$$S_b = \frac{FC}{1 - \frac{VC}{S}} \tag{3.1}$$

Where: S_b is break-even sales
FC is the volume of operating fixed costs
VC is the variable cost per unit of sales
S is the selling price per unit

It is unnecessary to know the break-even volume in terms of units for most purposes. In the variable cost ratio, the unit expression drops out. Thus, if the selling price is $10 per unit and the variable cost per unit is $8, the VC ratio is .8. This ratio could also have been determined from an income statement by comparing total variable costs to total sales.

In order to explore the impact of operating leverage on the riskiness of the firm a bit further, let us consider another example. Assume that a firm has a high degree of operating leverage. Let VC/S = .2 and operating fixed costs equal $80,000. The break-even point for this corporation would be:

$$S_b = \frac{\$80,000}{1 - .2} = \$100,000$$

Thus, the break-even point for this firm is the same as for the company in the previous example. The firms are distinctly different, however, in that the latter firm is far more levered operationally. Let us assume several possible sales levels with the ensuing income statements for the latter corporation:

---

[2]Assuming that the variable cost ratio $\leqslant$ 1.

Sales	$120,000	$140,000	$160,000
VC	24,000	28,000	32,000
FC	80,000	80,000	80,000
Earnings	$ 16,000	$ 32,000	$ 48,000

Let us further assume that $140,000 is the expected sales figure but that there is a possibility that sales could be $120,000 or $160,000. If sales turned out to be $160,000, actual sales would have exceeded expected sales by $20,000, or 20/140 = 14.3 percent. Earnings, however, would have been $16,000 larger, or 16/32 = 50 percent! This percentage difference in Δ Earnings, given any Δ Sales is the essence of operating leverage. Leverage may also work unfavorably. Had sales been 14.3 percent *under* the estimate ($120,000 instead of $140,000), earnings would have been cut in half! These examples illustrate the effects of operating leverage given differences in actual sales from expected sales. Similar examples could illustrate changes in earnings given changes in actual sales over time. Of course, if these sales changes were known with certainty, the earnings stream could also be predicted with certainty.

Returning to our initial example where $\frac{VC}{S}$ = .8 and operating fixed costs = $20,000, let us assume a profit of $32,000 as in the previous case. The projected income statement would be:

Sales	$260,000
VC	208,000
FC	20,000
Earnings	$ 32,000

Now, let us vary sales positively and negatively by 14.3 percent as in the previous example (14.3% X $260,000 = $37,200):

Sales	$222,800	$260,000	$297,200
VC	178,240	208,000	237,760
FC	20,000	20,000	20,000
Earnings	$ 24,560	$ 32,000	$ 39,440

The change in earnings, given a ΔS = 14.3 percent, is $7,440, or 7,440/32,000 = 23.3 percent. Thus, the leverage factor is roughly half of that in the previous case.

SOLVED PROBLEMS

1. The Wexter Corporation sells its only product for $5. In order to earn

$50,000, the firm must sell 100,000 units. If variable costs are $4 per unit, what fixed costs must the Wexter Corporation meet?

SOLUTION

$$S_{b+p} = \frac{FC + \text{Profit}}{1 - \dfrac{VC}{S}}$$

$$500,000 = \frac{FC + 50,000}{1 - \dfrac{4}{5}} = \frac{FC + 50,000}{.2}$$

$$(.2)(500,000) = FC + 50,000$$

$$FC = \$50,000$$

2. For the Wexter Corporation above, if sales increased by 20 percent, by what percentage would profits increase?

SOLUTION

Sales	$500,000	$600,000
VC	400,000	480,000
FC	50,000	50,000
Earnings	$ 50,000	$ 70,000

Profits would increase by 40 percent.

UNSOLVED PROBLEMS

1. The Westminster Corporation has no fixed costs. Its variable cost ratio is .7.

   (a) What is the break-even point for Westminster?

   (b) What profit would Westminster generate with a sales volume of $100,000?

   (c) Given a sales level of $100,000, if sales increased by 20 percent by what percentage would profits increase?

2. The Symington Cement Company sells cement for $1 per bag. The firm earns a profit of $.20 per bag at a sales volume of $100,000. The firm has fixed costs of $20,000 per year.

   (a) What is the variable cost ratio for Symington?

(b) Calculate the break-even sales level for Symington.

(c) Assuming the price per bag of cement did not change, what effect would a change in the firm's sales volume have on its break-even point?

(d) If Symington raised its price per bag to $1.20, what effect would this have on the break-even point?

3. Given the original assumptions about the Symington Cement Company (number 2 above),

(a) What would happen to dollar profits if sales increased by 10 percent?

(b) What percentage increase in profits would result?

(c) Answer (a) and (b) assuming a 10 percent decrease in sales.

4. Analyze the impact of the following on the operating leverage characteristics of a firm:

(a) The firm foresees a less volatile pattern for the business cycle.

(b) The firm has just secured a large govenment contract which will account for over half of all future sales.

(c) The firm has become more capital intensive (using more capital inputs relative to labor inputs).

(d) The firm has recently initiated a guaranteed annual wage.

5. The Gemini Corporation sells its only product for $20. The firm has a variable cost ratio of .75.

(a) If Gemini sells $88,000 worth of this product per year, what are the firm's total variable costs? Variable cost per unit?

(b) Assume that Gemini has an average tax rate of 40 percent and earns an after tax profit of $2,400. What are the firm's fixed costs?

(c) Determine the break-even point for Gemini in dollars and in units.

(d) What impact would a decrease in variable costs of $1 per unit and an increase in fixed costs of $6,000 have on the firm's break-even point?

SECTION 3.2

The manner in which a firm is financed may affect the riskiness of the enterprise. In our examples of operating leverage, we made an implicit assumption that the firm was financed entirely by equity sources. However, a firm may also be financed by debt (or preferred stock). When a firm uses funds obtained at a fixed cost in the hope of increasing the return to common stockholders, the firm is said to be trading on its equity. The results of trading on the equity are similar to those indicated for operational leverage. The term financial leverage is often applied to the magnification of net income produced as earnings before interest and taxes (E.B.I.T.) vary. Strictly speaking, operating leverage refers to the magnification of E.B.I.T. as sales vary.

To illustrate the combined impacts of operating and financial leverage, consider a firm with the following sales possibilities:

Sales	Probability
$120,000	.3
100,000	.4
80,000	.3

If this firm is financed entirely by equity (no debt or preferred stock), with operating fixed costs of $20,000 and a variable cost ratio of .5, the resulting income statements would be:

Sales	$120,000	$100,000	$80,000
Variable Costs	60,000	50,000	40,000
Operating Fixed Costs	20,000	20,000	20,000
E.B.I.T.	$ 40,000	$ 30,000	$20,000
Interest Payments	-0-	-0-	-0-
E.B.T.	$ 40,000	$ 30,000	$20,000
Taxes (50%)	20,000	15,000	10,000
Net Income	$ 20,000	$ 15,000	$10,000

Given an expected sales level of $100,000, a 20 percent variation from that level would produce a $33\frac{1}{3}$ percent change in net income. If this firm is financed entirely by common stock, a possible simplified balance sheet for the firm might be:

Balance Sheet

Assets $100,000	Common Stock, 10,000 shares @ $10 $100,000

If there are 10,000 shares outstanding, possible earnings per share would be: $2.00, $1.50, or $1.00. Now let us suppose that the $100,000 asset investment of the firm is financed one-quarter by bonds (at a 6 percent cost) and three-quarters by equity. The new balance sheet would be:

Balance Sheet

Assets $100,000	Bonds @ 6% $ 25,000 Common Stock, 7500 shares @ $10 75,000 $100,000

The new income statements would be:

Sales	$120,000	$100,000	$ 80,000
Variable Costs	60,000	50,000	40,000
Operating Fixed Costs	20,000	20,000	20,000
E.B.I.T.	$ 40,000	$ 30,000	$ 20,000
Interest Payments	1,500	1,500	1,500
E.B. T.	$ 38,500	$ 28,500	$ 18,500
Taxes (50%)	19,250	14,250	9,250
Net Income	$ 19,250	$ 14,250	$ 9,250

Given an expected sales level of $100,000, a 20 percent variation from that level would produce a Δ E.B.I.T. of $33\frac{1}{3}$ percent, and a Δ net income of 35 percent (5000/14250). Although the leverage effect from debt use is not large, the impact on earnings per share is substantial:

Sales	EPS (no debt)*	EPS (with debt)**
$120,000	$2.00	$2.57
100,000	1.50	1.90
80,000	1.00	1.23

*Net income divided by 10,000 shares.
**Net income divided by 7,500 shares.

The upshot of using debt sources of financing in this case is to increase earnings per share at each level of sales considered. Nevertheless, the volatility of the firm's earnings has increased (increasing risk), and the firm's break-even point is higher. The break-even point when financing included only common stock was:

$$S_b = \frac{FC}{1 - VC/S} = \frac{\$20,000}{.5} = \$40,000$$

The effect of having to pay $1,500 in interest payments is to increase fixed costs by $1,500. Thus, when debt financing is included, the break-even point becomes:

$$S_b = \frac{FC + i}{1 - (VC/S)} = \frac{\$21,500}{.5} = \$43,000$$

The impact of an even larger dose of debt (say 50 percent) would produce the following income statements:

Sales	$120,000	$100,000	$ 80,000
Variable Costs	60,000	50,000	40,000
Operating Fixed Costs	20,000	20,000	20,000
E.B.I.T.	$ 40,000	$ 30,000	$ 20,000
Interest Payments	3,000	3,000	3,000
E.B.T.	$ 37,000	$ 27,000	$ 17,000
Taxes (50%)	18,500	13,500	8,500
Net Income	$ 18,500	$ 13,500	$ 8,500
# Shares	5,000	5,000	5,000
E.P.S.	$ 3.70	$ 2.70	$ 1.70

The favorable leverage (operating and financial) in the above example results from the fact that the firm is far away from its break-even point. If the firm were closer to break-even sales, the impact of leverage could be quite unfavorable. Let possible sales be $60,000; $50,000; and $40,000:

Sales	$60,000	$50,000	$40,000
Variable Costs	30,000	25,000	20,000
Operating Fixed Costs	20,000	20,000	20,000
E.B.I.T.	$10,000	$ 5,000	$ 0
Interest Payments	3,000	3,000	3,000
E.B.T.	$ 7,000	$ 2,000	($ 3,000)
Taxes (50%)	3,500	1,000	0
Net Income	$ 3,500	$ 1,000	($ 3,000)
# Shares	5,000	5,000	5,000
E.P.S.	$ .70	$ .20	($ .60)

A comparison of sales and EPS for levered (debt) and non-levered (no debt) capital structures indicates:

Sales	E.P.S. (no debt)	E.P.S. (25% debt)	E.P.S. (50% debt)
$60,000	$.50	$.57	$.70
50,000	.25	.23	.20
40,000	.00	(.20)	(.60)

Thus, if sales were $50,000, financial leverage would actually reduce E.P.S. If sales were $40,000, a break-even position (with no debt) would be forced into a position of moderate loss (25 percent debt). The picture portrayed here might be even more dismal, since percentage debt costs tend to rise as a firm borrows more, and as a firm operates with a smaller profit cushion away from its break-even point.

SOLVED PROBLEMS

1. The Hynak Corporation is considering the use of borrowed funds in order to increase its rate of return to stockholders. The firm presently has 100,000 shares outstanding @ $10, or a $1,000,000 capitalization. It has been suggested that the firm borrow $500,000 (at 6 percent) and retire 50,000 of its shares. If the firm expects an E.B.I.T. of $60,000 in the future, would this be a good idea? (Assume taxes of 50 percent).

SOLUTION

	No Debt	With Debt	
E.B.I.T.	$ 60,000	$60,000	
Interest	0	30,000	(6% of $500,000)
E.B.T.	$ 60,000	$30,000	
Taxes	30,000	15,000	
Net Income	$ 30,000	$15,000	
# Shares	100,000	50,000	
E.P.S.	$ .30	$ .30	

The firm should reject the idea. E.P.S. does not increase, although the firm has taken on debt and become riskier.

2. Suppose the Hynak Corporation above had fixed costs (from operations) of $10,000 and a variable cost ratio of .3. If sales could vary ±10 percent from $100,000, would you recommend the use of debt?

SOLUTION

Sales	$90,000	$100,000	$110,000
V.C.	27,000	30,000	33,000
F.C.	10,000	10,000	10,000
E.B.I.T.	$53,000	$ 60,000	$ 67,000

	No Debt	With Debt	No Debt	With Debt	No Debt	With Debt
Interest	$ 0	$ 30,000	$ 0	$ 30,000	$ 0	$ 30,000
E.B.T.	53,000	23,000	60,000	30,000	67,000	37,000
Taxes	26,500	11,500	30,000	15,000	33,500	18,500
N.I.	$ 26,500	$ 11,500	$ 30,000	$ 15,000	$ 33,500	$ 18,500
# Shares	100,000	50,000	100,000	50,000	100,000	50,000
E.P.S.	$ .265	$ .230	$ .300	$ .300	$ .335	$ .370

The answer would depend on the relative probabilities assigned to the sales figure. If $90,000 or $100,000 were stronger possibilities than $110,000, the recommendation should be against borrowing $500,000.

UNSOLVED PROBLEMS

1. Brown, Jones, and Smith have decided to go into business. It has been determined that they will need $1,000,000 for the venture. All details concerning the business have been decided except the plan of financing. Brown, who is conservative, believes that the entire $1,000,000 should be raised from the sale of common stock (100,000 shares @ $10). Smith, on the other hand, is a speculator of sorts. He believes that the firm should be financed with .75 debt and only .25 common stock (25,000 shares @ $10). He claims that $750,000 can be borrowed easily at 7 percent. Jones, a moderate, has suggested a compromise by which half of the funds would be obtained from the sale of stock (50,000 shares @ $10) and half borrowed. Jones has observed that this smaller loan could be secured at a 6 percent rate since the risk to the lender would be less.

(a) Assume that the firm earns $20,000 (E.B.I.T.) and has an average tax rate of 40 percent. What are the EPS under each financing plan?

(b) What is the rate of return on total assets (E.B.I.T./Total Assets) under each plan?

(c) What is the rate of return on equity (net income/equity) under each plan?

(d) Which alternative would you recommend?

2. Answer number 1 above assuming an E.B.I.T. of $100,000.

3. Answer number 1 above assuming an E.B.I.T. of $200,000.

4. Brown, Jones, and Smith (see above) are venturing into the oil and gas exploration business. They have estimated their operating fixed costs to be $100,000 per year.

(a) Determine the three possible sales levels (corresponding to the E.B.I.T. figures above) if their variable cost ratio is expected to be .1.

(b) What arguments might you raise against Smith's proposal even if E.B.I.T. were anticipated to be high?

(c) Under the circumstances would Jones' proposal for "moderation" necessarily be the optimum plan?

COMPREHENSIVE PROBLEM

The Amalgamated Fisheries Company is contemplating the purchase of a new boat. The boat will cost $100,000 and will have a life of about 5 years (no salvage). The firm plans to depreciate the vessel on a straight-line basis.

1. If the firm has a variable cost ratio of .75, how much added annual revenue must the boat generate for the firm to maintain the same annual dollar profit as before the purchase?

2. Assume that the vessel generates the volume of annual revenue determined in (a). Further, assume that cash charges associated with operating the vessel are equal to variable costs, that the firm pays 40 percent of its earnings in taxes, and that Amalgamated has an opportunity use of funds of 10 percent. In what way may it be said that this project does not "break-even" even though its acceptance does not reduce profits?

3. Would acceptance of this project change Amalgamated's rate of return on investment?

4 TAX FACTORS
AFFECTING FINANCIAL ADMINISTRATION [1]

SECTION 4.1   For the purposes of taxation, an organization may qualify as a corporation even if it is not incorporated. The basic rule is whether the organization possesses the characteristics of a corporation, which include such things as long or unlimited life, limited liability, ease of ownership transfer, etc. If an organization so qualifies, then it is subject to income taxation as a corporate entity.[2] Taxable income is generally equal to gross income less deductions allowed to corporations.

The gross income of a corporation is generally derived from sources such as the following: gross profit from sales; dividends, interest, rent, and royalties received; and net gains on the sale of capital assets. A contribution of capital is not income. Corporations may usually exclude from their taxable income 85 percent of the dividends which they receive on common or preferred stock of other corporations;[3] they may not exclude any of the interest received on debt that they hold. If the corporation sustains a net loss on capital asset transactions for the year, this may not be deducted from other income but may be carried forward for up to five years as a short-term capital loss and used to offset any capital gains that occur during that time. On the other hand, should the corporation end the year with net long-term capital gains (on assets held more than six months) that exceed net short-term capital losses, the net long-term capital gain in excess of net short-term losses may either be included in ordinary income or may be taxed separately at a 25 percent rate.[4] Finally, the corporation may also receive capital gains treatment on

---

[1] For further information, the student is directed to one of the loose-leaf tax services such as those published by Prentice-Hall.

[2] For an exception, see the provisions of Subchapter S of the Internal Revenue Code.

[3] Individuals may exclude from taxable income the first $100 of dividends that they receive each year.

[4] This corporate treatment is to be distinguished from that of individuals, who have the option of including one-half of net long-term gains in excess of short-term losses in ordinary income or taking the 25 percent tax separately on the total amount. Individuals may also deduct $1,000 of

certain depreciable property and real property that is used in trade or business (Sec. 1231 property) if it is held over six months and recognized gains exceed recognized losses.[5] Net losses for the year on Sec. 1231 property may be deducted as ordinary losses.

The corporation is allowed to deduct expenses from gross income to determine taxable income. There is no set list of these expenses, but the corporation is usually on strongest ground in claiming a deduction if the expense is an ordinary and necessary business expense and if it is reasonable in amount. Typical deductions claimed by corporations include the following: costs (such as wages, raw materials, rent, repairs, and depreciation) of goods sold, other selling expenses (such as salaries, advertising, bad debts, and certain taxes), interest, amortization and depletion, contributions to pension and profit-sharing plans, the inter-corporate dividend exclusion (described above), and net operating losses carried over from other years. Deduction for charitable contributions is only allowed up to 5 percent of the sum (taxable income and contributions made); any excess may be carried forward five years. Should a corporation sustain a net operating loss during the year (this determination is very complicated) it may, if it meets certain conditions (provided that there has been no substantial change in ownership or business), carry this loss back three years and, if it is still not exhausted, forward five years; the resulting recomputation of taxable income in other years should result in either a recovery of taxes paid in earlier years or a lower tax burden in subsequent years.

After subtracting the deductions from gross income to determine taxable income, we are ready to apply the tax rates. All corporate taxable income is subject to a normal tax rate which, at this writing, is 22 percent. In addition, taxable income above $25,000 is subject to a surtax, currently 26 percent. Thus, we could say that the first $25,000 of corporate income is taxed at 22 percent (as a sop to small business) and the rest at 48 percent.

SOLVED PROBLEMS

1. In 1969, Johnson Company had gross income of $170,000, which included dividends from taxable domestic industrial companies of $20,000. Its expenses included costs of goods sold, $50,000; salaries and selling expenses, $30,000; and depreciation, $20,000. Compute the taxes that the Johnson Company owes.

---

capital losses from ordinary income each year and carry the capital losses forward indefinitely.

[5] Subject to depreciation recapture discussed below.

SOLUTION

Gross Income		$170,000
Less: Itemized deductions		
Cost of goods sold	$50,000	
Salaries and SE	30,000	
Depreciation	20,000	100,000
Difference		70,000
Less: special deduction		
Dividends received (85% of 20,000)		17,000
Taxable Income		$ 53,000
Normal tax (22% X 53,000)		$ 11,660
Surtax [26% (53,000 – 25,000)]		7,280
Total tax		18,940

2. Suppose that part of the Johnson Company's gross income was composed as follows:

Short-term capital gain	$ 5,000	
Short-term capital loss	10,000	
Net short-term capital loss		$ 5,000
Long-term capital gain	20,000	
Long-term capital loss	5,000	
Net long-term capital gain		15,000
Excess of net long-term capital gain		
Over net short-term capital loss		10,000

Compute the tax for the Johnson Company using the alternative treatment of net long-term capital gains.

SOLUTION

Taxable income (from above)	$ 53,000
Less: Excess of net long-term capital gain	
over net short-term capital loss (incl. above)	10,000
Ordinary taxable income	43,000
Normal tax (22% of 43,000)	9,460
Surtax [26% (43,000 – 25,000)]	4,680
Subtotal	14,140
Add: 25% of excess of long term gains over	
short-term losses (25% X 10,000)	2,500
Total alternate tax	$ 16,640

The Johnson Company, therefore, should use the alternate method because it results in a lower tax.

UNSOLVED PROBLEM

The Mills Company had a 1969 gross income of $200,000, which included $25,000 in dividends, $5,000 in interest, $10,000 in net short-term capital gains, and $20,000 in net long-term capital gains. Expenses included $70,000 cost of goods sold, $30,000 salaries and selling expenses, $20,000 depreciation, and a $50,000 payment to the Mafia for protection. Determine the taxes for the Mills Company under both the regular and alternative methods.

SECTION
4.2
The student may now be wondering why all corporations do not subdivide themselves into many different corporations to take advantage of the preferential tax rate on the first $25,000 of income. The answer is that many still do, although the advantages may not be as great as they seem. The Internal Revenue Code defines an affiliated group of corporations as (very roughly) those which are owned 80 percent or more by a common parent. If such a controlled group elects to file separate returns for each corporation in order to gain multiple surtax exemptions, they are taxed an additional 6 percent on the first $25,000 of each corporation's income. In addition, by not filing a consolidated return, the group loses the opportunity to offset the losses or loss carry forwards of one member against the gains of another. Further, affiliated corporations filing consolidated returns are allowed a 100 percent exclusion of dividends paid from one member to another, while only 85 percent may be excluded if separate returns are filed. Thus, increasing numbers of corporations are electing to file consolidated returns.[6]

From a tax viewpoint, the proportionate share of income from a proprietorship or partnership is included in full on each taxpayer's return, while the corporation pays taxes on its own income and its stockholders pay taxes on the dividends which they receive. It should be noted, however, that Subchapter S of the Code allows corporations of ten or fewer shareholders, if they meet certain other conditions, to be taxed as partnerships. This arrangement has the disadvantage of making each owner pay taxes at his personal rate on his full share of corporate income, instead of on just the amount distributed as dividends. On the other hand, it does eliminate the double taxation of income and the possibility of an accumulated earnings tax (see below). Such an approach has several

---

[6]Taxation as a determinant of the optimal form of organization is analyzed by Edward E. Williams, "Selecting the Appropriate Form of Business Organization: A Decision Model," *Engineering Economist,* (July-August, 1969), pp. 221-227.

advantages over an unincorporated organization. Aside from the limited liability and ease of ownership transfer, it is possible to pass through to the stockholders the operating losses and capital gains of the corporation and, importantly, to deduct various fringe benefits (pension, medical, profit-sharing) which an unincorporated business often may not deduct.

Since the tax rates for individuals now go as high as 70 percent, another question that might arise concerns the use of a corporate shell by high-bracket taxpayers to avoid taxes. The IRS has several tools to prevent this. In the first place, if a company is owned and controlled by a few people ("closely held") and receives most of its income in the form of interest, dividends, royalties, etc., it may be classified as a personal holding company and be subject to a tax of 70 percent on the amount of personal holding company income not paid out in dividends to stockholders. Even if a company is involved in a trade or business, it may be subject to penalty if it fails to pay dividends in order to avoid a tax liability for its stockholders. If such a company accumulates earnings beyond the reasonable needs of the business for the purpose of avoiding taxes on its stockholders, it may be subject to a tax of 27.5 percent on the second $100,000 so accumulated (there is a $100,000 exemption) and 38.5 percent on the remainder. In practice, this law is usually applied only to closely held corporations which are, in effect, personal holding companies in disguise.

SECTION 4.3   Some of the implications of taxation for the operation of a business have already been suggested. For example, corporate management finds debt a more attractive source of funds than equity because interest is a deductible expense but dividends on common and preferred stock are not. In addition, since dividends are taxable to stockholders but earnings retained are not, there is a definite advantage to retaining earnings for new projects rather than paying dividends and attempting to issue new stock. Even if the retention results in a higher price for the stock, the stockholder is taxed at the favorable capital gains rates and only when he sells the stock.

A major goal in dealing with the Internal Revenue Service is to put all possible expenses into the current period, so that taxable income is lower; thus, taxes are reduced. One should not adopt the "Well, I am going to have to pay them sooner or later" attitude. In Chapter 1 we stressed that money has time value, so the longer the payment of taxes may be deferred, the longer one is able to use the money. If the rate of interest is 10 percent and it is possible to defer the payment of $1 in taxes for a year, the tax bill has been effectively cut to $.91.

A very simple application of this method can be shown using inventory valuation. Under the first-in-first-out (Fifo) method, it is assumed that the units which have been in inventory the longest are the first sold, whereas under last-in-first-out (Lifo) method it is assumed that the most recently acquired units are the first sold. Note the implications:

Year 1	*FIFO*		*LIFO*	
Sales, 10,000 units @ $100		1,000,000		1,000,000
Cost of sales:				
Opening inventory, 10,000 @ $50	500,000		500,000	
Purchases, 10,000 @ $70	700,000		700,000	
Total	1,200,000		1,200,000	
Less: closing inventory				
(Fifo) 10,000 @ $70	700,000	500,000		
(Lifo) 10,000 @ $50			500,000	700,000
Gross profit		500,000		300,000
Less: other expenses		100,000		100,000
Earnings before taxes		400,000		200,000
Less: taxes (50%)		200,000		100,000
N.I.		200,000		100,000
Year 2				
Sales, 10,000 @ $100		1,000,000		1,000,000
Opening inventory	700,000		500,000	
Purchases	-0-		-0-	
Less: closing inventory	-0-	700,000	-0-	500,000
Gross profit		300,000		500,000
Less: other		100,000		100,000
E.B.T.		200,000		400,000
Taxes (50%)		100,000		200,000
N.I.		$ 100,000		$ 200,000

Although total taxes were $300,000 in both cases, the company was able to defer $100,000 for a year by using Lifo during a period of rising inventory prices.

A somewhat more complicated problem, often dealt with in finance, concerns depreciation. Whenever there is a choice between treating a cost as an expense of the current period or adding it to the cost basis of an asset to be depreciated over time, the former alternative is usually better.[7] Several methods of computing depreciation may be available to the taxpayer:

---

[7]One exception would be the corporation with inadequate income to offset the increased expenses.

1. *Straight—line Method.* The cost or other basis of the property, less salvage value, is allocated evenly over the remaining useful life of the property. Salvage value less than 10 percent on personal property having a three-year life or more may be ignored.

2. *Declining Balance Method.*

   a. Double declining balance—depreciation at twice the straight line rate is applied to the remaining value of the asset, unadjusted for salvage; may switch to straight line at any time; and usually applies to new or rebuilt property with at least a three-year life.

   b. Limited declining balance—1½ times straight line rate; it is often allowed for used tangible property with a three-year life or more.

3. *Sum-of-the-years digits Method.* Cost or other basis, less salvage, is allocated according to a fraction whose numerator is the number of years' useful life remaining and whose denominator is the sum of the numbers representing the number of years of useful life of the property. It is generally applied to the same type of property as double declining balance.

4. *Unit of Production Method.* The difference between cost and salvage value is allocated by the fraction (units produced during period/estimated units to be produced over useful life).

To illustrate the more common methods, let us suppose that a machine costs $35,000, with a 5 year useful life and a $5,000 salvage value at the end of its life. Depreciation would be as follows:

Year	Straight-Line	DDB	S of YD
1	$ 6,000	$14,000	$10,000
2	6,000	8,400	8,000
3	6,000	5,040	6,000
4	6,000	2,560	4,000
5	6,000	-0-	2,000
Total	30,000	30,000	30,000

It should be apparent that the accelerated methods, by allocating a greater part of the expense to the earlier years (since the machine has already been paid for, this expense allocation is merely a bookkeeping exercise) reduce taxable income and thus reduce taxes in these years. Furthermore, some observers are taking the position that, as long as a firm continues to grow and buy new assets, it may never need to worry about the higher taxes in later years when the accelerated methods provide lower depreciation charges because there will be new assets to depreciate and shield income from taxation.

The existence of accelerated depreciation allowed some persons to buy a Section 1231 asset (see above), depreciate it rapidly in order to recognize little taxable income, and then sell at a profit, which was taxed at capital gains rates. To correct this abuse Congress passed Section 1245 of the Internal Revenue Code, which states that gains on the disposition of depreciable property (except livestock, buildings and their structural components) shall be taxed as ordinary income to the full extent of depreciation taken since 1961; only that part of the gain in excess of this depreciation may receive capital gains treatment under Section 1231. Section 1250 allows increasing capital gains treatment of depreciable real property with regard to holding period, up to the point that all gains on depreciable real property held over 10 years receive the favorable capital gains treatment under Section 1231.

SOLVED PROBLEMS

1. The True Company has an inventory of 10,000 units of item "X" at a cost of $10 at the beginning of 1968. It plans to buy 10,000 additional units @ $8 during the year and sell 10,000 units at $20 in 1968 and in 1969, after which time it will discontinue item "X". If the company pays taxes at a 50 percent rate and has a 10 percent after-tax opportunity cost of funds, which method of inventory valuation (Fifo or Lifo) is more advantageous and what is the present value of the advantage?

SOLUTION

1968	*FIFO*		*LIFO*	
Sales of "X"		$200,000		$200,000
Opening inventory				
(10,000 @ $10)	100,000		100,000	
Purchases (10,000 @ $8)	80,000		80,000	
Total	180,000		180,000	
Less: ending inventory				
Fifo (10,000 @ $8)	80,000	100,000		
Lifo (10,000 @ $10)			100,000	80,000
Gross income		100,000		120,000
1969				
Sales of "X"		200,000		200,000
Opening inventory	80,000		100,000	
Purchases	-0-		-0-	
Less: ending inventory	-0-	80,000	-0-	100,000
Gross income		120,000		100,000

In the case of declining inventory prices, Fifo has the advantage of deferring the recognition of income.

Year	Fifo	Lifo	Difference	Tax Difference	Present Value Factor @ 10%	Present Value
1968	$100,000	$120,000	−20,000	+10,000	1.00	$10,000
1969	120,000	100,000	20,000	−10,000	.91	− 9,100
				P.V. of Fifo advantage $		900

2. The Cairnes Company has purchased a new machine for $125,000 with additional freight-in costs of $10,000 and installation costs of $15,000. The machine will have a 5-year useful life, with no salvage value.

(a) Show the amounts of depreciation to be taken in each year under straight-line, double declining balance, and sum-of-the-years-digits methods.

(b) If the firm has a 10 percent after-tax cost of funds and is taxed at a 40 percent rate, what is the present value of each method of depreciation?

SOLUTION

(a) and (b)

STRAIGHT LINE

Year	Depreciation	Taxes Saved	Present Value Factor @ 10%	Present Value
1	30,000	12,000	.91	$10,920
2	30,000	12,000	.83	9,960
3	30,000	12,000	.75	9,000
4	30,000	12,000	.68	8,160
5	30,000	12,000	.62	7,440
				$45,480

DOUBLE DECLINING BALANCE

Year	Depreciation	Taxes Saved	Present Value Factor @ 10%	Present Value
1	60,000	24,000	.91	$21,840
2	36,000	14,400	.83	11,952
3	21,600	8,640	.75	6,480
4	16,200	6,480	.68	4,406
5	16,200	6,480	.62	4,018
				$48,696

SUM-OF-THE-YEARS-DIGITS

Year	Depreciation	Taxes Saved	Present Value Factor @ 10%	Present Value
1	50,000	20,000	.91	$18,200
2	40,000	16,000	.83	13,280
3	30,000	12,000	.75	9,000
4	20,000	8,000	.68	5,440
5	10,000	4,000	.62	2,480
				$48,400

UNSOLVED PROBLEMS

1. Rework Solved Problem number 1 above, under the assumption that the 10,000 units purchased in 1968 are bought at $12 each instead of $8.

2. Rework Solved Problem number 2 above, under the assumption that the machine has an eight-year life and $25,000 salvage value and that the company has a 60 percent tax rate.

COMPREHENSIVE CASE

The Trident Company has the following income and expenses for 1969 and all later years:

Sales	$100,000
Dividend income	5,000
Long-term capital gains	20,000
Short-term capital gains	10,000
Short-term capital losses	5,000
Cost of goods sold	50,000
Salaries and selling expense	10,000
Interest expense	5,000
Depreciation	10,000

1. If the Trident Company pays a normal tax of 22 percent and a surtax of 26 percent, what is its net income after taxes? (Remember to give the more favorable treatment to capital gains.)

2. If Trident has 10,000 common shares outstanding, what is its net income per share for 1969 and all future years?

3. Trident pays dividends per share that are equal to net income per share. Trident shareholders pay taxes on these dividends at a 30 percent rate. If

Trident shareholders evaluate their stock by discounting dividend receipts, net of taxes, at 10 percent, what should be the price of Trident stock?

In 1970, Trident is offered the opportunity to buy a new machine, which would change the future income and expenses of the company. This machine would have a total cost of $100,000, a 10-year useful life with no salvage, would add $50,000 a year to sales and $20,000 to cost of goods sold. A similar machine could be purchased at the end of each ten-year period for the same price and with the same impact on costs and sales. For the sake of simplicity, assume that the machine would be depreciated on a straight-line basis.

4. How would the purchase of this machine affect the corporation's net income after taxes in 1970 and subsequent years?

5. If the machine were financed by the sale of stock at the current market price, how many new shares would be issued?

6. If the machine were bought and the new shares issued, what would Trident's earnings per share be in 1970 and subsequent years?

7. If stockholders continued to discount net dividend receipts at 10 percent, what would the purchase of the machine do to the price of the stock?

5 CAPITAL PROJECT ANALYSIS

Optimal corporate investment policy is essential to the firm's survival and growth. In turn, the growth and prosperity of the nation are dependent upon the existence of the large volume of savings that the corporate sector efficiently channels into the most desirable investment opportunities. Thus, the investment decision not only affects the well-being of the shareholders, but also the well-being of the nation.

Unit I (the investment subsystem) is designed to reduce the number of variables to be considered in the investment decision. We assume that funds are available to the firm in unlimited quantities at a known and constant cost. (This assumption is relaxed in the Unit II, in which the cost of funds is considered.) In addition, we give little attention to the means by which the firm generates investment proposals, although a good financial information system is crucial to the growth of a firm. Finally, we assume that some estimate of the cash flows associated with a project may be made. As a rule, cost estimates based upon existing capital goods prices, wage rates, and engineering standards may be fairly accurate, but sales estimates, especially for products not presently on the market, can be fraught with error. Financial analysis cannot provide solutions which are more accurate than the data upon which they are based. Indeed, if accurate cash flow estimates could be made, the entire capital budgeting problem would become rather trivial. The last section of this chapter presents some approaches to the problems of risk and uncertainty, but first we must consider the standard techniques of project analysis. Five major techniques are discussed below.

1. Payback Analysis. The *payback period* for a project indicates the number of years required to recover the initial investment. In the case of a project having a cash outflow in the present followed by uniform cash inflows in subsequent years, the payback period may be determined by simple division (Initial Investment/Annual Cash Inflow). In the case of varying flows, the analyst must subtract each cash inflow from the investment until the entire sum is returned (interpolating in the last year if

54

necessary). Payback analysis gives no consideration to the timing of flows (and, hence, the time value of money) within the payback period nor to any cash flows that might accrue after the payback period. At best then, payback is a break-even, not a profitability, measurement. Its proponents would claim that payback analysis does give management a limited view of the risk exposure and liquidity of various projects, but, as we shall see later, there are far superior measures of these considerations.

2.   *Average Rate of Return Analysis. Average* (or, *accounting*) *rate of return* is defined as (Average Net Income/Average Investment).[1] The application of this measure to past company data by external analysts (discussed in Chap. 8) may be justified on the basis that it is the best they can do with the materials at hand, but its usefulness to company analysts as a planning tool is open to serious question.[2] One of the few rationalizations for its use may be that the results of projects undertaken will eventually appear in the firm's financial statements and be subjected to this measurement by external analysts. If the result does not appear to be favorable, the company's securities' prices may be penalized. The company must thus be certain that projects undertaken will "look good on the books." To the extent that project lives are long and annual flows are relatively constant, the method provides reasonably accurate solutions (so, for that matter, does the payback). When these conditions do not hold, however, problems arise. The numerator of the above fraction (average net income) ignores the time value of money by the use of a simple average and ignores the actual timing of inflows by employing net income rather than cash flow data. The denominator (average investment) also ignores the actual timing of capital returns and the time value of money (for essentially the same reasons given above). In addition, both terms of the fraction require the assumption of some depreciation scheme.

SOLVED PROBLEM

The Miller Company must choose between two mutually exclusive investment proposals. Each would cost $6,000, have a 4-year life, be depreciated on a straight-line basis, and generate earnings before depreciation as shown below. Ignoring taxes, use the payback and average rate of return methods to determine the better alternative.

	PROJECT	
Year	A	B
1	$1,000	$2,000
2	2,000	2,000
3	3,000	2,000
4	2,000	2,000

[1] Some analysts also use the rate of return on initial investment (Average Income/Initial Investment).

[2] See Edward E. Williams, "A Note on Accounting Practice, Investor Rationality, and Capital Resource Allocation," *Financial Analysts Journal,* July-August, 1969. pp.37-40.

SOLUTION

(a) Payback: A = 3 years, B = 3 years

(b) Average rate of return (depreciation = $1,500 per year):

$$A = \frac{\dfrac{-\$500 + \$500 + \$1{,}500 + \$500}{4}}{\dfrac{\$6{,}000}{2}} = \frac{\$500}{\$3{,}000} = 16\frac{2}{3}\%$$

$$B = \frac{\dfrac{\$500 + \$500 + \$500 + \$500}{4}}{\dfrac{\$6{,}000}{2}} = \frac{\$500}{\$3{,}000} = 16\frac{2}{3}\%$$

Thus, the two projects would appear to be equally desirable by either method. Yet Project B is clearly superior because it returns $1,000 two years earlier than Project A. This difference is not detected by either method, however, because each ignores the time value of money.

3. Net Present Value Method. The net present value method simply requires the analyst to discount at the cost of funds to the firm all cash inflows and outflows associated with a project and take the algebraic sum of the result (which is the net present value of the project). The theory states that a project having a positive net present value (N.P.V.) will increase the value of the firm by that amount and should be undertaken. Projects having a zero net present value probably should not be undertaken, and those with a negative net present value definitely should not be undertaken.[3] The major criticisms of the net present value approach are that it is difficult to use in a capital rationing environment (considered in Chap. 18) and that its accuracy is directly dependent upon the accuracy of the cost of capital estimate. The latter criticism is especially telling, for only in textbooks may a firm's cost of capital be exactly determined or, in many cases, closely approximated.

4. Internal Rate of Return Method. The internal rate of return (I.R.R.) is that rate of discount which will cause the present value of all cash inflows to equal the present value of all cash outflows or, viewed another way, that rate of discount which will cause the net present value of the project to be zero. It is expressed by formula:

$$\sum_{t=0}^{n}\left(\frac{F_t}{(1+r)^t}\right) = 0 \tag{5.1}$$

Where: F_t = Net cash flow in period t

r = Internal rate of return

---

[3] We define at this point and will consider in a later chapter the allied concept, the *profitability index* (P. I.), which is the present value of cash inflows, discounted at cost of capital/present value of cash outflows, similarly discounted. It should follow that the acceptance criterion in this case is P. I. > 1.

The theory states that any project which has an internal rate of return greater than the cost of capital will earn more than it will cost and should thus be accepted. This method is consistent with the net present value insofar that any project which has a positive net present value when discounted at the cost of capital will also have an internal rate of return which is greater than the cost of capital. If a project's cash flows are constant, its internal rate of return may be found easily by use of the tables in Appendix D; if the flows vary, however, a trial-and-error approach using the tables in Appendix C must be employed (the mechanics of these computations were discussed in Chap. 1).

Discount tables are constructed under the assumption that compounding takes place at the rate of discount. For example we may say that, at a 10 percent rate of discount, $1 to be received in a year is worth 91¢ today only if the 91¢ may indeed be invested at 10 percent; if the best yield available is only 5 percent, the statement and the entire process are obviously inaccurate. This technical problem does not arise with the net present value method because the discount rate employed is the cost of capital; it is assumed that the firm will invest at or above the cost of capital or else distribute the funds to those who supplied them and who have alternate opportunities at this rate of return. With the internal rate of return approach, however, it is assumed that funds returned early in the life of the project can be reinvested at whatever the internal rate of return happens to be. At very high internal rates of return, this assumption is obviously not valid and causes the method to give inaccurate answers. As long as the internal rate of return method is used strictly for acceptance or rejection decisions based on the cost of capital, the above problem does not impair its effectiveness.

The internal rate of return method has also been criticised because it may provide multiple solutions. This problem may occur if the net cash flow in different years alternates between inflows and outflows. The difficulty is rooted in the compounding assumption discussed above. An experienced executive, however, when presented with a proposal which has internal rates of return of −200 percent, 25 percent, and 4,000 percent, can usually select the appropriate figure.

5. Terminal Value Method. The terminal value approach avoids some of the problems encountered above. Under this method, each cash inflow would be compounded at whatever rate it was felt could be earned on the funds (often the cost of capital but sometimes the Treasury bill rate) for the remaining life of the project. The project would then be analyzed as though it involved a single cash outflow (in the current period) and a single cash inflow at the end of its life or some other time (this inflow would include compounded interest on funds returned earlier). The future inflow could be discounted at the cost of capital to obtain a net present value or equated with the outflow to obtain an internal rate of return.[4] The advantages of this modification are that the compounding assumption is avoided and projects of different lives may be placed on a comparable basis (considered in the next section).

Finally, it is possible to array all investment projects available to the firm at a given point in time in descending order of their internal rates of return. Such a schedule, which would actually resemble a step function but may be approximated by a smooth line, is called a marginal efficiency

---

[4]Unless a compounding rate other than the cost of capital were used, this method would give the same net present value as the regular approach.

THE MARGINAL EFFICIENCY OF CAPITAL
SCHEDULE FOR THE FIRM

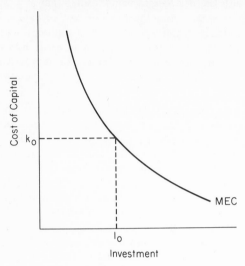

Figure 5.1

of capital (*MEC*) schedule and is depicted in Fig. 5.1. A major function of the first unit of this book is the determination of the *MEC* curve for a given firm. The second unit attempts to determine the cost of funds to the firm (sketched as k_0 in Fig. 5.1). The intersection of these curves determines the optimal level of investment (I_0) for the firm. This level may in turn be compared to the amount of funds available to determine whether additional financing will be required or whether larger dividends should be paid or reductions of indebtedness effected. It should follow that increases in the general level of interest rates or the riskiness of the firm will cause the k_0 curve to shift upward; improvements in technology, the opening of new markets, improved business conditions, etc., will cause the *MEC* curve to shift outward; and all of these changes will affect the optimal level of investment for the firm.

SOLVED PROBLEMS

1. The Bela Corporation, which has a 50 percent tax rate and a 10 percent after-tax cost of capital, is evaluating a project which will cost $100,000 and will also require an increase in the level of inventories and receivables of $50,000 over its life.[5] The project will generate additional sales of $100,000

---

[5] Any increases in working capital required by a project should be included in the cash flow analysis, as funds are required to be employed at a zero return.

and cash expenses of $30,000 in each year of its 5-year life. It will be depreciated on a straight-line basis. What are the net present value and internal rate of return for the project?

SOLUTION

	Years 1-5	
Sales	100,000	100,000
Cash Expenses	30,000	30,000
Depreciation	20,000	
Earnings before Taxes	50,000	
Taxes	25,000	25,000
Net Income	$ 25,000	
Cash Flow		$ 45,000

(a)   NET PRESENT VALUE

Year	Cash Flow	Present Value Factor @ 10%	Present Value
0	−150,000	1.000	−150,000
1-4	+ 45,000	3.170	+142,650
5	+ 95,000	.621	+ 58,995
			NPV = + 51,645

(b)   INTERNAL RATE OF RETURN

Year	Cash Flow	Present Value @ 20%	Present Value	Present Value @ 24%	Present Value
0	−150,000	1.000	−150,000	1.000	−150,000
1-4	+ 45,000	2.589	+116,505	2.404	+108,180
5	+ 95,000	0.402	+ 38,190	0.341	+ 32,390
			4,695		− 9,425

I.R.R. ≃ 21%

2. Assume that Bela (see number 1 above) could only invest funds generated by the project at the cost of capital. What is the internal rate of return of the project based upon a terminal value?

SOLUTION

Year	Years to End of Project	Cash Flow	Compound Factor @ 10% End of Project	Terminal Value
1	4	+45,000	1.464	65,880
2	3	+45,000	1.331	59,895
3	2	+45,000	1.210	54,450
4	1	+45,000	1.100	49,500
5	0	+95,000	1.000	95,000
				$324,725

$$\$150,000 = \frac{\$324,725}{(1+r)^5}$$

$$\frac{1}{(1+r)^5} = \frac{\$150,000}{\$324,725}$$

$$F_5 = .46$$

Where: F_5 is the factor for year 5 from Appendix C
          I.R.R. = 17%

UNSOLVED PROBLEMS

1. The Birdsey Corporation is choosing between two mutually exclusive investment alternatives. The proposals have an expected 5-year life and will be depreciated on a straight-line basis. The net cash flows generated by each proposal are given below.

	PROJECT	
Year	A	B
0	-$5,000	-$5,000
1	1,000	2,000
2	1,000	1,000
3	2,000	1,000
4	2,000	3,000
5	2,000	2,000

(a) Calculate the net income generated by each project.

(b) Determine the payback and average rate of return for each project.

2. The Dexter Company has a 50 percent tax rate and a 12 percent after-tax cost of capital. Dexter is considering the purchase of a machine which would cost $50,000, have freight-in and setup expenses of $10,000, and $10,000 salvage value. The machine would have a 5-year useful life and be depreciated on a straight-line basis. Purchase of the machine would result in increased sales of $70,000 and cash expenses of $30,000 during each of the 5 years. Furthermore, an additional investment of $25,000 in current assets will be required during the life of the project. Determine the payback period, average rate of return, net present value, and internal rate of return for this project.

3. Suppose that Dexter (see number 2 above) discovers that it can reinvest funds generated from the project at an after-tax return of only 6 percent. Using a terminal value approach, determine the new net present value and internal rate of return.

4. The Benjamin Corporation is considering the addition of a new product line. It is expected that the new line will increase sales by $500,000 forever. Cash expenses associated with the project will be about $100,000 per year. The firm pays 50% of its E.B.T. in federal income taxes. It should cost the firm about $1,000,000 to establish the new line.

(a) Determine the payback for the project. Compute the reciprocal of the payback (i.e., 1/payback).

(b) Calculate the average rate of return and the internal rate of return for the project.

(c) Using the internal rate of return you computed above, capitalize the net income stream generated by the project.

(d) Compute the present value of the inflows. (Let $n = 30$ as a limit.)

(e) Do you find any of the above conclusions surprising? Why do the answers to (c) and (d) differ?

SECTION 5.2

Frequently, projects may be undertaken only if certain other projects are undertaken; the former are called contingent proposals. We introduced one type of contingent proposal in Section 5.1 when we discussed the working capital requirements of various projects: A given machine could be purchased only if the firm were willing to employ funds at a zero return. These funds were invested in increased inventories and receivables that were required to support the expanded level of operations. As implied in the last section, the appropriate approach to contingent proposals is to treat all of the projects which must be undertaken together as a package and combine their flows for purposes of analysis.

In other cases several projects may be proposed, only one of which may be accepted; these are called mutually exclusive proposals. The first problem, of course, is to determine whether any of the proposals should be undertaken. If two or more mutually exclusive projects exceed the minimum acceptance criteria, then differential cash flow analysis is employed to select the best of the projects. Under this method, the acceptable proposal involving the smallest outlay is adopted as a standard and compared to the proposal involving the second-smallest outlay. The object is to determine whether the additional outlay required by the second proposal is justified by the present value of the additional inflows. The superior proposal becomes the standard for comparison with the next larger proposal. The proposal which is the standard after all of the mutually exclusive projects have been evaluated is the one which should be adopted.

The differential flow analysis is the general method for evaluating mutually-exclusive projects. If complete revenue and expense data are given and certain restrictive assumptions are made, the net present value method will provide the same answer. The internal rate of return method (see solved problem) will not necessarily provide the correct answer. Differential cash flow analysis may only be employed upon those mutually exclusive proposals which have first passed the general test of investment acceptance. Financial managers should resist the temptation to immediately analyze the mutually exclusive projects in order to find the best one before they have determined whether any of the alternatives are worthy of acceptance. The replacement decision usually involves mutually exclusive proposals; a machine has worn out and attention focuses upon which new machine should be bought to replace it. Overlooked in the confusion is the fact that not replacing the machine is a valid alternative and should be given at least passing consideration. In a very real sense, every day that the manager opens the plant gates and turns on the lights, he is making an investment decision (the implications of this philosophy are covered in greater detail in Unit III of this book).

Mutually exclusive projects may often have different lives. This condition tends to complicate comparison. In the world of simplified theory, where asset prices do not change and all reinvestment takes place at the cost of capital, the foregoing presents no difficulty. In a more realistic world, however, it may be that the shorter-lived assets can only be replaced at a higher cost, thus giving an advantage to the longer-lived proposal. This may not be reflected in the computation. On the other hand, in a world where future projections are subject to risk and uncertainty, the shorter-lived asset does involve less risk exposure to the firm. It may also be the case that the funds released by the shorter-lived project can be employed at very lucrative rates of return in the future, or only at very low rates. For all of these reasons, the analyst must be very careful in comparing projects of unequal lives; it is quite possible that either a terminal value approach (using the longest life of any proposal as the terminal point) or one of the methods of dealing with risk discussed in the next section will be required.

SOLVED PROBLEM

The Popov Corporation has an after-tax cost of capital of 10 percent. The corporation is currently evaluating the three proposals whose after-tax cash flows are listed below. Only one may be accepted. Which should it be?

Year	A	B	C
0	-21,000	-27,540	-34,430
1-5	+ 7,000	+ 9,000	+11,000
I.R.R.	20%	19%	18%

SOLUTION

Year	B vs. A	Present Value @ 10%	Present Value
0	-6,540	1.00	-6,540
1-5	+2,000	3.79	+7,580
			+$ 1,040

Year	C vs. B	Present Value @ 10%	Present Value
0	-6,890	1.00	-6,890
1-5	+2,000	3.79	+7,580
			+$ 690

Project C should be undertaken. Under the restrictive assumptions above, the net present value approach could also have been used.

	A	B	C
Years 1-5	+7,000	+9,000	+11,000
Present Value @ 10%	3.79	3.79	3.79
	26,530	35,110	41,690
Less Year 0	-21,000	-27,540	-34,430
Net Present Value	$+ 5,530	$+ 6,570	$+ 7,260

It should be noted that Project C is the optimal choice even though it has the lowest I.R.R. Project C has the largest net present value and the lowest I.R.R. because of the differences in required initial outlay. Project C requires a $34,430 outlay, while Project A requires only a $21,000 outlay. Under the assumption that the firm may obtain all funds desired at the cost of capital (an assumption which we relax later in this book), the selection criterion is maximization of net present value. Under capital rationing conditions, Project C would not necessarily be the optimal choice (see Chap. 18).

UNSOLVED PROBLEMS

1. The Reskov Company must replace one of its machines; the alternative to replacement would be too expensive to consider seriously. One possible replacement, the Moscow machine, would cost $18,000 and involve cash

operating expenses of $7,500 per year. The other alternative, the Prague machine, would cost $12,000 and have cash operating expenses of $9,000 per year. Either machine would be depreciated on a straight-line basis over a 12-year life. The Reskov Company has a 50 percent tax rate and a 14 percent after-tax cost of capital. Which machine should it buy?

2. Suppose the Reskov Corporation (see number 1 above) had an after-tax cost of capital of 12 percent. What would your answer be now? Given the contingency of this answer on an accurate estimate of the firm's cost of capital, can you make any suggestions as to how the analysis might be improved?

SECTION 5.3

Thus far in our discussion, projects have been treated as though their returns were certain. The flows have been analyzed with regard to a measure of central tendency but any possible dispersion about the central point has been ignored. We must now take cognizance of the fact that all projects are subject to risk and different projects are subject to different degrees of risk.[6] Although concepts of risk and uncertainty have existed for a long time, their application to specific problems remains rather crude and subject to qualification.

1. Risk-Adjusted Discount Rate Method. Perhaps the simplest approach is the risk-adjusted discount rate. In this approach, the required rate of return is allowed to vary directly with the perceived risk of the project. Thus, the firm may require new products and other projects of high perceived risk to exhibit say, a 15 percent return, while replacement of equipment for existing products and other low-to-normal risk projects must only earn a 10 percent rate of return. Some firms have several of these risk-return classifications.

It should be apparent that both the selection of a required return for a given risk class of projects and the assignment of individual projects to a class are highly subjective and variable among decision makers and over a period of time. In addition, the mathematics of the method are such that the penalty imposed upon risky projects (by the use of a discount rate greater than the cost of capital) will systematically increase as flows become more distantly removed from the present (assuming that a constant or increasing discount rate is used). Although it may be true that more distant flows are subject to greater risk, this matter should be judged on its own merits in each case. For these reasons, the risk-adjusted rates method is generally felt to be a rather crude method of dealing with risk.

2. The Certainty-Equivalent Method. The certainty-equivalent approach may be depicted as follows:

---

[6] Another important consideration, the relationship between the risk of a given project and the overall risk of the firm, is discussed in Unit III.

$$PV = \sum_{t=0}^{n} \frac{\alpha_t F_t}{(1+i)^t} \tag{5.2}$$

Where: F_t = Cash flow in period t

i = Pure (risk-free) rate of interest

α_t = Certainty-equivalent coefficient $(0 \leqslant \alpha \leqslant 1)$ which varies inversely with perceived risk of flow in period t

As indicated by the formula, this approach reduces the flow in each year to account for risk but, since the resulting number $(\alpha_t F_t)$ is viewed as a certain flow, discounting takes place at the pure rate of interest.[7]

Problems arise in the determination of the coefficient (α_t). For example, if a particular project were expected to return $400,000 in year 4 ($F_4$ = $400,000), management would be asked what absolutely certain flow in year 4 it views as being equally desirable to the risky $400,000. If the answer were $200,000, then the coefficient (α_4) would be 0.5 and $200,000 would be discounted at the pure rate of interest to represent year 4 of the project. A cynic would be tempted to suggest that α_4 is 0.5 solely because F_4 = $400,000 and it is desired that $\alpha_4 F_4$ = $200,000. At the very least, it should be noted that not one of the variables $(\alpha_t, F_t, i$ or even $n)$ in the above formula can be known with certainty.

3. Probability Distribution Method. Probability distributions may be brought into the analysis in several ways, of which we will only consider the simplest at this point. (More involved formulations are presented in Unit III.) For our purposes, we will assume that future outcomes are normally distributed and that an expected outcome and standard deviation (see Chap. 2) may be determined for each future period. These are bold assumptions in view of data limitations (in any discipline, the data are invariably less accurate than the tools used to manipulate them), but they are necessary for our explication.

Given the above assumptions, suppose that we have determined that the cash flows for a project in year 3 are normally distributed about an expected value (μ) of $400,000, with a standard deviation (σ) of $100,000. By definition, the actual cash flow in year 3 (F_3) may be expected to be equal to or greater than $400,000 for 50 percent of the time and equal to or less than $400,000 the other 50 percent of the time. If the decision maker were completely indifferent to risk (risk neutral), then $400,000 would be the appropriate value to use for year 3 in the analysis of the project.

It is quite likely, however, that the possibility of outcomes below $400,000 would outweigh the equal likelihood of outcomes above $400,000. In this case the decision maker is risk-averse; the degree of risk-averseness is a function of *how much more* the low outcomes weigh on his mind. Suppose that he would be willing to tolerate the actual outcome falling below the estimate only about 16 percent of the time. The tables in Appendix E indicate that about 84 percent of the outcomes would exceed a

---

[7]See Alexander A. Robichek and Stewart C. Myers, *Optimal Financing Decisions* (Englewood Cliffs, N.J.: Prentice-Hall, Inc. 1965), pp. 79-93.

value of $\mu-1\sigma$ (or \$300,000 in our case). If the decision maker were less risk-averse and he were willing to tolerate a shortfall 31 percent of the time, then $\mu-0.5\sigma$ (or \$350,000) could be used as the appropriate flow for year 3. Were he more risk-averse, however, and would tolerate only a 2 percent shortfall, then $\mu-2\sigma$ (or \$200,000) would be the appropriate value.

In addition to the disadvantages of this method that have already been indicated, it must be determined whose risk preferences will be used and how they will be measured. An advantage of the method, however, is that once the rule for adjusting flows ($\mu-1\sigma$, $\mu-0.5\sigma$, or whatever) has been determined, it may be applied to all projects without alteration of the discount rate. The riskier projects, which by definition will have a larger σ relative to μ, will be automatically penalized.

4. Cardinal Utility Method. Up to this point, we have carefully avoided being too specific as to whose risk preferences shall be used in these models. Some argue that the stockholders' preferences are the important ones and, since no meaningful measurement or aggregation may be made, the entire matter should be dropped. Others take the position that the risk preferences of management are controlling but, since great variation will exist in the management of the same company and no meaningful aggregation can be made, the matter should be dropped. Many authorities contend that utility cannot be measured, interpersonal comparisons cannot be made, and that the whole matter should be dropped. Granting these limitations, we will now present a short cardinal utility approach.

Mr. Grimes is the sole owner and manager of a firm. We will attempt to chart the utility of positive sums of money to Mr. Grimes on an arbitrary scale by which \$0 = 0 units of utility (utiles) and \$1,000,000 = 1,000 utiles, We ask Mr. Grimes how much he would pay for a 50 percent chance of receiving \$1,000,000 and a 50 percent chance of nothing; the response is \$250,000. Thus,

$$\$250,000 = 0.5 \, (1,000 \text{ utiles}) + 0.5 \, (0 \text{ utiles})$$
$$\$250,000 = 500 \text{ utiles}$$

We next ask how much he would pay for a 50-50 chance of \$250,000 or nothing; the response is \$62,500. Thus,

$$\$62,500 = .5 \, (500 \text{ utiles}) + .5 \, (0 \text{ utiles})$$
$$\$62,500 = 250 \text{ utiles}$$

The value of positive sums of money to Mr. Grimes may be stated as follows:[8]

$$\text{If } M > 0, \text{ then } U = \sqrt{M}$$

Where: M = Sums of money
U = Utility

---

[8]The relationship between M and U is highly variable among individuals and over time. Thus $U = \sqrt{M}$ is unique to Grimes at this point in time.

Mr. Grimes is now faced with an investment proposal which has the following possible cash inflows in year 2.

Flow	Probability	Expected Value
$1,000,000	0.3	$300,000
490,000	0.4	196,000
360,000	0.3	108,000
	1.0	$604,000

As indicated above, the expected value of the flow that would normally be used in the analysis is $604,000. It is possible, however, to make use of Mr. Grimes' utility function ($U = \sqrt{M}$):

M	$U = \sqrt{M}$ (utiles)	Probability	Expected Value (utiles)
$1,000,000	1,000	0.3	300
490,000	700	0.4	280
360,000	600	0.3	180
			760

Since $M = U^2$, then $(760)^2 = \$577,600$ is the value to be discounted for year 2.

UNSOLVED PROBLEMS

1. Reconsider the Bela Corporation (solved problems numbers 1 and 2, Sec. 5.1). Suppose that the risk of the project required that a 15 percent discount rate be used. How would this affect the answers given?

2. Suppose instead that the flows given for Bela (solved problem number 1, Sec. 5.1) were subject to the following certainty equivalents and the pure rate of interest were 4 percent. How would this affect the answer?

t	α_t
0	1.0
1	0.9
2	0.8
3	0.7
4	0.6
5	0.5

3. Suppose instead that the flows given for Bela were only expected values (μ) and that the coefficient of variation (σ/μ) in each case (except the initial outlay) were 0.25. If management wished to have the actual outcome in each

year fall short of the estimate no more than 16 percent of the time, how would the answers to solved problem number 1 of Sec. 5.1 be affected?

4. Reconsider the project that was offered to Mr. Grimes (see Sec. 5.3). Suppose that the data for the other years in the life of the project were as follows:

Initial Outlay = $950,000

Outcomes	Probability
Year 1	
10,000	0.3
40,000	0.3
90,000	0.4
	1.0
Year 3	
250,000	0.3
640,000	0.5
810,000	0.2
	1.0

If Mr. Grimes requires a 10 percent return, compute the net present value of this project using (a) a normal expected value and then (b) an expected value modified for utility considerations.

COMPREHENSIVE CASE

The Grant Company has a tax rate of 50 percent. It currently owns an N.C. lathe which it bought 4 years ago at a cost of $50,000. The lathe has a 20-year, straight-line depreciation schedule and could be sold for its current book value. The N.C. lathe is expected to contribute $10,000 per year to earnings before depreciation and taxes.

The Grant Company could trade its N.C. lathe plus $30,000 for a new S.C. lathe, which would have a 20-year life and be depreciated on a straight-line basis. The S.C. lathe would be expected to contribute $15,000 per year in earnings before depreciation and taxes.

1. What are the payback period, average rate of return and internal rate of return on both the old and the new lathes? On these bases alone, should the new lathe be purchased?

2. If the Grant Company has an after-tax cost of capital of 10 percent, what

is the net present value of keeping the old lathe? Of purchasing the new lathe?

3. Reconsider the decision under the assumption that the risk of the S.C. lathe requires that a 16 percent discount rate be used.

4. Reconsider the above under the assumption that the N.C. contribution has a certainty-equivalent coefficient of 0.9, while the S.C. coefficient is 0.7. Assume that the pure rate of interest is 4 percent.

6 MANAGEMENT OF ACCOUNTS RECEIVABLE AND INVENTORIES *

SECTION 6.1   In the previous chapter, investment in current assets was subsumed as a part of the capital budgeting decision. It is clear that an investment in receivables, inventories, and cash is a necessary complement to the purchase of most fixed plant and equipment. However, the more specific decision as to the optimum investment level of current and fixed assets (i.e., the optimum asset mix) requires additional analysis. In this chapter, optimal receivables and inventory policy are considered.

A firm grants credit terms for one reason: to maintain or increase sales. In many industries, terms are set on an industry-wide basis and the firm can do little to change them. For other industries, terms are flexible and the individual firm can attempt to vary its credit policies in order to attract additional business. Since most firms operate in monopolistically competitive environments (neither perfect competition nor monopoly), the firm must consider the possibility of retaliation from competitors if they seek a larger market share by offering more favorable credit terms. Also, elasticity of demand for the product involved must be considered. If demand is relatively inelastic, more favorable credit terms (which amount to a price cut) may not increase revenues.

The accounts receivable turnover gives a general measure of the productivity of the receivables investment:

$$R_t = \frac{S_c}{A/R} \qquad (6.1)$$

Where: R_t is the receivables turnover
S_c is the volume of credit sales
A/R is average accounts receivable

---

*Portions of this chapter have been adapted from James C. Van Horne, *Financial Management and Policy*. Chaps. 17-18.

As a measure of the liquidity of the receivables investment, the turnover may be converted into the average age of receivables. This is accomplished by dividing the turnover into the number of days in the year (assumed to be 360 for sake of convenience).[1]

The object of the firm is to attain an optimum R_t. If R_t is too high, the firm may be sacrificing profitability for liquidity. If R_t is too low, the firm may be endangering its liquidity position, hence increasing the possibility of technical insolvency.[2] An excessively high R_t may mean that the credit terms offered by the firm are overly stringent. Such stringency may deprive the firm of sales (both in the present and in the future). A high R_t may also imply the intensive use of expensive credit checking and collection procedures. A low R_t may increase the risk of account delinquency. Furthermore, the larger the investment in receivables (resulting from a low turnover), the greater the cost of financing the investment. In each case, a decision to grant credit or make credit terms more liberal must balance the benefits (higher sales, etc.) against the costs (risk of nonpayment, cost of capital, etc.).

SOLVED PROBLEMS

1. The W. P. Smith Company hopes to increase annual sales by granting more liberal credit terms. Current credit sales are $120,000. The average collection period is 30 days. It is expected that sales will rise by the following amounts if the collection period is lengthened:

Increase in Collection Period (days)	Δ Sales
15	$ 8,000
30	12,000
45	14,000
60	15,000

The firm sells its only product for $1.00. Variables costs per unit (before taxes) are $0.50. Average unit costs at the current sales level are $0.60. If the firm requires a 20 percent pre-tax return on investment, which credit policy should be adopted? (Assume a 360-day year.)

---

[1] These measures are discussed more specifically in Chap. 8 as financial ratios pertinent to the liquidity and profitability of the firm.

[2] A firm is technically insolvent when it does not have the cash to meet its bills. It is possible for a firm to have a positive net worth and still be technically insolvent.

SOLUTION

(a)

Sales Level			Average Cost
120,000 Units			
$FC =$	12,000		
$VC = 120,000 \times .50 =$	60,000		
	72,000/120,000 =		$.60
128,000 Units			
$FC =$	12,000		
$VC = 128,000 \times .50 =$	64,000		
	76,000/128,000 =		$.59
132,000 Units			
$FC =$	12,000		
$VC = 132,000 \times .50 =$	66,000		
	78,000/132,000 =		$.59
134,000 Units			
$FC =$	12,000		
$VC = 134,000 \times .50 =$	67,000		
	79,000/134,000 =		$.59
135,000 Units			
$FC =$	12,000		
$VC = 135,000 \times .50 =$	67,500		
	79,500/135,000 =		$.59

(b)

Policy	Turnover	Sales	A/R	Invest-ment*	ΔI	Req. Ret. on ΔI**
Present	12x	$120,000	$10,000	$ 6,000	–	–
Δ 15 days	8x	128,000	16,000	9,440	$3,440	$688
Δ 30 days	6x	132,000	22,000	12,980	3,540	708
Δ 45 days	4.8x	134,000	27,917	16,471	3,491	698
Δ 60 days	4x	135,000	33,750	19,913	3,442	688

(c)

	15 Days	30 Days	45 Days	60 Days
Incremental Sales	8,000	4,000	2,000	1,000
Marg. Profit on Incre. Sales	4,000	2,000	1,000	500
Req. Return on Incre. A/R	688	708	698	688
Incremental Worth	3,312	1,292	302	(188)

*(A/R) × (Average Cost/Selling Price)
**(ΔI) × (Pre-tax Req. Return)

Increasing terms by fifteen days produces $4,000 of added profit, although the required marginal return on investment is only $688. Similarly, a thirty day increase results in $2,000 of added profit (beyond the $4,000 produced by Δ 15 days). The marginal required return on Δ 30 is $708. Thus, $\Delta P > \Delta C$. At $\Delta 45$, $\Delta P = \$1,000$ and $\Delta C = \$698$. Increasing terms by 45 days appears to be optimal. At Δ60, only $500 is added to profit, although required marginal return is $688.

2. The Smith Company (above) will also experience the following bad debt losses if terms are increased:

Δ Collection Period	Percent Default (on Total Sales)
15 days	0.5
30 days	1.0
45 days	1.5
60 days	2.0

The firm currently has no bad debt loss. How do these additional data influence your decision?

SOLUTION

		INCREASE IN COLLECTION PERIOD*		
	Present Policy	15 Days	30 Days	45 Days
Total Sales	120,000	128,000	132,000	134,000
Bad Debt Loss	0	640	1,320	2,010
Marginal B D Loss	0	640	680	690
Cost of Marginal B D Loss**	0	378	401	407
Incremental Sales	0	8,000	4,000	2,000
Marg. Profit on Incre. Sales	0	4,000	2,000	1,000
Less: Cost of Marginal B D Loss	0	378	401	407
		3,622	1,599	593
Less: Req. Return on Incre. A/R	0	688	708	698
Incremental Worth	0	2,934	891	(105)

*Δ 60 days was eliminated from consideration since the marginal return was under the required amount. Allowing for bad-debt expense will lower the marginal return. Thus, Δ 60 would fare even worse than before.

**(Bad-debt Loss) × (Average Cost Per Unit/Selling Price Per Unit).

The added information eliminates Δ 45 days, since the large bad debt experience with those terms actually reduces profits. At Δ 30 days, marginal profit after bad debts is $1,599 while the required marginal return is only $708; this therefore is the optimal solution.

UNSOLVED PROBLEMS

1. The Quando Corporation believes that its credit policy is too generous. The firm currently grants terms net 60 and experiences a 4 percent bad debt loss. It is expected that a reduction in credit terms will reduce the bad debt experience. It should also reduce the sales volume.

Decrease in Collection Period (Days)	Default on Total Sales (Percent)	Δ Sales
15	3	$-10,000
30	2	-25,000
45	1	-50,000

Current credit sales are $200,000. The firm sells its only product for $2. Variable costs are $1 per unit. Average unit costs at current sales levels are $1.50. Any reduction in investment may be used to reduce financing. Financing costs are 10 percent. Which collection period is optimal?

2. The Zander Company is considering extending credit to the Cenco Corporation. The credit manager of Zander has discovered that Cenco has a Dun and Bradstreet rating of A+1½, and that the firm generally maintains a bank balance in the low six figures. Contact with other suppliers indicates that Cenco does not take advantage of trade discounts and is generally slow in paying when terms are less than net 90. Zander terms are net 30. Financial statements from Cenco are included below. Should the credit be granted?

CENCO CORPORATION
BALANCE SHEET

(thousands)

	19-0	19-1	19-2	19-3
Assets				
Cash	$ 152	$ 156	$ 160	$ 170
Receivables	100	85	90	100
Inventories	140	180	140	120
Fixed Assets (net)	1,000	960	940	920
Total Assets	$1,392	$1,381	$1,330	$1,310
Liabilities				
Payables	346	382	412	490
Term Loan (9%)	200	150	100	0
Common Stock	500	500	500	500
Retained Earnings	346	349	318	320
Total Liab. & Equities	$1,392	$1,381	$1,330	$1,310

CENCO CORPORATION
INCOME STATEMENT

(thousands)

	19-0	19-1	19-2	19-3
Sales (all credit)	$2,680	$2,670	$2,660	$2,620
Cost of Goods Sold	2,412	2,483	2,474	2,489
Gross Profit	$ 268	$ 187	$ 186	$ 131
Operating Expenses	250	175	217	129
Net Profit before Taxes	$ 18	$ 12	$ (31)	$ 2
Income Taxes	9	6	0	0
Net Income	$ 9	$ 6	$ (31)	$ 2
Dividends	4	3	0	0
To Retained Earnings	$ 5	$ 3	$ (31)	$ 2

3. The Sampson Company wishes to purchase about $200,000 worth of raw materials from the Enterprise Corporation. It has been determined by the Enterprise credit manager that Sampson will be able to meet its obligations to Enterprise according to the following distribution:

Payment on time (net 30)	.10
Payment one month late	.40
Payment two months late	.20
Payment four months late	.20
No payment (bad debt)	.10

Enterprise has a variable cost ratio of 0.80 and an opportunity cost of funds of 1 percent per month. It is estimated that Sampson would buy $100,000 worth of materials if credit were not extended. Should Enterprise extend credit to Sampson?

SECTION 6.2

The optimal inventory policy of the firm may be approached in a fashion similar to that of receivables policy. A firm incurs certain costs when inventories are maintained, and certain other costs develop due to a lack of inventories. It is the balancing of these costs that determines the optimal level of inventory.

Inventories are stocked for two reasons. Raw materials inventories and work-in-process inventories are necessary to smooth the production process. The maintenance of sufficient raw materials prevents the firm from operating on a hand-to-mouth basis, which is typically expensive. Finished goods inventories are stocked so that the current demands of customers may be met. In many industries, present (and future) sales depend upon carrying an adequate volume of products to satisfy customer requests immediately.

A general measure of the productivity of the inventory investment is the inventory turnover, which is given by:

$$I_t = \frac{CGS}{\bar{I}} \tag{6.2}$$

Where: I_t is the inventory turnover
CGS is the cost of goods sold
$\bar{I}$ is the average level of inventories

As a liquidity measure, I_t may be converted into the number of days' sales represented by inventories by dividing it into the number of days in the year.[3]

---

[3] See Chap. 8.

The firm seeks to attain an optimal I_t. If I_t is too low, the firm is incurring excessive inventory carrying costs. Such costs include: (1) storage, (2) servicing, taxes, insurance, etc., (3) risk of loss associated with inventory price changes, spoilage, obsolescence, etc., and (4) the financing costs associated with the investment in inventories. If I_t is too high, the firm is carrying too little inventory. Costs associated with carrying insufficient inventories include: (1) loss of present and future sales as a result of not being able to fill orders promptly, (2) downtiming and perhaps shutdown costs, and (3) the loss of discounts that might accrue from quantity purchases.

An important partial optimization model in inventory management is the efficient order quantity (EOQ). This model indicates the appropriate volume of raw materials or goods to purchase, the efficient frequency of purchase, and the optimal volume of inventories to carry.[4] To illustrate, we shall use the following set of symbols:

Q = order quantity (number of items purchased per order)
R = inventory requirements per period
S = purchasing cost per order
C = carrying costs per unit of inventory held per period
T = total cost of inventory investment per period
R/Q = number of orders per period

As the order quantity of inventory (Q) becomes larger, discounts, reduced handling expenses, etc. lower the purchasing costs per order (S). Thus, the total ordering cost per period ($R/Q \times S$) becomes smaller as Q becomes greater. This is depicted by function RS/Q in Fig. 6.1. Conversely, as the order quantity increases in size, the carrying costs increase. Total carrying costs are given by multiplying the carrying cost per unit (C) times the average inventory held ($Q/2$). Function ($CQ/2$) illustrates this relationship. Total inventory costs (T) are total ordering costs plus total carrying costs, or

$$T = \frac{CQ}{2} + \frac{RS}{Q} \tag{6.3}$$

The optimal order quantity (Q^*) is found where total costs are minimized. The minimum point on function T may be found by differentiating T

---

[4]If S is defined to include set up costs, this model will also determine the efficient production run.

with respect to Q. When this derivative is set equal to zero, T is mini-mized.[5] Thus,

$$\frac{dT}{dQ} = \frac{C}{2} - \frac{RS}{Q^2}$$

$$0 = \frac{C}{2} - \frac{RS}{Q^2}$$

$$\frac{RS}{Q^2} = \frac{C}{2}$$

$$Q^2 = \frac{2RS}{C}$$

$$Q^* = \sqrt{\frac{2RS}{C}} \qquad (6.4)$$

INVENTORY COSTS AND EFFICIENT ORDER QUANTITY

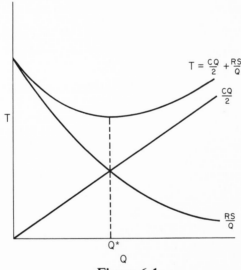

Figure 6.1

SOLVED PROBLEMS

1. The Airline Company uses 1,800,000 widgets per year in the production

---

[5] A function is either at a peak, trough, or horizontal to the abscissa when its first derivation is zero. A trough (low point) prevails if the second derivative is positive.

of zops. The demand for zops varies widely during the year, but constant production levels are maintained by building and then reducing finished goods inventories. Each time widgets are ordered it costs the firm $200. Carrying costs are $8 per unit.

(a) What is the *EOQ* for widgets?

SOLUTION

$$Q^* = \sqrt{\frac{(2)(1,800,000)(200)}{8}}$$

$$= \sqrt{90,000,000} = 9,487 \text{ units}$$

(b) What are the total inventory carrying costs for widgets?

SOLUTION

$$T = \frac{CQ}{2} + \frac{RS}{Q}$$

$$T = \frac{(8)(9487)}{2} + \frac{(1,800,000)(200)}{9,487}$$

$$T = \$37,948 + \$37,948 = \$75,896$$

(c) How many times per year would inventory be ordered?

SOLUTION

$$\frac{1,800,000}{9,487} = 190 \text{ times, or about every 2 days.}$$

UNSOLVED PROBLEM

The Cinco Seis Centavo corporation produces pesos, a very useful product in several countries. The only raw material required to produce pesos is the centavo, which C.S.C. mines from the ground. In order to produce one peso, one hundred centavos are required. The demand for pesos is steady throughout the year and about 5,000 are sold per month. The costs of mining centavos are fixed. Each time the mine is used, it costs the firm $10,000. Carrying costs are $0.01 per centavo per month.

1. How often should the mine be used?
2. What is the total inventory cost for the period?

SECTION 6.3

The *EOQ* formula is a partial optimizing formula since several variables are omitted from consideration. Most importantly, the benefits and costs associated with safety stocks are ignored. Clearly, the carrying costs of maintaining inventories increase as the size of the safety stock grows. On the other hand, stockouts of raw materials may result in downtiming or perhaps even a shutdown. Stockouts of finished goods may reduce the volume of present (and future) sales.

SOLVED PROBLEMS

1. The Aesop Company has an *EOQ* of 5,000 units and orders every twenty days. The firm knows with certainty that five days are required to order and receive shipments. Orders are placed on the fifteenth day for receipt on the twentieth. Stockouts have been estimated to cost the firm $2.00 per unit. Average carrying costs over the optimal twenty-day period are $0.50 per unit. Inventory usage has been estimated to be steady and is given by the following probability distribution for each twenty-day cycle:

Usage	Probability
4,500	.02
4,600	.04
4,700	.07
4,800	.12
4,900	.18
5,000	.20
5,100	.16
5,200	.10
5,300	.08
5,400	.02
5,500	.01

(a) Determine the optimal safety stock to be carried by the firm in addition to normal inventories.

SOLUTION

It should be noted initially that no stockout occurs if usage is 5,000 units or less. Stockouts, consequently, may be 100 (if usage is 5,100), 200 (if usage is 5,200), 300, 400, or 500. The costs of a stockout are given on the next page:

Safety Stock	Stockout	Cost @ $2	Probability	Expected Cost	Total
500	0	0	0	0	0
400	100	$ 200	.01	$ 2	$ 2
300	200	400	.01	4	
	100	200	.02	4	8
200	300	600	.01	6	
	200	400	.02	8	
	100	200	.08	16	30
100	400	800	.01	8	
	300	600	.02	12	
	200	400	.08	32	
	100	200	.10	20	72
0	500	1,000	.01	10	
	400	800	.02	16	
	300	600	.08	48	
	200	400	.10	40	
	100	200	.16	32	146

Total costs, including carrying costs (@ $0.50), are:

Safety Stock	Stockout	Carrying Cost	Total Cost
0	$146	$ 0	$146
100	72	50	122
200	30	100	130
300	8	150	158
400	2	200	202
500	0	250	250

The optimal (lowest total cost) safety stock is 100 units.

    (b)   What is the probability of being out of stock?

SOLUTION

$$(P_u = 5,500) + (P_u = 5,400) + (P_u = 5,300) + (P_u = 5,200)$$
$$(.01) + (.02) + (.08) + (.10) = (.21)$$

2. Aesop (above) has found that the lead time required for procurement is not known with certainty but is subject to the following probability distribution:

Lead Time (Days)	Probability
4	0.2
5	0.6
6	0.2

It is believed that the distribution for usage and lead time are independent. Daily usage does not vary appreciably, and 5,000 units were on hand at the beginning of the most recent twenty-day cycle.[6] Given these added data, what is the new optimal safety stock?

USAGE		LEAD TIME		Joint	Expected
Units	Probability	Days	Probability	Probability	Stockout
4,500	.02	4	.2	.004	NONE
		5	.6	.012	NONE
		6	.2	.004	NONE
4,600	.04	4	.2	.008	NONE
		5	.6	.024	NONE
		6	.2	.008	NONE
4,700	.07	4	.2	.014	NONE
		5	.6	.042	NONE
		6	.2	.014	NONE
4,800	.12	4	.2	.024	NONE
		5	.6	.072	NONE
		6	.2	.024	40
4,900	.18	4	.2	.036	NONE
		5	.6	.108	NONE
		6	.2	.036	145
5,000	.20	4	.2	.040	NONE
		5	.6	.120	NONE
		6	.2	.040	250
5,100	.16	4	.2	.032	NONE
		5	.6	.096	100
		6	.2	.032	355
5,200	.10	4	.2	.020	NONE
		5	.6	.060	200
		6	.2	.020	460
5,300	.08	4	.2	.016	35
		5	.6	.048	300
		6	.2	.016	565
5,400	.02	4	.2	.004	130
		5	.6	.012	400
		6	.2	.004	670
5,500	.01	4	.2	.002	225
		5	.6	.006	500
		6	.2	.002	775

SOLUTION

In determining the expected stockout, it is observed that no stockout occurs until the usage equals 4,800 and the lead time exceeds the expected five days. At usage 4,800, lead time six days, usage is 240 per day (4,800 ÷ 20). If the order arrives one day late, the stockout would be 40 (i.e., 5,000 − 4,800 = 200; 240 − 200 = 40). At usage 4,900, lead time six days, usage is 245 a day

---

[6]This and the previous problem are somewhat changed if safety stock buildups (and reductions) from previous cycles are considered.

(4,900 ÷ 20). If the order arrives on day late, the stockout would be 145 (5,000 – 4,900 = 100; 245 – 100 = 145). At usage 5,000, lead time six days, usage is 250 per day (5,000 ÷ 20). With the order arriving one day late, the stockout would be 250. At usage 5,100, usage stockout is 100. But if the shipment arrives one day early (lead time four days), with daily usage at 255 (i.e., 5,100 ÷ 20), only 4,845 units (255 × 19) of the 5,000 in inventory will have been used, thus no actual stockout occurs. If the order arrives on time, the stockout is simply 100. If the shipment arrives one day late (lead time six days), the stockout is 100 plus the usage for the late day, or 355 units. This process is repeated until all possible stockout values are determined.

Given the above calculations, the following safety stock-stockout cost table may be prepared:

Safety Stock	Incremental Stockout	Incremental Stockout Cost @ $2	Cumulative Probability	Incremental Expected Stockout Cost	Total Cost Cumulative
775	–	$ –	–	$ –	$ –
670	105	210	.002	0.42	0.42
565	105	210	.006	1.26	1.68
500	65	130	.022	2.86	4.54
460	40	80	.028	2.24	6.78
400	60	120	.048	5.76	12.54
355	45	90	.060	5.40	17.94
300	55	110	.092	10.12	28.06
250	50	100	.140	14.00	42.06
225	25	50	.180	9.00	51.06
200	25	50	.182	9.10	60.16
145	55	110	.242	26.62	86.78
130	15	30	.278	8.34	95.12
100	30	60	.282	16.92	112.04
40	60	120	.378	45.36	157.40
35	5	10	.402	4.02	161.42
0	35	70	.418	29.26	190.68

Combining the stockout cost with the carrying cost, we obtain:

Safety Stock	Stockout Cost	Carrying Cost ($.50)	Total Cost
0	$190.68	$ –	$190.68
35	161.42	17.50	178.92
40	157.40	20.00	177.40
100	112.04	50.00	162.04
130	95.12	65.00	160.12
145	86.78	72.50	159.28
200	60.16	100.00	160.16
225	51.06	112.50	163.56
250	42.06	125.00	167.06
300	28.06	150.00	178.06

Safety Stock	Stockout Cost	Carrying Cost ($.50)	Total Cost
355	17.94	177.50	195.44
400	12.54	200.00	212.54
460	6.78	230.00	236.78
500	4.54	250.00	254.54
565	1.68	282.50	284.18
670	0.42	335.00	335.42
775	–	387.50	387.50

Total costs are minimized at safety stock = 145.

UNSOLVED PROBLEM

The Bellaire Corporation uses 36,000 units of raw material X per year. The firm uses this raw material continuously and evenly during the year. Each time orders are placed for X, it costs the firm $13.89. Carrying costs are $1 per unit. Stockouts have been estimated to cost the firm $3 per unit. Inventory usage is described by the following probability distribution:

Usage (EOQ)	Probability
0.8	.08
0.9	.12
1.0	.30
1.1	.25
1.2	.20
1.3	.05

Lead time required for procurement has been found to be about 4 days, but either 3- or 5-day waits are possible. It is estimated that P (3 days) = 0.1, P (4 days) = 0.8, and P (5 days) = 0.1 and that this distribution has no relationship to the usage distribution. Daily usage of inventories is about constant, and the firm orders 4 days before inventories are expected to be depleted. It is assumed that the volume EOQ is on hand at the beginning of each order period.

1. Determine the EOQ for Bellaire.
2. What is the optimal safety stock for Bellaire?
3. What is the probability of being out of stock?

7 CASH

BUDGETING AND MANAGEMENT

SECTION
7.1
Once the firm has determined its receivables and inventory requirements and has estimated capital expenditures, a cash budget may be prepared. For the financial manager, the cash budget is a very significant short-run planning tool. Whereas the capital budget determines the long-run course of the firm, the cash budget makes it possible for the firm to be prepared for daily, weekly, and monthly events.

The cash budget summarizes the cash cycle for the firm. The major source of cash to the firm is sales. Cash sales produce cash immediately, whereas credit sales produce cash upon collection. Other sources of cash to the firm include revenues secured from auxiliary activities, funds secured from financing (sale of stock, bonds, etc.), and the conversion of assets (sale of plant and equipment, for example).

Cash disbursements arise from the revenue producing activities of the firm. The purchase of materials, labor, etc. is an important use of cash for most manufacturing firms, whereas wholesaling and retailing concerns employ funds to purchase inventories. Salaries, other general and administrative expenses, interest payments, and taxes constitute major uses of cash. Disbursements are also made when dividends are paid, when loans are repaid (or treasury stock purchased), and when plant and equipment are purchased.

The preparation of the cash budget allows the financial manager to be aware of any potential cash deficiencies or surpluses which may develop. Prospective cash deficiencies may be met through short-term borrowing, speeding the cash cycle, postponement of payment on purchases, or the liquidation of assets. Cash surpluses may be invested in short-term marketable securities.

Since most items in the cash budget are projections subject to variation (risk), it is reasonable for the firm to maintain sufficient cash reserves to mitigate the possibility of an overestimation of revenues (i.e., cash inflows lower than expected) or an underestimation of expenses (i.e., cash outflows greater than anticipated). The greater the uncertainty associated with items in the budget, the larger should be the volume of cash reserves. Firms also maintain cash balances to meet bank compensating balance requirements (see Chap. 9) and to satisfy constraints imposed by other creditors.

SOLVED PROBLEM

The financial manager for the Wolfe Company is preparing a cash budget for the second quarter (April, May, and June). The firm is required by its bank to maintain a compensating balance of $10,000 on deposit. It is felt that the risk associated with the cash projections necessitates the maintenance of another $10,000 in cash. Sums in excess of the reserve may be held in marketable securities which yield 0.5 percent per month (ignore transactions costs and other costs associated with purchasing and selling securities). Cash deficiencies (i.e., a balance under $20,000) may be borrowed from the bank at a cost of 1 percent per month. As of March 30, the firm had $25,000 in cash balances. Prepare the cash budget for the second quarter, given the following data:

Actual Sales					
January	$100,000	April	$140,000	July	$130,000
February	120,000	May	150,000	August	110,000
March	140,000	June	150,000	September	100,000

Accounts Receivable: about 40 percent of sales are for cash. The remaining 60 percent are on credit with terms net 30. Virtually all accounts are collected within the month after sale.

Other Revenues: the firm collects $40,000 per month in interest and rents.

Cost of Goods Manufactured: 80 percent of sales. 90 percent of the cost is paid during the month of incurrence. The balance is paid during the following month.

Selling and Administrative Expenses: $20,000 per month plus 20 percent of sales, which is paid during the month of incurrence.

Interest Payments: A semiannual payment on a $1,000,000 outstanding bond issue (@ 7 percent) is made on June 30. Five percent of the outstanding amount of the issue is purchased to satisfy sinking fund requirements. The current price of the bonds is 80.

Taxes: An income tax payment of $10,000 is made on April 14.

Dividends: None are distributed by the firm.

Capital Expenditures: a $50,000 lathe will be purchased for cash in April.

SOLUTION

SCHEDULE #1: CASH RECEIPTS

	March	*April*	*May*	*June*
Cash Sales (a)	$ 56,000	$ 56,000	$ 60,000	$ 60,000
Credit Sales Collections (b)	84,000	84,000 84,000	90,000 84,000	90,000 90,000
Other Revenues (c)		40,000	40,000	40,000
Total (a + b + c)		$180,000	$184,000	$190,000

SCHEDULE #2: CASH DISBURSEMENTS

	March	*April*	*May*	*June*
Cost of Goods Manufactured	$112,000	$112,000	$120,000	$120,000
Cash Payment (a)	100,800	100,800	108,000	108,000
Balance payment (b)		11,200	11,200	12,000
S & A payment (c)		48,000	50,000	50,000
Interest payment (d)				35,000
Sinking fund (e)				40,000
Taxes (f)		10,000		
Capital Outlay (g)		50,000		
Total (a. . .g)		$220,000	$169,200	$245,000

SCHEDULE #3: CASH BALANCE

	April	*May*	*June*
Total Receipts	$180,000	$184,000	$190,000
Total Disbursements	220,000	169,200	245,000
Net Cash Flow	(40,000)	14,800	(55,000)
Beginning Balance	25,000	20,000	20,000
Monthly Borrowing	35,000	(14,450)	55,206
Interest Charges (on previous month's loan)	(0)	(350)	(206)
Cash Balance	$ 20,000	$ 20,000	$ 20,000
Cumulative Borrowing	$ 35,000	$ 20,550	$ 75,756

UNSOLVED PROBLEM

1.   Prepare a cash budget for the Apex Appliance Company for the first three months of 1970.

(a)

Sales (actual)		Sales (Forecasted)	
October	$250,000	January	$100,000
November	350,000	February	150,000
December	500,000	March	200,000
		April	225,000

(b) Sales are 1/4 cash and 3/4 credit. Sixty percent of credit sales are collected one month after sale. Forty percent are collected two months after sale.

(c) The store has a cash gross margin of 40 percent. Purchases are made one month before anticipated sales and are paid for two months after purchase.

(d) Wages and salaries are $10,000 per month plus 1 percent of all sales over $300,000, paid as incurred.

(e) Rent is $2,500 per month plus 1 percent of all sales over $300,000 paid as incurred.

(f) One-tenth of cash gross margin for each quarter is paid at the end of the quarter in income tax prepayments.

(g) Dividends of $10,000 are paid at the end of each quarter.

(h) The firm has a cash balance of $25,000 on December 31, 1969, and prefers to maintain a balance of at least $25,000. Balances larger than $25,000 are automatically invested by the firm's bank in negotiable certificates of deposit which yield .4 percent per month. Cash deficiences are met by selling certificates of deposit or from short-term bank borrowing, which costs the firm .6 percent per month.

2. As a financial consultant, what advice would you give the Wolfe Company? (See solved problem above.)

SECTION 7.2

When the cash balances of the firm becomes larger than is desired in the short-run, it often pays the firm to invest surplus balances in marketable securities, negotiable certificates of deposit, or some other highly liquid money market instrument. In the investment of temporarily idle funds, liquidity (i.e., convertibility into cash with little or no market price risk and small transactions costs) is of prime importance, since the firm's short-term securities investment serves as a cash reserve which may be needed on short notice.

Approaches to the appropriate division of funds between cash and marketable securities have been formulated in several cash inventory models.[1] Assume that the Wizard Corporation will pay out a stream of T

---

[1] Cf. William J. Baumol, "The Transactions Demand for Cash: An Inventory Theoretic Approach," *Quarterly Journal of Economics,* November, 1952, pp. 545-56.

dollars evenly over a period of time. Cash is obtained either through selling securities or borrowing. The opportunity investment rate and the borrowing rate are assumed, for simplicity, to be equal. Let i be this rate. Cash is obtained immediately in lots of C at a fixed cost b. The cost of being liquid, i.e., holding cash, is given by $iC/2$ which is the opportunity investment (borrowing) rate times the average balance held in cash. The cost of not being liquid, i.e., having to sell securities, is bT/C which is the fixed cost of selling securities times the number of occasions securities are sold. The total cost associated with cash maintenance is given by:

$$\frac{bT}{C} + \frac{iC}{2} \tag{7.1}$$

Differentiating and setting the result equal to zero, we obtain:[2]

$$C^* = \sqrt{\frac{2bT}{i}} \tag{7.2}$$

C^* is the optimal cash withdrawal lot.

UNSOLVED PROBLEMS

1.   The Henderson Company will spend about $640,000 in cash next year. The firm can earn 5 percent from purchasing marketable securities, but incurs a cost of $10 each time securities are sold.

   (a) What is the optimal cash withdrawal lot?

   (b) What is the average cash balance held by the firm?

   (c) What is the total cost associated with cash maintenance?

   (d) Determine the optimal cash velocity for the firm.

2.   Assume Henderson (above) began the year with $640,000 in cash.

   (a) How much would be invested in marketable securities initially?

   (b) How much would be invested in securities after 6 months?

3.   What assumptions are made implicitly and explicitly in the model described in Eq. (7.2)? Which assumption is especially unrealistic?

---

[2]The mathematics of this process are the same as for the materials inventory decision. See Chap. 6.

SECTION   The model encompassed in Eq. (7.2) is a nice theoretical
7.3   formulation, but more variables must be encompassed
for it to be useful as a managerial decision-making tool. In particular, the
assumption that there are no cash inflows must be relaxed, Furthermore,
it is unrealistic to assume that b is entirely a fixed cost and is not a
function of the volume of securities sold.

A working model may be constructed which employs these relaxed
assumptions. This model focuses on the optimum volume of securities to
hold, given a desired minimum cash balance. It is assumed that anticipated
cash inflows are subject to risk.[3]

SOLVED PROBLEM

The Wilfred Company prepares a cash budget each week. The firm determines
its cash needs and invests surplus cash in commercial paper, which yields .14
percent per week. Commercial paper may be purchased in minimum lots of
$100,000. A fixed cost of $40 and a variable cost of .03 percent are incurred
on each transaction. The firm must maintain a minimum cash balance of
$200,000.

On February 1, the firm had $300,000 in cash and $200,000 in commercial
paper. The cash budget for the week of February 1-7 indicates the following
distribution of net receipts:

Probability	Amount
0.1	–$200,000
0.2	– 100,000
0.4	0
0.3	+ 100,000

Assume that the firm will sell commercial paper rather than borrow in order
to maintain the desired cash balance until the supply of commercial paper is
depleted. The sale of securities during the week results in the loss of 1/2 of
the weekly interest which would be earned if securities were not sold.
Determine the optimal level of commercial paper holdings for the week.

SOLUTION

EXPECTED CASH
BALANCE FEB. 7

Probability	Balance
0.1	$100,000
0.2	200,000
0.4	300,000
0.3	400,000

---

[3] Adapted from James C. Van Horne, *Financial Management and Policy*, pp. 341-6.

WILFRED COMPANY
OPTIMAL LEVEL OF COMMERCIAL PAPER HOLDINGS

Commercial Paper Level	Gross Earnings for Week	Cost of Buying Securities, Beginning of Week	Probability of Having to Sell Prob. Amt.	Cost of Selling Securities, Beginning of Week	Expected Costs and Earnings Lost due to Sale before End of Week*	Total Expected Selling Costs	Total Expected Costs	Total Expected Net Earnings
$100,000	140	—	—	70	—	70	70	70
200,000	280	—	(.1) 100,000	—	(.1)(140) = 14	14	14	266
300,000	420	70	(.1) 200,000 (.2) 100,000	—	(.1)(240) = 24 (.2)(140) = 28	52	122	298
400,000	560	100	(.1) 300,000 (.2) 200,000 (.4) 100,000	—	(.1)(340) = 34 (.2)(240) = 48 (.4)(140) = 56	138	238	322
500,000	700	130	(.1) 400,000 (.2) 300,000 (.4) 200,000 (.3) 100,000	—	(.1)(440) = 44 (.2)(340) = 68 (.4)(240) = 96 (.3)(140) = 42	250	380	320

*Includes fixed costs, commissions, and interest opportunity costs.

Given the fact that the firm now holds $300,000 in cash, the worst possible outcome for net receipts (i.e., – $200,000) would require the sale of $100,000 worth of paper. Since the firm now has $200,000 in paper, the minimum possible level of commercial paper holdings is $100,000. At this level, there is no probability that the cash balance will be under $200,000 on February 7. The optimal level of commercial paper holdings is $400,000. The firm should buy $200,000 of additional paper.

UNSOLVED PROBLEMS

1. Rework the solved problem (above). Let the rate on commercial paper rise to .16 percent. How does this affect your decision? Suppose the rate were .12 percent. How would this change affect your decision?

2. Determine the optimal level of commercial paper for the Wilfred Company (above) during the week of February 8-15. Assume that the firm holds $300,000 in commercial paper and $200,000 in cash as of February 8. The yield on commercial paper is .10 percent. Transactions costs have not changed. The cash budget for February 8-15, indicates the following distribution of net receipts:

Probability	Amount
0.2	–$100,000
0.3	0
0.2	+ 100,000
0.2	+ 200,000
0.1	+ 300,000

II THE FINANCING SUBSYSTEM

8 FINANCIAL STATEMENT ANALYSIS

SECTION
8.1

The analysis of financial statements, although a moderately old and well-institutionalized art, is quite open to question. There is serious doubt that the manipulation of poorly defined and measured historical data, regardless of how skillfully performed, will yield meaningful predictions of future events. No matter how accurately ratios are computed, they must be used with great care. A ratio standing alone usually means little. Comparison with the ratios of similar companies, however, will often point to specific areas of strength or weakness and the ratios of the same company may also be compared over time to determine trends.

Financial analysis is very important to potential lenders and investors and is therefore important to the financial manager, who must keep abreast of what his creditors and stockholders are seeing and thinking. The manager uses financial analysis in making projections because he wants to be sure that future financial statements will present the corporation in as favorable a light as possible. Such analysis is often instrumental to detecting inefficiency within the firm and to directing policy.

Since many interest groups are involved, it should not be surprising that many aspects of the firm are analyzed. Short-term creditors usually are primarily interested in the liquidity of the firm. It is generally assumed that no major change in the firm's position will occur over the life of the credit; thus, the only cause for concern is whether the firm will have adequate funds available for repayment. Long-term creditors must be interested in everything that short-term creditors are, and more. Because many things can happen to a firm over the life of a long-term loan, the fundamental income position must be analyzed, and specific protection for the creditor (often in the form of minimum ratios which must be maintained) may be included in the loan agreement. The stockholder must be concerned with everything that the creditors are (because creditors must be satisfied before there is any residual for the equity interest) and with the profitability of his investment as well.

SECTION 8.2   It should be obvious that the first step in statement analysis is to secure the statements; this is sometimes not as easy as it sounds. Closely held companies often do not emit statements to outsiders. Many publicly held companies do not reveal any more than they must, although in recent years the government and the accounting profession have been doing a good job of encouraging corporations to publish more complete statements. Even the financial manager may have a problem in analyzing his own company, not because of unavailability of data, but rather because data are often collected for other purposes and are thus not completely suitable for analysis.

Once the statements are obtained, certain adjustments must often be made. Some of the more common are listed below:

1. For short-term analysis, nonrecurring items should be eliminated, for the simple reason that they cannot be expected to recur in the future. This category would include large nonbusiness or extraordinary income or expense.

2. The use of liability and equity reserve accounts should be examined. The special segregation of equity reserves should almost always be ignored (this would include "reserve for contingencies" or "reserve for replacement of plant"). Even liability reserves, such as the account for deferred taxes caused by the use of accelerated depreciation, should be examined. (There is a good chance that the taxes will never be paid and thus do not constitute a true liability.)

3. Attempts to offset specific assets and liabilities should be scrutinized, because a distortion of the ratios may result. One common example of this practice is the netting of the current asset "government securities held in anticipation of taxes" against the current liability "accrued taxes," which tends to increase the current ratio.

4. Intangible assets (patents, goodwill, etc.) should be treated with great care, as their value on the books often has no relation to their market value or future income-generating capacity.

5. If a company leases a substantial amount of its assets (which may often be detected by the presence of sizable leasing expenses on the income statement) it may appear to have little debt and yet be heavily obligated by leasing contracts. To make the financial statements of different companies comparable, many analysts capitalize leases and treat them as debt. For example, if a company had annual leasing expenses of $100,000 and the analyst wished to capitalize it at 10 percent, he would add $1 million to the fixed asset and long-term debt accounts of the company's balance sheet.

THE EXAMPLE CORPORATION
DECEMBER 31

(thousands)	1968	1969
Current Assets		
Cash	$ 10,000	$ 8,000
Marketable Securities	10,000	5,000
Accounts Receivable	30,000	33,000
Inventory	40,000	44,000
Total Current Assets	$ 90,000	$ 90,000
Fixed Assets:		
Plant and Equipment	$200,000	$220,000
Less: Reserve for Depreciation	100,000	110,000
Net Plant	100,000	110,000
Other Assets	10,000	10,000
Total Assets	$200,000	$210,000
Current Liabilities		
Notes Payable (7%)	$ 10,000	$ 10,000
Accounts Payable	10,000	15,000
Accrued Wages and Taxes	20,000	24,000
Total Current Liabilities	$ 40,000	$ 49,000
Long-Term Debt		
3% - First Mortgage Bonds of 1980	$ 40,000	$ 38,000
4% Subordinated Debts of 1990	20,000	19,000
Total	$ 60,000	$ 57,000
Preferred Stock		
5% Preferred	$ 20,000	$ 20,000
Common Stock (1,000,000 shares, par $10)	10,000	10,000
Capital Surplus	30,000	30,000
Retained Earnings	40,000	44,000
Total Liabilities and Net Worth	$200,000	$210,000

THE EXAMPLE CORPORATION
YEAR ENDED 12/31/69
(thousands)

Sales		$200,000
Less: Cost of Goods Sold	$120,000	
Selling, Gen., and Adm. Exp.	40,000	
Depreciation	10,000	
Interest	2,650	172,650
Net Income before Taxes		27,350
Less: Taxes @ 50%		13,675
Net Income before Preferred		13,675
Less: Preferred Dividend		1,000
Net Income available to Common		12,675
Less: Common Dividends		8,675
Earnings Retained		$ 4,000

SECTION 8.3   One of the first things to be computed by the analyst, if it is not already provided with the financial statements, is a funds flow analysis (or, as it is often called, a sources and uses of funds statement). Since this statement only compares balance sheets at two points in time, it does not truly trace the flow of funds through the firm and for this reason is of limited usefulness.

For funds-flow statements, the cash account generally acts as the residual. In other words, various sources provide funds that are employed for various uses and the difference is reflected by a change in the cash account. Accordingly, sources of funds include: (1) a decrease in any asset (other than cash); (2) an increase in any liability; (3) proceeds from the sale of stock; (4) net income after taxes; and (5) noncash expenses, such as depletion, depreciation, and amortization. Uses of funds consist of: (1) an increase in any asset other than cash; (2) a decrease in any liability; (3) a reduction in stock; and (4) cash dividends.

A source and use of funds statement for the Example Corporation for 1969 would thus appear as follows:

THE EXAMPLE CORPORATION
SOURCES AND USES OF FUNDS STATEMENT
YEAR ENDED 12/31/69
(thousands)

Sources of Funds		Uses of Funds	
Net Income	$13,675	Dividends	$ 9,675
Depreciation	10,000	Increase-Acc. Rec.	3,000
Decrease-Marketable Securities	5,000	Increase-Inventory	4,000
Increase-Accounts Payable	5,000	Increase-Plant	20,000
Increase-Accruals	4,000	Decrease-Long-term debt	3,000
	37,675		$39,675
Add: Decrease in Cash	2,000		
	$39,675		

SECTION 8.4   As we pointed out earlier, short-term creditors of the firm are primarily interested in liquidity. We shall now consider several ratios that aid in liquidity determination.

1. Percentage Breakdown of Balance Sheet (Common Size Statement). This is probably the simplest way to determine liquidity trends over time. A modified breakdown of the Example Corporation would appear as follows:

	1968	1969
Current Assets:		
Cash and Marketable Securities	10%	6%
Accounts Receivable	15	16
Inventory	20	21
Total Current	45	43
Fixed	50	52
Other	5	5
Total Assets	100%	100%
Current Liabilities	20%	23%
Long-Term Debt	30	27
Preferred	10	10
Common and Surplus	40	40
Total	100%	100%

Just as a crude overview, this breakdown shows that the firm has become less liquid, with current assets (and, most importantly, cash and marketable securities) declining and current liabilities rising.

2. Current Ratio. The current ratio is defined as (current assets/current liabilities). For the Example Corporation, the current ratio was 2.25 (90/40) in 1968 and 1.84 (90/49) in 1969. This ratio is supposed to give some notion of how well the firm is able to pay its obligations when they come due. Thus, a ratio of 1 would imply that the firm has adequate current assets at a particular point in time (if liquidated at book value) to meet the liabilities due within one year. A current ratio of 2 (which many writers during the 1930's felt was a desirable minimum for industrial companies) would imply that the liquidation value of all current assets could uniformly decline to one-half of book value and the firm would still be able to meet its obligations. Furthermore, it may be assumed that if all firms in the same industry have identical cash cycles, then the current ratio may be used as a measure of relative liquidity. This approach to liquidity determination is more than a little crude; nevertheless, the level and the trend of the current ratio of the Example Corporation lend further weight to our suspicion that liquidity is deteriorating.

3. Quick (Acid Test) Ratio. One of the many criticisms of the current ratio is the fact that it assumes that inventories represent available funds, when in fact many inventories are highly illiquid, especially during recessions.[1] Thus, the quick ratio has been devised to include only the relatively more liquid current assets. The quick ratio is often defined in one of the following ways:

$$\frac{\text{Current assets} - \text{inventories}}{\text{Current liabilities}} \quad \text{or} \quad \frac{\text{Cash} + \text{marketable securities} + \text{accounts receivable}}{\text{Current liabilities}} \tag{8.1}$$

---

[1] The student should not adopt a doctrinaire approach to ratios. The inventories of some companies are adequately liquid to be included, although the receivables of others are too illiquid to be included.

For the Example Corporation, the quick ratio was 1.25 in 1968 (50/40) and 0.94 in 1969 (46/49). This trend further substantiates our notion of reducing liquidity.

4. Receivables Turnover-Average Collection Period. The pool of cash must be constantly replenished from the collection of receivables in order to pay the short-term creditor. It is therefore of interest to know how rapidly the receivables are being collected.

The receivables turnover is given by the fraction (annual credit sales/average receivables outstanding). It is often necessary to use year-end receivables instead of the average and also to assume that all sales are for credit if no breakdown is given. The receivables turnover for the Example Corporation in 1969 was thus 6.4 times (200 /31.5). This ratio could then be compared with that of previous years or those of similar companies.

A somewhat more useful approach is the average collection period, which is defined as:[2]

$$\frac{\text{Average (or year-end) level of receivables} \times 365 \text{ (or 360)}}{\text{Annual credit sales (or annual sales)}}$$

For Example, the collection period in 1969 was [(31.5/200) X 365] = 58 days. Not only might historical and intercompany comparisons be made, but also this average collection period could be compared to the terms in the industry to see whether Example's customers are taking their discounts, paying when due, or stretching their payments (see Chaps. 6 and 9).

5. Inventory Turnover-Average Days' Inventory. Inventory must be sold to replenish the pool of receivables. A slow-moving inventory might well indicate that first receivables, and then cash will decline; it might also suggest that the inventory is obsolete, so that price reductions will be required before it can be sold. In extreme cases, this would further imply that the inventory is over-valued on the books.

The two approaches to determining inventory liquidity are the inventory turnover, which is defined as (cost of goods sold/average inventory), and the average days' inventory, defined as (average inventory x 365/cost of goods sold). In the Example case, the turnover is 2.9 times (120/42) and the average days' inventory is 128 days (or, viewed another way, if production ceased immediately, sales at the current rate could be satisfied out of inventory for 128 days).

6. Basic Defensive Interval.[3] Just as it was argued that all current assets were not equally liquid, it may also be stated that all current liabilities are not equally pressing. The basic defensive interval is an attempt to see how long the firm could continue to meet its cash obligations from liquid assets. The basic defensive interval is defined as (cash + marketable securities + receivables/daily operating expenditures). For this

---

[2] Various analysts will use 360 or 365 for the number of days in the year. The easier figure with which to work is 360; however, 365 is the more accurate figure. When making comparisons, one should be consistent in using one or the other of these numbers.

[3] C.f. G.H. Sorter and George Benston, "Appraising the Defensive Position of a Firm: The Interval Measure," *The Accounting Review,* (October, 1960), pp. 633-40.

purpose, daily operating expenditures are determined by summing all cash operating expenses for the year (cost of goods sold + selling, general, and administrative expenses) and dividing by 365. The basic defensive interval for Example Corporation in 1969 was about 105 days (46/0.438).

SECTION
8.5

Since profitability is of interest to bondholders and to stockholders, we will treat it separately here.

1. Margins. The gross profit margin is defined as (sales-cost of goods sold/sales) and the net profit margin is (net profit after taxes/sales). The gross margin for Example is 40 percent (80/200) and the net margin is 6.8 percent (13.7/200). Margins will vary greatly from industry to industry, but again historical and intercompany comparisons will be useful. It should be noted that the two ratios are used together. If the net margin is low and/or declining but the gross margin is in line, the conclusion is that the problem is with overhead, interest, etc.; if, however, the gross margin is also low, this could imply that the raw material, wage, or production costs are too high.

2. Turnover. The turnover ratio attempts to relate the level of assets with output. It is defined as (sales/total assets). For Example, the turnover is 1.0 times (200/200). A relatively low level or declining trend in turnover normally implies either that sales have fallen or that the company has been adding capacity more rapidly than it has been generating sales to utilize the capacity.

3. Earning Power. Earning power (net income after taxes/total assets) is merely the net margin times the turnover.[4] Although the margins and turnovers of firms differ greatly, there is a tendency for their earning powers to be more nearly the same. The earning power of Example is (1.0 X 6.8%) = 6.8%

4. Rates of Return. The rate of return on total investment is defined as (net profit after taxes + interest on long-term debt/long-term debt + stockholders' equity)[5] and the rate of return on stockholders' equity is (net income available to common stockholders/common stockholders' equity). For the Example Corporation, rate of return on total investment is (15.625/161) = 9.7%, while the return on common equity is (12.675/84) = 15.1%. A comparison with the past or with other companies' ratios would have to be made before it could be determined what these levels indicate.

SECTION
8.6

The ratios of especial interest to long-term, fixed liability holders shall now be considered.

1. Debt-equity Ratio. The debt-equity ratio (long term debt/stockholders' equity) is often used as an indicator of the risk of a bond, although it does not serve this purpose

---

[4]Also defined as (net operating income/total assets).

[5]Some authorities reduce the numerator of this fraction by the amount of taxes saved through the payment of interest.

very well. The ability of a firm to make interest and sinking fund payments does not relate very closely to the amount of debt it has contracted (unless one assumes that all assets have the same return for all firms) and even in liquidation this ratio is not very good because it relies upon book values, rather than market or liquidation values. For the Example Corporation, the debt-equity ratio is 55% (57/104) and the debt to total capitalization ratio (debt/debt + equity) is 35% (57/161).

2. *Coverage Ratios.* Interest coverage ratios attempt to tell how many times the interest requirement on long-term debt is being met. There are several different ways of computing these ratios. We shall consider two:

a. The overall coverage method adopts the "going concern" proposition that no bond is more secure than the most junior issue, because a default on that issue will throw the whole company into bankruptcy. The overall coverage is defined as (net income before taxes and interest on long-term debt/long-term debt interest requirement) and for the Example Corporation this is (29.3/1.9) = 15.4 times.

b. The cumulative deduction method attempts to differentiate between bonds on the basis of their seniority and, thus, to show a higher coverage for the more secure obligations.[6] This ratio is defined as (net income before taxes and interest on long-term debt/interest requirement for bond issue being considered and for all debt of equal or prior seniority). Thus, the mortgage bonds of Example would have a coverage of (29.3/1.14) = 25.7 times and only the debentures would have coverage of 15.4 times. The student should note that coverage for the least-senior bond under the cumulative deduction method will also be the overall coverage.

Preferred stock may also be considered within this framework. The preferred dividend coverage, if there is no long-term debt, is simply (net income after taxes/preferred dividend requirement). If, however, there is debt, the preferred stock must be treated as a junior after-tax debt issue and its coverage is computed as follows:

$$\frac{\text{net income before taxes and interest on long-term debt}}{\text{interest requirement on long-term debt} + \dfrac{\text{preferred dividend requirement}}{1 - \text{tax rate}}} \tag{8.3}$$

---

[6]Coverage figures computed by the cumulative deduction method may affect bond ratings and thus the cost and availability of long-term debt funds to the firm.

For the Example Corporation, the preferred coverage would be:

$$\frac{29.3}{\dfrac{1.9 + 1.0}{1 - 0.5}} = \frac{29.3}{1.9 + 2.0} = \frac{29.3}{3.9} \cong 7.5 \text{ times}$$

SECTION 8.7   Very few equity ratios remain. They are:

1. Earnings Per Share. (Net income available to common shareholders/number of common shares outstanding.) For the Example Corporation, E.P.S. = $12,675,000/1,000,000) = $12.675.

2. Dividends Per Share. (Common dividends paid/number of common shares outstanding.) For the Example Corporation, D.P.S. = ($8,675,000/1,000,000) = $8.675.

3. Payout. (Dividends/earnings.) Thus, either ($8,675,000/$12,675,000) or $8.675/$12.675) = 68%.

4. Price-Earnings (P/E) Ratio. (Price per share/earnings per share.) If Example Corporation common were selling for $150 per share, the *P/E* ratio would be ($150/$12.675) $\cong$ 11.8 times.

5. Yield on Common. (Dividends per share/price per share.) For Example, it is ($8.675/$150) = 5.8%.

6. Book Value Per Share. (Common stockholders' equity/number of common shares outstanding.) Book value per share for Example is ($84/1) = $84. If shareholders' equity is reduced by the amount of any intangible assets before dividing by the number of shares, the resulting figure is net tangible assets per share.

UNSOLVED PROBLEMS

1. The long-term debt section of the balance sheet of the FLN Corporation shows the following:

6% First Mortgage Bonds of 1987	$10,000,000
$6\frac{3}{8}$% Second Mortgage Bonds of 1977	8,000,000
$7\frac{1}{8}$% Senior Debentures of 1982	15,000,000
8% Subordinated Debentures of 1990	10,000,000
$9\frac{1}{4}$% Jr. Sub. Debs. of 1985	5,000,000
	$48,000,000

Net income before interest and taxes for the FLN Corporation is $10 million.

(a) Compute the overall interest coverage.

(b) Using the cumulative deduction method, compute the coverage for each issue.

2.

THE ZERO COMPANY
DECEMBER 31

(thousands)	*1970*	*1971*
Current Assets		
Cash	$ 50	$ 100
Marketable Securities	130	130
Accounts Receivable	120	200
Inventory	100	170
Total Current	$ 400	$ 600
Fixed Assets		
Gross Plant	$1,000	$1,000
Less: Accumulated Depreciation	500	550
Net Plant	500	450
Other Assets	100	150
Total Assets	$1,000	$1,200
Current Liabilities		
Notes Payable (8%)	$ 50	$ 50
Accounts Payable	100	150
Accrued Wages and Taxes	50	100
Total Current	$ 200	$ 300
Long-term Debt		
7% First Mortgage Bonds	$ 100	$ 100
8% Debentures	100	100
Preferred Stock - 7%	100	100
Common Stock (10,000 shares - par $10)	100	100
Capital Surplus	100	100
Retained Earnings	300	400
Total Liabilities and Net Worth	$1,000	$1,200

THE ZERO COMPANY
DECEMBER 31

(thousands)		*1971*
Sales		$600
Less: Cost of Goods Sold	$217	
Selling, Gen. and Admin. Expenses	40	
Depreciation	50	307
Net Income before Interest and Taxes		293
Less: Interest		19
Net Income before Taxes		274
Less: Taxes (50%)		137
Net Income		137
Less: Preferred		7
Net Income to Common		130
Less: Common Dividends		30
Earnings Retained		$100

(a) Compute a source and use of funds statement.

(b) Compute the following ratios:
    (1) Percentage breakdown of balance sheet
    (2) Current ratio
    (3) Quick ratio
    (4) Average collection period
    (5) Average days' inventory
    (6) BDI
    (7) Gross Margin
    (8) Net margin
    (9) Turnover
   (10) Earning power
   (11) Rate of return on total investment
   (12) Rate of return on common equity
   (13) Debt/total capitalization
   (14) Overall interest coverage
   (15) Preferred dividend coverage
   (16) Earnings per share
   (17) Dividends per share
   (18) Payout
   (19) *P/E* ratio—if the price is $150/share
   (20) Yield on common—if the price is $150/share
   (21) Book value per share

(c) Analyze the position of Zero from the viewpoint of:
    (1) Short-term creditor
    (2) Long-term creditor
    (3) Stockholder
    (4) Management

COMPREHENSIVE CASE

THE BACH BRAKE COMPANY
COMPARATIVE BALANCE SHEETS
FOR YEARS 1968-69

(thousands)

	1968	1969
Assets		
Cash	$ 5,000	$ 4,000
Receivables, Net	25,000	15,000
Inventories	22,000	34,000
Current Assets	$ 52,000	$ 53,000
Fixed Assets (net)	27,000	27,000
Total Assets	$ 79,000	$ 80,000

THE BACH BRAKE COMPANY
COMPARATIVE BALANCE SHEETS
FOR YEARS 1968-69

(thousands)

Liabilities and Net Worth		
Accounts Payable	$ 10,000	$ 12,000
Notes Payable (5%)	7,000	7,000
Other Current Liabilities	3,000	1,000
Current Liabilities	$ 20,000	$ 20,000
Long-Term Debt (6%)	15,000	15,000
Common Stock (Par $10)	10,000	10,000
Retained Earnings	34,000	35,000
	$ 79,000	$ 80,000

THE BACH BRAKE COMPANY
COMPARATIVE INCOME STATEMENTS
FOR YEARS ENDED 1968-69

(thousands)

	1968	*1969*
Sales (All Credit)	$120,000	$110,000
Materials	45,000	39,000
Labor	40,500	37,000
Heat, Light, Power	9,000	9,000
Depreciation	1,500	1,500
Total Cost of Goods Sold	$ 96,000	$ 86,500
Gross Profit	$ 24,000	$ 23,500
Selling Expense	10,000	10,000
General and Administrative	9,500	9,250
E.B.I.T.	$ 4,500	$ 4,250
Interest Expense	1,250	1,250
Net Before Tax	$ 3,250	$ 3,000
Federal Income Tax	1,625	1,500
Net Income	$ 1,625	$ 1,500

Other Data:

(a) Average Price of Common Stock

1968	*1969*
$16¼	$12

(b) The balance sheet and income statement data for 1968 and 1969 are representative of the condition and performance of the past ten years. The firm is cyclical in nature with sales fluctuating between $100,000,000 and $130,000,000. Bach's share of the brake industry market was 4.0 percent in 1968 and 3.6 percent in 1969.

(c) The fixed assets of the company have a current market of $25,000,000.

(d) Assume a 360-day year.

1. Compute a sources and uses of funds statement for 1969.
2. Fill in the blanks in the following matrix of financial ratios.

		1968		1969	
		Bach	Industry	Bach	Industry
(a)	Current Ratio	2.6	2.5	_____	2.6
(b)	Acid-Test Ratio	1.5	1.5	_____	1.6
(c)	Inventory Turnover	4.4x	4.6x	_____	4.8x
(d)	A/R Turnover	4.8x	6.8x	_____	7.0x
(e)	BDI	96 days	110 days	_____	120 days
(f)	Gross Margin	20.0%	20.0%	_____	21.6%
(g)	Net Margin	1.4%	3.4%	_____	3.5%
(h)	Total Asset Turnover	1.5x	1.8x	_____	1.6x
(i)	Rate of Return on Total Investment	4.3%	8.9%	_____	10.0%
(j)	Rate of Return on Equity $\frac{\text{Net Income}}{\text{Net Worth}}$	3.7%	10.0%	_____	10.2%
(k)	Times Interest Earned	4.6x	4.8x	_____	4.7x
(l)	$\frac{\text{Shareholders Equity}}{\text{Total Liabilities & Net Worth}}$	56%	40%	_____	42%
(m)	Earnings per Share	$1.625		_____	
(n)	Dividends per Share	$ .675		_____	
(o)	P/E Multiple	10x	14x	_____	13x

3. Analyze and evaluate the position of the company. Cite specific ratio levels and trends as evidence. What major problem areas are apparent?

4. The Bach Company is contemplating a major expansion which will result in a 50 percent increase in production and sales of their present lines. To expand, they must invest $15,000,000 in plant and equipment. Once the expansion is completed, it is expected that an additional $55,000,000 in sales and an additional $12,000,000 in gross profits (after annual straight line depreciation of $750,000) will result. Selling, general, and administrative expenses will increase by approximately $8,000,000. As a financial consultant to the firm, you are asked to:

(a) Make recommendations with regard to the financial policies of the firm that would be applicable whether or not the expansion is undertaken.

(b) Determine the approximate total amount of funds needed to accomplish the expansion.

(c) Recommend sources for these funds.

(d) Evaluate the desirability of the proposed expansion.

9 SHORT-TERM
SOURCES OF FUNDS

SECTION
9.1

The banking system represents a major source of funds for American corporations. Although many firms will wait until a project is almost under way before discussing matters with their bankers, modern planning (and bargaining) techniques indicate that the availability of funds should be ascertained well in advance. A business will normally keep some minimum balance in the bank, since this is an important first step toward obtaining a loan. It is also desirable periodically to file financial statements with the bank, so that it has a running record of the condition of the business. If these two prerequisites are met satisfactorily, the firm should be able to obtain a line of credit. A line of credit is merely an informal agreement on the part of the bank that, other things being equal, it would be willing to lend the firm amounts up to some stated ceiling at some stated interest rate. The interest rate charged would usually be tied to the prime rate (that minimum rate charged to borrowers of unquestioned credit worthiness), such as prime plus 1 percent. The borrower may also be required to be out of debt to the bank (or the banking system) for some period during the year to show his liquidity (the "clean-up" provisions). Although a line of credit arrangement is of some help to a prospective borrower, it is not legally binding upon the bank and might be greatly reduced if credit conditions were to tighten.

If the prospective borrower cannot afford to take the chance of having the size of his borrowings reduced, the more formal revolving credit arrangement might be appropriate. This arrangement involves a binding commitment covering a stated period (often a year) on the part of the bank to lend up to some set maximum amount at a set interest charge (usually stated in terms of prime). As in the case of the line of credit, the bank can extract itself from this commitment if the financial condition of the borrower deteriorates substantially during the period, but it may not dishonor the obligation merely because credit conditions tighten (in which case the prime rate, and thus the rate charged under the revolving credit

108

agreement, would rise anyway). In return for undertaking this obligation, the bank will require that a fee (often .5 percent, but sometimes .75 percent, per year) be paid on the unborrowed balance and may also require an additional fee (this will depend upon the relative bargaining position of borrower and lender). To illustrate, let prime be 8 percent and assume that the Wombat Corporation had a $1 million revolving credit arrangement at prime plus one percent, one-half percent paid on the unborrowed balance, and average borrowings of $600,000 over the year. The total cost of the revolving credit arrangement would be:

$$(\$600,000)\,(.09) + (\$400,000)\,(.005) = \$54,000 + 2,000 = \$56,000.$$

As we have indicated above, bankers will examine closely the balances of prospective borrowers. In the first place, there is a greater tendency for banks to lend to their own depositors than to non-depositors. Part of this inclination reflects a feeling of responsibility, but it cannot be ignored that banks make their profits by lending and investing funds deposited with them and therefore wish to reward and encourage the loyalty of their depositors. Many bankers feel that their depositors have the right, in normal times, to look to them for loans of four to five times the depositor's normal balance. In return, the banker expects a certain portion of a loan (usually 15-20 percent) to be left on deposit in the form of a compensating balance. The size of this balance will rise during tight money periods when the banker has more bargaining power. The compensating balance requirement may well raise the effective cost of the loan to the borrower. It may be possible, however, to leave this compensating balance in the form of an interest-bearing time deposit (thus cutting the cost of these idle funds) or to arrange for a third party to provide the compensating balance for a fee (link financing).[1]

The impact of these various banker obfuscations upon the true rate of interest shall now be considered. For our examples, we will take a time period of one year, a nominal interest rate of 6 percent, and a principal of $100.

1. *Simple advance*—borrow $100 January 1, repay $106 December 31.

True rate = 6/100 = 6.0%

2. *Advance with compensating balance*—borrow $100 January 1, keep minimum of $20 in bank at all times, which would not otherwise be done, repay $106 on December 31.

---

[1] Although beyond the scope of this book, it should be noted that dealer-placed commercial paper is an attractive source of funds for strong corporations, especially when banks are scaling down their lending. Normally, the rates on this paper are some 0.5 percent below prime.

$$\text{True rate} = 6/100\text{–}20 = 6/80 = 7.5\%$$

3. *Advance with compensating balance (alternative)*—borrow $100 January 1, keep minimum of $20 in bank at all times, only $10 of which would normally be maintained, repay $106 December 31.

$$\text{True rate} = 6/100 - 10 = 6/90 = 6.7\%$$

4. *Advance with time deposit compensating balance*—borrow $100 January 1, put $20 in one year time deposit at 4 percent earning $0.80, repay $106 on December 31.

$$\text{True rate} = 6\text{–}\ .80/100 - 20 = 5.20/80 = 6.5\%$$

5. *Advance with link financing*—borrow $100 January 1, pay 1 percent premium to third party to supply $20 time deposit compensating balance, repay $106 December 31.

$$\text{True rate} = (6 + .20)/100 = 6.20/100 = 6.2\%$$

6. *Discount*—borrow $94 January 1, repay $100 December 31.

$$\text{True rate} = 6/94 = 6.4\%$$

7. *Discount installment*—borrow $94 January 1, repay $8.33 every month for a year ($8.33 X 12 = $100)[2]

$$\text{True rate} = \frac{(2)\ (12)\ (\$6)}{(\$94)\ (13)} \cong 11.8\%$$

8. *Add-on installment*—borrow $100 January 1, repay $8.83 every month for a year ($8.83 X 12 = $106).

$$\text{True rate} = \frac{(2)\ (12)\ (\$6)}{(\$100)\ (13)} \cong 11.1\%$$

The bankers are thus able to appear to charge everyone about the same nominal rate of interest. They simply compute the charge differently for different classes of borrowers. Indeed, there are formulas even more involved than those we have illustrated. The prospective borrower, therefore, must inform himself not only as to the nominal rate but also as to the method of "computation" of this rate.

---

[2]The approximation formula for the true charge on an installment is:

$$\text{True rate} = \frac{(2)\ (\text{number of payments in 1 year})\ (\text{interest charge in dollars})}{(\text{cash advance})\ (\text{total number of payments} + 1)}$$

UNSOLVED PROBLEMS

1. Assuming a time period of one year, a nominal interest rate of 10 percent, a principal of $500, a time deposit rate of 5 percent, a compensating balance of 20 percent, and a link financing premium of 2 percent, recompute the eight interest rates illustrated above.

2. Assume that the May Company has a $5 million revolving credit arrangement at prime plus 2 percent, prime is 7 percent, there is a .5 percent charge on the unborrowed balance, the bank required a flat fee of $50,000 to negotiate the agreement, and the May Company will have average borrowing of $3 million.

(a) What is the total interest cost for the year?

(b) What is the effective interest rate to the May Company?

(c) What would the effective cost and rate on another $1 million be if the May company raised its borrowings to $4 million?

SECTION
9.2
Another major source of funds can be the firm's own suppliers, including some that are rarely considered. For example, to the extent that employees provide useful services prior to the time at which they are paid for these services, they are supplying funds to the firm at no cost. In addition, a firm earns profits continuously but must only pay taxes quarterly; in the interim, the government is a free source of funds.

Discussions of this sort, however, rather rapidly turn to trade credit, which is granted on raw materials, merchandise, or whatever else the firm purchases. A certain amount of this credit may seem to be costless, for if term are *n*/10, *EOM* (payment for this month's purchases are due by the 10th of next month) it would appear that the purchaser is getting from 10 to 40 days' (depending upon when the purchase was made) free use of funds. An economist might suggest that the credit is not free at all but that the seller may have raised his prices to cover the cost of this credit. We would not argue with this position, but the fact remains that in most cases the purchaser cannot obtain any reduction in price by early payment.[3]

A very common feature in most trade credit arrangements is the use of a discount period. If the terms are 2/10, *n*/30 (a 2 percent discount is allowed if payment is made within 10 days, but payment must be made within 30 days in any case), then the purchaser may pay 98 percent of his

---

[3] In some lines an "anticipation rate" is granted, which means that a purchaser may get an interest rate credit by prepayment.

bill on any of days 1-10 or 100 percent on days 11-30. It should be immediately apparent that the only two feasible choices are 98 percent on day 10 or 100 percent on day 30.[4] To choose between these alternatives we need only note that to wait the full 30 days implies that we are paying 2 percent of our bill to borrow 98 percent for 20 days, or an effective rate of $(2/98 \times 360/20) = 36.8\%$. Put more rigorously, the formula for the cost of trade credit is as follows:

$$\frac{\text{Percentage Discount}}{100\% - \text{Percentage Discount}} \times \frac{360}{\text{Total period} - \text{discount period}} \tag{9.1}$$

Trade credit costs, as computed above, only apply when the discounts are not taken; in our example, the first 10 days of credit are free and only the next 20 days bear a rate of 36.8 percent. It should be obvious in this case that the supplier expects the firm to take its discounts; otherwise, the purchaser might not be able to compete. It should therefore follow, under the exception principle, that purchases should be carried net of discount and an account for discounts not taken should be initiated. In other words, management should assume that all discounts will be taken and should be informed if they are not.

Suppose that the terms of trade credit are 2/10, n/90. In this case, the cost of paying in 90 days instead of 10 is $(2/98 \times 360/80) = 9.2\%$. Such a rate is comparable to the cost of other sources of funds and may merit investigation should the purchasing firm require short-term funds.

Finally, although a purchaser should pay by the end of the assigned period, some do not. This procedure is known as "stretching" payables and is followed by weak, cash-deficient firms at most times and by many firms during periods of tight money. The costs of such a policy in terms of deterioration of credit rating, reluctance of suppliers to sell again on credit, etc. are difficult to quantify but are very real nevertheless. Whenever possible, it is best to apprise suppliers of the problems causing the delay and of when they may expect payment.

UNSOLVED PROBLEMS

1. Compute the cost of not taking discounts in the case of each of the following terms:

---

[4]Payment before day 10 or on days 11-29 would be shortsighted, since funds may be used for the remaining period (until day 10 or day 30) at no additional cost.

    (a) $1/10, n/30$

    (b) $3/30, n/90$

    (c) $2/10, n/60$

2. The Roybok Company is able to invest funds at 10 percent after taxes of 50 percent. It is currently purchasing $100,000 of raw materials a month on terms of $1/10, n/30$ and not taking the discount. Evaluate this policy.

3. The Roybok Company (see number 2 above) is considering stretching this month's $100,000 payment an extra 30 days. In doing so, however, there is a 25% chance that the supplier will lose patience and force Roybok to pay cash on delivery for raw materials for the next year. Should Roybok try to stretch its payables?

4. The local bank is willing to lend Roybok enough to pay this month's raw materials bill at 10 percent with a 20 percent compensating balance and to make an additional loan for Roybok to take the discount on next month's bill at 12 percent with a 25 percent compensating balance. What should Roybok do now?

SECTION 9.3   For the sake of completeness, we might note that the firm may often obtain additional short-term funds on a secured basis. It is possible to obtain a loan secured by the accounts receivable. The loan value will depend upon the quality and liquidity of the receivables, but will often vary from 50-90 percent of their face value. If the loan is arranged with a bank, the rate charged may be some 2 to 3 percent over prime, with an additional charge for handling the receivables of 1-2 percent. If the borrowing is from a commercial finance company, the rate may be appreciably higher. On a non-notification basis, the customer represented by the receivable would continue to make his payments to the company, and the company would forward them to the lender. This method is preferred by the company because it need not inform its customer that a third party has been brought into the relationship. It is not favored by the lender because he has less control over the money. On a notification basis, the customer would make his payment directly to the lender.

    It is also possible to sell (or factor) receivables. This method has the advantage to the company of shifting the responsibility of credit department costs and bad debt losses (assuming that the receivables are sold without recourse to the seller) to the factors who, it should be noted, charge for all of this. The factor's fee (often in the range of 2 percent of the receivables purchased) only covers the credit and collection function in that the company selling the receivables must still wait until they are collected before it receives its money. Should the company want its money sooner, it may obtain an advance at some stated rate of interest. Should the company keep its money on deposit with the factor after the receivables are collected, it may receive interest.

It is possible for a firm to borrow on the basis of its inventory. Marketability and volatility in market price are important considerations in determining the loan value of inventory. In addition, great care must be taken to see that security is maintained and that the inventory cannot be sold without the lender being paid.

UNSOLVED PROBLEMS

1. The Alda Company has annual sales of $3 million (80 percent on credit) and an average collection period of 30 days. The credit department costs $30,000 a year to maintain and bad debts run 1 percent of receivables. A factor is willing to buy the receivables of the Alda Company at a 2 percent discount. Should the offer be accepted?

2. If Alda keeps its present arrangement, it may use its receivables for collateral and borrow from the bank $100,000 for a year at 8 percent with a 20 percent compensating balance. The factor, on the other hand, will grant an advance of up to 80 percent of the value of receivables which it holds and will charge 14 percent interest on advances. Assuming that Alda will require at least $80,000 of short-term funds for the year, which means of obtaining them appears to be cheaper?

COMPREHENSIVE CASE

The Mahoney Company is a manufacturer of aircraft parts, with relatively constant sales. As a result of expanding business, it will need an additional $1 million of working capital to carry enlarged inventories and receivables. For several reasons, not the least of which is that the expanded level of business may not continue beyond the expiration of current contracts, it is desired that these funds be obtained from short-term sources. The firm, therefore, may look to the following alternatives:

1. Bank loan—The bank will loan $1.25 million at 10 percent, with a 20 percent compensating balance.

2. Trade credit—The company buys about $800,000 of raw materials a month on terms of 3/10, n/60 and takes the discount. It could forego the discount on certain of its purchases.

3. Factoring—A financial intermediary which deals in factoring has offered to buy the company's receivables (an average of $2 million per month) which have a 30 day collection period at a 2 percent discount from face value. The factor will make an advance of up to 75 percent of the face amount of receivables purchased. The factor will charge 10 percent interest on advances. By factoring, the company will be relieved of its .5 percent bad debt losses and the $100,000 per year expense of running a credit department.

Which of these alternatives is superior? Why?

10 TERM
DEBT AND LEASING

Term debt (short for "intermediate term debt") is generally defined as those loans with a maturity greater than one year and less than seven to ten years (the upper boundary, separating term debt from long-term debt, is not too clear). In strict violation of our attempts to separate the financing and investment decisions, management often selects the maturity of debt to be issued with an eye to the life of the assets to be purchased with the proceeds. It is often felt, therefore, that seasonal or other short-run increases in inventory of receivables should be financed with short-term debt; a plant with a 20- or 30-year life should be financed with long-term debt; and equipment and the like having a 1-10 year life ought to be financed with term debt. Such equipment can also be leased, which is the reason that both topics are considered together. Perhaps a more constructive rationalization for term debt is that management desires to structure the package of securities to be sold by maturity as well as by type. Thus, payment may be geared to cash inflows. This reduces the likelihood that the firm would be forced into a possibly unfavorable market to refund the securities.

The repayment provisions on term debt generally require that the loan be amortized over its life, either with equal annual repayments or equal payments with a larger repayment ("balloon" payment) in the final year of the loan. If a firm suffers erratic cash flows, it may be possible to negotiate a more flexible repayment schedule. There is often, however, a penalty provided if the borrower desires to repay the loan prior to maturity. Using the tables in the back of this book, it is possible to compute the amortization schedule for a term loan.

1. *Equal Annual Repayments.* Suppose that the firm desires a $1,000 loan, to be repaid in equal installments over 8 years, and the lenders require an 8 percent return. What annual payment must be made? This question can be rephrased as: What annual cash flow, lasting 8 years, will have a present value of $1,000 when discounted at 8 percent?

Appendix D provides the present value of $1 per year for n years discounted at r percent. In this case, $n = 8$ years and $r = 8$ percent. Checking the table, we discover that the present value is $5.75. For the present value to be $1,000, the annual payment would be ($1,000/$5.75) = 174 times $1, or $174. Stated more rigorously, this formula is:

$$\text{Annual payment} = \frac{\text{Amount borrowed}}{PV \text{ of } \$1 \text{ per year for } n \text{ yrs at } r\%} \qquad (10.1)$$

Where: n = number of years to maturity of loan
$\qquad\quad r$ = desired interest rate

Thus, a $174 payment per year for 8 years will completely repay a $1,000 loan and provide the lender an 8 percent return on the unpaid balance every year.

2. *Equal Repayments with Balloon.*
    (a) *When size of annual payment is known.* Suppose the firm decides that a $174 payment per year will put too great a strain on cash flows during the early years and that $125 per year is all that they can afford. In this case a larger repayment would be scheduled for the last year, which the firm could attempt to refinance at that time should they still be unable to meet the larger payments. Our task is to determine the size of the balloon payment due in year 8.
    Appendix D shows that the present value of $1 per year for 7 years at 8 percent is $5.21. The seven years of $125 payments will thus have a present value of (125 × 5.21) = $651.25, leaving a present value of ($1,000 − $651.25) = $348.75, to be satisfied by the payment at the end of year 8. Appendix C indicates that $1 to be received in year 8, discounted at 8 percent, has a present value of $0.54. To have a present value of $348.75 the balloon payment at the end of year 8 must therefore be ($348.75/54) ≃ $646.
    (b) *When size of balloon is known.* Suppose that, instead of the above assumption, the borrower wants to make a $300 balloon payment at the end of year 8 and wants to know what the annual payments for the first 7 years will be. From the above analysis, we know that $300 in year 8 has a present value of ($300 × .54) = $162, which leaves a present value of ($1,000 − $162) = $838 to be amortized by the 7 annual payments. The present value of $1 per year for 7 years, discounted at 8 percent, was given above as

$5.21. Substituting into our formula, the required annual payment is $838/5.21) $\simeq$ $161 for the first 7 years.

The lenders of term debt are generally banks, insurance companies and, to a lesser degree, pension funds. Even here, however, there is some specialization. Banks, with their desire to keep their portfolios liquid, tend to concentrate in shorter maturities (1-5 years); insurance companies, with a greater desire to keep their vast amount of funds employed, often take the longer maturities. Currently, a practice has developed of splitting loans between banks and insurance companies; for example, if a business desires a 15 year amortized loan, a bank may take the first 5 years of the loan and an insurance company the remaining 10 years.

In the cases we have illustrated thus far, term debt bears a fixed rate of interest over its life. It is also possible for the interest rate to vary over the life of the loan, with the rate charged each year geared to the prime rate or Federal Reserve discount rate for the area in which the firm operates. In such a case, there would normally be both a floor and a ceiling for the rate charged. If the prime rate (or whatever money market indicator was being used) changed during the year, a weighted average would be employed to determine the interest charge for the year.

SOLVED PROBLEM

The Swisher Company has borrowed $10,000 for 5 years from the local bank. The principal is to be amortized evenly over the period and the interest charged each year is to be prime plus 1 percent, but at no time less than 6 percent nor more than 10 percent. During the third year of the loan, prime is 8 percent for four months, 9 percent for four months and 10 percent for four months. What is the total payment Swisher must make to the bank in year three?

SOLUTION

The interest charge to Swisher would be 9 percent for one-third of the year and 10 percent for the other two-thirds (because it cannot be more than this rate), giving a weighted average of $[(\frac{1}{3})(.09) + (\frac{2}{3} \times .10)] = 9.67\%$. The annual principal repayment is ($10,000/5) = $2,000, implying that $4,000 would have been repaid during the first two years and the balance in year 3 would be $6,000. The interest due is thus ($6,000 $\times$ 9.67%) = $580. The total payment due consists of the $580 interest and the $2,000 principal amortization, or $2,580.

SECTION
10.2
Because the time period involved in term lending is sufficiently great for the financial condition of the firm to deteriorate markedly, specific provisions are usually inserted in the loan agreement for the protection of the lender. Invariably, one requirement will be that financial statements be provided periodically to the lender and another will be some sort of acceleration clause, stating that a violation of any of the loan agreement provisions will cause the entire amount of the note to be due immediately. Other provisions, which may or may not appear in any given loan agreement, are outlined below:

1. Minimum working capital or current ratio that must be maintained, limits on capital expenditures—minimum liquidity required by lenders so that the firm will be able to meet its obligations.

2. Limits on dividends, salaries, stock repurchases and sale of assets—to protect lenders against the withdrawal of assets from the firm.

3. Limits to the amount of additional debt and leasing that may be undertaken, provisions preventing other creditors from obtaining senior status with regard to assets or income—to protect the lender's position *vis-à-vis* other creditors.

4. Requirements that the company have long term contracts with and insurance on the lines of key people in the organization—to protect the loan against loss should the borrower lose key personnel.

There is little argument that a certain amount of lender protection is essential, but some of these restrictions become so detailed that management must check its loan agreement every time it makes a move. This often reaches the point that lenders are running the company by remote control. It is usually desirable to allow management the maximum freedom consistent with lender protection. Whenever a lender has so little confidence in the borrower that a very detailed and restrictive loan agreement is required, it would perhaps be best for the lender to reconsider whether he really wants to make the loan.

SOLVED PROBLEM

The Lutz Company has a 10 percent pretax opportunity cost of funds. It has obtained a nonamortized 3-year term loan for $10 million at 7 percent. The loan agreement contains certain restrictive provisions, including working capital and dividend limitations. As a result of the working capital requirement, the firm will hold $1 million more of non-income-earning current assets than it otherwise would. The dividend restriction will force the firm to retain $2 million which it otherwise would not. The Lutz Company has found a 3-year $1 million project with an 8 percent pretax return. What is the effective cost of the loan?

SOLUTION [1]

One way to approach this problem is to take the dividend restriction first. This would imply that an additional $2 million must be employed within the firm at a net opportunity loss of 2 percent. The working capital restriction, however, indicates that $1 million of this must be employed at a zero return, or a net opportunity loss of 10 percent. Thus we have:

$$
\begin{array}{rcl}
\$10 \text{ million} \times 7\% &=& \$700{,}000 \\
1 \text{ million} \times 2\% &=& 20{,}000 \\
1 \text{ million} \times 10\% &=& \underline{100{,}000} \\
&& \$820{,}000
\end{array}
$$

$820,000/$10 million = 8.2% (Approximation of cost of term debt)

UNSOLVED PROBLEMS

1. (a) If the lender requires a 10 percent return, what annual payment would be made to amortize a $3,000 loan over 6 years?

(b) What payment would be left for year 6 if the borrower could afford to pay only $500 in each of the first 5 years?

(c) What payment would be made in each of the first 5 years if the borrower wanted a $1,000 "balloon" in year 6?

2. The Ajax Company borrowed $20,000 for 4 years, with equal principal amortizations each year. The interest rate charged is the Federal Reserve discount rate for Ajax' district plus 3 percent. During the last year of the loan, the discount rate was 6 percent for four months and 6.5 percent the other eight months. Compute the total payment made by Ajax during year 4 of the loan.

3. The Braze Company has a 20 percent pre-tax opportunity cost of funds. It has obtained a 5-year term loan for $100,000 at 9 percent. The loan agreement requires the firm to maintain $20,000 of working capital in excess of what it would normally keep and retain $30,000 a year which would otherwise be paid as dividends. The Braze Company has 5-year investment

---

[1] It must be stated at the outset that this approach to quantification of the costs of restrictive covenants is very crude and is subject to numerous theoretical arguments. It is felt, however, that the effort is worthwhile because it gives the student some awareness of these costs.

projects available which return 15 percent and can obtain Treasury bills (91 day maturities) at a 6 percent yield. What is the effective cost of this term loan?

SECTION 10.3   Leases may be classified in several ways. *A maintenance lease* involves a package deal in which the lessee makes one payment and the lessor acquires, provides, and maintains the article being leased. In the case of a *financial lease,* the lessor does little more than finance the transaction; the responsibility for maintenance lies with the lessee. If the lease is drawn for less than the useful life of the asset so that the lessor's investment will not be fully amortized by the lease payments, it is then important to determine which party will be responsible if the value of the asset at the end of the lease differs from what it was estimated to be at the beginning. Although the terminology becomes muddy at this point, the term *operating lease* generally refers to the case where the lessor assumes this risk.

The determination of lease payments is similar to the term loan amortization schedules we constructed in the previous section. Thus, if a piece of equipment costs $1,000, has an 8-year life, and the lessor desires an 8 percent pre-tax return, the annual payment would be $174, as we computed earlier. Also, if the equipment has a life greater than 8 years such that its market value is $139 at the end of the lease, then 8 annual payments of $161 will satisfy the lessor's requirements (see Sec. 10.1).

The cost of leasing as a source of funds is determined by reversing the above process. If a lessor is willing to lease a piece of equipment with an 8-year life and a $1,000 cost for $174 a year, the cost of funds from this source is 8 percent. Similarly, if the lessor is willing to lease a $1,000 piece of equipment for 8 years that will be worth $139 at the end of that time for $161 per year, the cost is also 8 percent.

A leasing arrangement may be undertaken in several ways. A firm may sell an asset it already owns to a lessor and then lease the asset (the "sale-leaseback" arrangement). A firm may contract with a lessor to lease a new asset, which the lessor then obtains from the manufacturer. The manufacturer of capital assets may have its own leasing agency, such that the lessee leases the asset directly from the manufacturer. The evaluation of the desirability of leasing which the prospective lessee must make is essentially the same in any case. There is one point, however, that cannot be emphasized too strongly: the alternative to leasing is *not* buying—it is *borrowing* and *buying.*

Bearing this fact in mind, let us consider some of the advantages which are claimed for leasing.

1. "A leasing agreement usually does not contain as many restrictive covenants as a loan agreement or bond indenture." This is true and therefore is an advantage to management. It must be borne in mind, however, that the lessor retains title to the asset, which is one of the most restrictive provisions of all. Furthermore, as indicated in the earlier section, the act of leasing may invoke the restrictive covenants of other debt agreements the firm has made.

2. "Leasing allows for 100 percent debt financing of the asset, whereas if one were to borrow and buy, the loan value of the asset would not be 100 percent of its cost." This is also true as far as it goes, but the fact remains that the lessor is only willing to make such an arrangement because of the financial strength of the lessee. The lessee is thus trading on its equity whether it likes it or not.

3. "Leasing allows for piecemeal financing in that the liabilities expand in unison with earning assets." No one would argue that it is practical to have a bond issue every time the firm buys a truck, but this piecemeal financing argument implies that no particular debt-equity relationship is optimal for the firm (a point to which we will return in Chap. 16).

4. "Leasing allows managers to evade budget restrictions, in that a manager might have the authority to approve a $10,000 per year lease but not a $100,000 purchase." This is also valid, but whether it constitutes an advantage of leasing is open to grave doubt.

5. "Leasing (especially sale-leaseback arrangements) frees cash." Selling an asset and leasing it back frees cash no more than keeping the asset and issuing obligations. Furthermore, the function of business is to employ cash, not to free it. One can always free cash by dissolving the enterprise.

6. "Leasing allows for the depreciation of land." If a firm sells its plant and leases it back, the lease payment will amortize the entire price paid by the lessor, including what he paid for the land. Since the lessee may deduct the entire lease payment for tax purposes, he is thus indirectly depreciating the land and reducing his taxes. At the termination of the lease, however, the land still belongs to the lessor and the lessee firm obtains none of the appreciation in value of the land.

7. "The accounting treatment of leasing is favorable." This is still true, although the accounting profession is moving toward change. Consider the following case:

SOLVED PROBLEM

The Able Company is considering the purchase of a $100 asset, which would have $10 depreciation per year. The acquisition would add $50 to sales and $20 to other expenses. The going rate of interest is 8 percent. The firm could either lease this asset or acquire a 10-year amortized term loan. Show the impacts of leasing vs. borrowing and buying on the following table.

SOLUTION

	Now	*Borrow and Buy*	*Lease*
Current Assets	$200	$200	$200
Fixed Asset	400	500	400
Total Assets	$600	$700	$600
Current Liabilities	$100	$100	$100
Debt	200	300	200
Equity	300	300	300
Total	$600	$700	$600
Sales	$150	$200	$200
Leasing Expense	–	–	18
Depreciation	40	50	40
Other Expenses	54	74	74
E.B.I.T.	56	76	68
Interest	16	24	16
E.B.T.	$ 40	$ 52	$ 52
Current assets/Total assets	–	.29	.33
Long term debt/Equity	–	1.00	.67
Asset turnover	–	.29	.33
Interest coverage	–	3.2x	4.3x
E.B.T./Total Assets		7.4%	8.7%

Note that the book expenses are $18 in both cases for the first year, as are the actual cash flow expenses ($18 leasing expense vs. $8 interest and $10 debt amortization). Despite this equality the leasing alternative makes the firm's ratios look better.

UNSOLVED PROBLEMS

1. If a company is to lease a $5,000 machine for its 10-year useful life and provide a 10 percent pre-tax return to the lessor, what annual payment must be made?

2. If the machine described above will have a $1,000 salvage value at the end of 10 years, what annual payment will now be required for the lessor to earn 10 percent?

3. If the machine, costing $5,000 and having no salvage, can be leased for $885 per year for 10 years, what pre-tax rate of return is the lessor demanding?

4. The Lease-All Company desires to earn a 20 percent pre-tax return on its investment. The Manor Company desires to lease a piece of equipment for 5 years which costs $1 million. The estimated value of this machine at the end of 5 years is normally distributed, with a mean of $300,000 and a standard deviation of $100,000. What annual charge should Lease-All make if it wishes to be 90 percent certain of earning its 20 percent pre-tax return?

COMPREHENSIVE CASE

The Ball Company currently owns a plant with a book value of $5 million, of which $1 million represents the land. The building will be depreciated on a straight-line basis with a 20-year life and no salvage assumed. Ball has a 10 percent after-tax cost of funds and a tax rate of 50 percent. The possible worth of the land at the end of 20 years is normally-distributed with a μ of $3 million and a σ of $1 million. The Ronson Leasing Company is prepared to buy the plant at its book value and lease it to Ball at a charge which would provide Ronson a 6 percent return after taxes of 50 percent; Ronson would use straight-line depreciation and assumes the land to be worth only its book value at the expiration of the lease.

1. What would the annual leasing charge be?

2. Assuming that Ball's estimates are accurate and that Ronson is risk-neutral, what actual after-tax rate of return would Ronson earn from the lease?

3. What is the net present value of the leasing proposal to Ball, assuming risk neutrality?

4. What is the probability that retention of the plant would have a greater present value to Ball than the sale-leaseback?

11 LONG-TERM DEBT AND RIGHTS OF CREDITORS

SECTION
11.1

As we indicated in the last chapter, long-term debt generally consists of those obligations with a maturity in excess of seven to ten years. In the case of corporations, long-term debt generally takes the form of either a privately-placed note (considered in Sec. 11.3) or a publicly-issued bond. Bond issues are similar in many respects to the term notes which we considered in the last chapter but are more formal in nature. The essential difference between the two is derived from the fact that a term loan is usually negotiated with one lender whereas a bond issue is generally sold to an investment banker who, in turn, distributes it to the general public. Because there are numerous lenders, it is necessary for them to have a representative—the "trustee," which is often the trust department of a bank—and a more specific statement of the rights and duties of lender and borrower—the "indenture," which is negotiated by the borrower and the trustee as representative of the lenders. The indenture will contain even more of the restrictive covenants discussed in Chap. 10.

For years, it was felt that the most secure type of bond was a mortgage, which contained a lien against specific property owned by the company. It has come to be appreciated, however, that interest and principal payments are made from income, not assets, and corporations are increasingly able to sell unsecured bonds (debentures) on favorable terms.[1] Subordinated and junior subordinated debentures have even lower income and asset priority than debentures; these bonds often have a conversion feature, which is considered in the next chapter. In general, the student should not rely on the classification of the bond (debenture, mortgage, etc.) to be descriptive of its asset or income security; only a careful study of the indenture will reveal such information.

---

[1] A partial exception applies to the railroads and certain other transportation companies. They must set up a separate company to acquire rolling stock by issuing equipment trust certificates (a form of secured debt) to investors. The railroad then leases the equipment or buys it under a conditional sales contract. The investors are protected against the railroad's default because the equipment is owned by the leasing company and may be repossessed and re-leased immediately.

The actual interest, or coupon payments on bonds, are generally made semiannually (although some have monthly, quarterly, or annual payments). Thus, a $1,000, 8 percent bond would pay interest of $40 every six months and would possess a coupon (or nominal) yield of 8 percent. Even when originally issued, however, bonds are often sold at a premium or discount from their par value; once they reach the market, their price obviously fluctuates continuously. Nominal yield is thus a concept of limited use to either the issuing company or the investor.

For these reasons, the notion of yield to maturity is generally given a central place in the discussion of bond returns. The yield to maturity is nothing more than an internal rate of return with semiannual compounding (to take account of the timing of interest payments). For example, if a 7 percent bond with 10 years to maturity were selling at 90 (bonds are quoted in percentages of their par, thus 90 = $900), the yield to maturity would show the actual rate of return earned on a $900 investment which paid $35 every 6 months for 10 years and $1,000 at the end of the period.[2] Either bond tables or very detailed present value tables must be consulted to obtain an accurate computation of the yield to maturity, but a fairly good estimate may be derived from the following formula:

$$\text{Yield to Maturity} = \frac{\text{Annual Coupon Payment} + \left(\dfrac{\text{Par Value} - \text{Current Price}}{\text{Remaining Life [in years]}}\right)}{\dfrac{\text{Par Value} + \text{Current Price}}{2}} \quad (11.1)$$

Thus, in the above case we have

$$Y \text{ to } M = \frac{\$70 + \left(\dfrac{\$1,000 - \$900}{10}\right)}{\dfrac{\$1,000 + \$900}{2}} = \frac{\$80}{\$950} = 8.4\%$$

Suppose that the market rate of interest on bonds of comparable risk declined until new bonds being issued were only bearing a 7.7 percent yield. For the bond described above to compete in the market place with these new bonds, it too would yield about 7.7 percent. The maturity and coupon of the bond were fixed at the time of issue and will not change over its life. The only variable which can affect yield therefore is price. The formula presented above may be used to estimate the price at which the bond would sell.

---

[2] Another concept of limited usefulness but occasionally applied to bonds is that of current yield, which is simply (current interest/current price). In the example cited, the current yield is ($70/$900) = 7.7%.

$$7.7\% = \frac{\$70 + \left(\dfrac{\$1,000 - x}{10}\right)}{\dfrac{\$1,000 + x}{2}}$$

$$X = \$950$$

It cannot be stressed too strongly that changes in the required yield on outstanding bonds must have an inverse effect upon their price (*the coupon payment does not change*).

UNSOLVED PROBLEMS

1. In 1965, the Allgood Company issued $10 million of 6 percent, 25 year debentures at 98.

   (a) What was the nominal (coupon) yield?

   (b) What was the current yield?

   (c) What was the yield to maturity?

   (d) Which of the above represented the cost of funds from this source to the company?

2. By 1970, the price of the Allgood debentures had declined to 80.

   '(a) What was the nominal (coupon) yield?

   (b) What was the current yield?

   (c) What was the yield to maturity?

   (d) Which yields are different from what they were in question 1? Why? Why did not current yield and yield to maturity change together?

   (e) In 1970, what was the cost of long-term, unsecured debt funds to Allgood? Why?

SECTION 11.2   During the latter part of the last century it was not uncommon for bonds, especially those of railroads, to be issued with maturities of 100 or 150 years; there were several issued for longer periods, including the West Shore R.R. 4% bonds due 2361 and the Elmira and Williamsport R.R. 5's of 2862.[3] More recently, however, most

---

[3]Everyone knew that railroads would grow and prosper forever. There appears to be a lesson here that the investing public must learn to its sorrow about every 20-30 years.

industrial companies' bonds have been issued with an original maturity of between 15 and 30 years and even public utilities have rarely gone beyond 40 or 50 years. In addition, almost all bonds contain some provision for an orderly retirement of part of the issue prior to maturity. Such provisions reduce the life of the average bond and, thus, the risk to the investor that the condition of the issuer will deteriorate. Perhaps even more important in a time of constantly rising interest rates, the investor is able to recover his money more quickly and reinvest for a higher return.

A serial issue is one way to provide for orderly retirement, although it is far more common in the case of municipal bonds. Such an issue would retire a certain number of specified bonds in each year. The investor would thus know at the time of issue exactly when his particular bonds would be retired. This arrangement allows the existence of different yields and even different coupons on different maturities of the same overall bond issue. Furthermore, the dollar amount of bonds to be retired each year can be set at the time of issue to correspond to the cash inflows of the project to be financed (which usually results in an initial period when no bonds are scheduled for retirement).

In the case of corporate bonds, however, the use of a sinking fund is the most common means of retirement prior to maturity.[4] A sinking fund provision usually states that, beginning in some year of the life of the issue, a certain percentage of the issue will be retired annually. For example, a 5 percent sinking fund beginning after 10 years on a 25-year, $10 million issue would require that $500,000 par value of bonds be retired in each of years 11-24, leaving $3 million to be retired at the end of year 25.

The mechanics of retirement are specified in the indenture of the bond issue, but the issuer invariably may satisfy his obligation by depositing the requisite sum with the trustee, who will determine by lot which bonds are to be called and redeemed at par. If the issuer is shrewd in indenture negotiation, he will also have the option of satisfying the sinking fund requirement by purchasing bonds in the market and submitting them to the trustee for cancellation. An indenture containing both options allows the issuer to pay the trustee at par if the bonds are selling at a premium over par in the market (e.g., if interest rates have declined since the bonds were issued) and to buy the bonds in the market if they are selling at a discount (if interest rates have risen).[5] Although these advantages to the issuer are disadvantages to the investor, the existence of a sinking fund does reduce the average life of a bond issue, which in turn reduces the risk

---

[4] Call provisions and conversion features are considered later.

[5] For tax purposes, the corporation has a deductable expense if it repurchases the bonds for more than their net amortized value on the books and ordinary income if it repurchases them for less than this amount.

exposure of the investor. In addition, the existence of a sinking fund tends to exert upward price pressure on bonds selling at a discount.[6]

Because of the essentially random nature of the redemption process under a sinking fund, an investor does not know when his bonds will be redeemed and thus cannot determine the yield to maturity by the means we have considered so far. Since the going rate of interest on debt instruments tends to be related to their maturity[7] the life of the bond is of more than academic interest to the investor. To prevent confusion, most investors will evaluate bonds on the basis of yield to average life, which is simply yield to maturity using the expected life of a bond instead of the total remaining life of the issue.

SOLVED PROBLEM

The Bock Company has just floated a 15-year, 8 percent bond issue, with a 10 percent sinking fund starting after the tenth year, at 95. Compute the yield to average life of the issue and compare it to the yield to maturity.

SOLUTION

There are several ways to compute average life, but the simplest is to assume that one owns a single bond and compute the following:

Year	Probability of Redemption	
1-10	0.0	0.0
11	0.1	1.1
12	0.1	1.2
13	0.1	1.3
14	0.1	1.4
15	0.6	9.0
	1.0	Average life 14.0 years

Thus, from the investor's viewpoint, the life of the average bond is 14 years and, from the issuer's position, the average life of the issue is 14 years. In sum, the market yield on these bonds should roughly be comparable to that of obligations maturing in 14 years.

---

[6]This phenomena may be explained either by the acceleration of redemption at par or by the impact of the issuer's demand for the bonds upon an imperfect market.

[7]The nature of this relationship is considered at length in the vast body of literature on the term structure of interest rates. Cf. Burton G. Malkiel, *The Term Structure of Interest Rates* (Princeton: Princeton University Press), 1966; and James Van Horne, "Interest-Rate Risk and the Term Structure of Interest Rates," *Journal of Political Economy,* August, 1965, pp. 344-51.

The yield to average life is determined by substituting average life for years to maturity in the yield to maturity formula. Thus:

$$\text{Yield to Maturity} \simeq \frac{\$80 + \left(\dfrac{\$1,000 - \$950}{15}\right)}{\dfrac{\$1,000 + \$950}{2}} \simeq \frac{\$83.3}{\$975} \simeq 8.54\%$$

$$\text{Yield to Average Life} \simeq \frac{\$80 + \left(\dfrac{\$1,000 - \$950}{14}\right)}{\dfrac{\$1,000 + \$950}{2}} \simeq \frac{\$83.6}{\$975} \simeq 8.57\%$$

Because some holders of $950 bonds will receive their $1,000 a few years before maturity, the yield to average life is higher than the yield to maturity. In more complicated illustrations, the difference between the two can be far greater than we have shown.

UNSOLVED PROBLEMS

1. Five years ago the Lippincott Corporation floated a 25-year, $10 million, 7 percent bond issue, with a 5 percent sinking fund beginning after the tenth year. The bonds were sold at 95. The bonds are currently selling at 90. What is the present yield to average life on these bonds?

2. The Lippincott Company (see unsolved problem above) pays a 40 percent tax rate and amortizes bond discounts evenly over the life of each bond. Illustrate the cash flow in each year associated with the bond issue.

3. The Willett Company is planning to offer a 10-year, 8 percent, $10 million bond issue at par, with a 20 percent sinking fund beginning after the fifth year. The trustee wishes to have the sinking fund satisfied only by calling the bonds at par, but the company wants to include the option of purchasing the bonds in the market. The trustee will only grant this option if the coupon is raised to 8.25 percent. The Willett Company is taxed at 50 percent and has a 10 percent after-tax opportunity cost of funds. Willett's expectations as to the price of the bonds at the end of years 6-9 (statistically independent of each other) are given on the next page. Which course should it follow? Why?

Price	Probability
96	0.2
98	0.2
100	0.2
102	0.2
104	0.2
	1.0

SECTION 11.3   In addition to the terms already discussed, most bond issues contain a call feature. This provision allows the debtor company to redeem the entire issue prior to maturity with funds secured by a new bond issue at a lower rate of interest. Such a provision tends to prevent bond prices from rising to a large premium over par no matter how low interest rates may go. To give some protection to the investor, there is often an initial period (frequently 5 or 10 years from issuance) during which the bonds may not be called for redemption. Also, a premium is typically paid when they are called. The call price is often par plus one year's interest in the first year that bonds are eligible for call, and it is scaled down to par by the final years of the issue.[8]

Since the existence of a call feature may cut short the scheduled life of the bond issue, it further complicates yield computations. This point is particularly apparent if a bond is still in its no-call period but interest rates have declined since it was issued. Everyone can be fairly confident that the issuer will call the bond as soon as it is able and, thus, an investor would be ill-advised to pay a large premium for the bonds. To account for the call feature, many analysts will compute a yield to first call date. Again, this is nothing more than a yield to maturity formulation under the assumption that the bonds will be called at the first possible opportunity. In many cases, analysts will compute both a yield to average life and a yield to first call date.

---

[8]Lest the student be confused, it should be noted that a bond indenture may contain several call price schedules. One schedule will give the price in various years at which bonds may be called for refunding purposes. Another schedule (which rapidly approaches par) may give the call price in future years for sinking fund purposes. There may be a third schedule giving the prices at which all or part of the issue may be called if the funds are not raised from a new issue at lower cost (as, for example, if the issuer sold some assets and wished to apply the proceeds to reducing its indebtedness).

SOLVED PROBLEM

A 9 percent, 20-year bond was issued 5 years ago. The bond had 10-year call protection and was callable in year 11 at 105. It is currently selling at 110. Compute yield to maturity and to first call.

SOLUTION

$$\text{Yield to Maturity} = \frac{\$90 + \left(\dfrac{\$1,000 - \$1,100}{15}\right)}{\dfrac{\$1,000 + \$1,100}{2}} = \frac{\$83.3}{\$1,050} = 7.93\%$$

$$\text{Yield to First Call} = \frac{\$90 + \left(\dfrac{\$1,050 - \$1,100}{5}\right)}{\dfrac{\$1,050 + \$1,100}{2}} = \frac{\$80}{\$1,075} = 7.44\%$$

To the corporation, the important decision is whether or not to refund an outstanding bond issue if interest rates decline. There are costs associated with a new bond issue, such as legal and printing expenses and perhaps double interest for the period between the sale of the new issue and the calling of the old. Of course, there are also expenses of calling the old issue, not the least of which is the call premium; fortunately this premium, as well as any unamortized issuing expense and discount associated with the old bonds, may be deducted for tax purposes. Thus, the refunding decision is a typical capital budgeting type problem in which a current outlay is made in order to effect future savings.

To analyze the problem in detail, the following framework is suggested.[9] For an example, we will assume that a company currently has $10 million of 9 percent bonds outstanding with 15 years left to maturity and a call price of 109. Unamortized discount on these bonds is $100,000, as is unamortized issuing expense. A new $10 million 15-year issue could be sold at 7.5 percent to return $9.7 million to the company after flotation costs. Additional issuing expenses would be $100,000 and the new bonds would be sold 60 days before the old bonds were called. The company pays taxes at 40 percent.

The initial outlay would be determined as follows:

---

[9] Adapted from James Van Horne, *Financial Management and Policy* (Englewood Cliffs, N.J.: Prentice-Hall, Inc., 1968), pp. 249-50

Cost of calling old bonds ($10 million @ 109)		10,900,000
Net proceeds of new issue		9,700,000
		$1,200,000
Issuing expense of new bonds		100,000
Interest on old bonds during overlap		150,000
		$1,450,000
Less: Tax savings		
Overlap interest	$ 150,000	
Call premium	900,000	
Unamortized discount on old	100,000	
Unamortized issuing expense on old	100,000	
	$1,250,000	
Tax savings (40% of above)		500,000
Net Initial Cash Outflow		$ 950,000

The annual savings would be determined as follows:

	Old Bonds		New Bonds	Difference
Interest expense	$900,000		$750,000	
Less: Tax Saving				
Interest	900,000		750,000	
Disc. Amor.	6,667		20,000	
Issuing Exp.	6,667		6,667	
Tax Saving (40% of above)	365,334		310,667	
Annual net cash outflow	$534,666		$439,333	$95,333

The problem now becomes the determination of whether annual after-tax savings of $95,333 per year for 15 years justify an expenditure of $950,000. Obviously, a discount rate is needed before a decision can be made. Most authorities suggest that the after-tax cost of the new bond issue provides the appropriate rate, which in our case would be (7.5% × 0.6) = 4.5%[10] Since our tables are not this refined, we shall use 5 percent. Appendix D gives the present value of $1 per year for 15 years as $10.38. This implies that the annual savings are worth $989,500 and the refunding has a net present value of $39,500 and should thus be undertaken.

---

[10]This argument is based upon the premise that the substitution of one form of debt for another is riskless to the firm and should not be penalized by a high required rate of return; if anything, the lower interest costs should reduce the risk of the firm. It might be argued that if the above were true, the pure rate of interest would be the appropriate rate. Furthermore, from a very pragmatic standpoint, it could be argued that firms always operate under a funds constraint and thus refunding should receive no more favorable treatment than any other possible use of funds.

UNSOLVED PROBLEMS

1. An 8 percent, 25-year bond was issued 3 years ago with 5 years' call protection. It may be called in the sixth year of its life at 108. It is currently selling at 110. Compute the yield to maturity and yield to first call.

2. The Hart Company currently has a 10 percent, $20 million bond issue outstanding with 20 years left to maturity and a call price of 106. The bonds were sold at par, but there is unamortized issuing expense of $200,000. A 20-year, $20 million issue could now be sold with a 9 percent coupon to net the company $19.5 million. Additional issuing expense would be $300,000 and a 90-day overlap would be required, but the idle funds could be invested in Treasury bills at 5 percent during this period. The Hart Company has a 50 percent tax rate. Should it refund the issue?

SECTION
11.4
As we have implied above, there are many expenses and delays involved in the sale of securities to the public. Starting from the moment the decision to secure funds is made, the company, in consultation with its investment banker, must assemble data and the opinions of accountants, lawyers, and engineers so that an accurate picture of the business may be presented to the public. These data are then submitted to the Securities and Exchange Commission (SEC) in the form of a registration statement.[11] The issue must also be approved by the state securities commissioner in each state in which attempts will be made to sell it (the "blue-sky" laws). As soon as the SEC is reasonably confident that full disclosure has been made (a period of several weeks to several months), the issue is sold to a syndicate led by the company's investment banker which marks the price up and proceeds to attempt to sell it.[12] The difference between the price to the public and the proceeds to the company (the "gross spread" which constitutes the profit and reimbursement of expenses to the investment banker) may vary from less than 1 percent to over 3 percent in the case of bonds and from 3 or 4 percent to over 20 percent in the case of common stock. The time lapse between the decision to sell securities and the actual receipt of the money will usually be at least six months and can be much longer.

A brief review of the above description should indicate that a public offering of securities involves (1) a vast loss of time, (2) numerous costs,

---

[11] Assuming the issue is over $300,000 or to be sold in interstate commerce. Full details of the Securities Act of 1933 and related matters may be found in any standard text on the securities markets or investments.

[12] In a "best-efforts" distribution, the investment banker would merely act as selling agent for the company and never take title to the securities.

including the gross spread, lawyers' and accountants' fees, etc., (3) greater disclosure of the operations of the business than would normally be made, and (4) aggravation from various levels of the government. It should not be surprising to learn, therefore, that an increasing amount of corporate debt is being sold in bulk to large institutional lenders without the formalities of a public sale. Such a distribution is called a private placement and is similar in most respects to the negotiation of a term loan. A corporation may borrow immediately and directly from one or a limited number (usually no more than 30-50) of institutions. There is no need for additional disclosure or government dealings. The underwriting spread is eliminated, although a borrower may pay a fee to an investment banker to have him find a lender and negotiate the loan agreement. The agreement may be constructed to meet the specific needs of borrower and lender. The major disadvantage is that since the lender is sacrificing marketability of the debt instrument, a higher rate of interest may be required.

UNSOLVED PROBLEM

The Argeles Company plans to issue $20 million of a 25-year debt. It may sell bonds with a 8 percent coupon, 2 percent gross spread, and $200,000 of issuing expenses or place a note privately at 8.25 percent, with a .25 percent fee to a banker and $25,000 of other expenses. Neither issue will be repaid prior to maturitity, interest is paid annually, and the company has a 16 percent pre-tax opportunity cost of funds. Which alternative is superior?

SECTION 11.5   To this point, the going-concern assumption has been followed fairly consistently. The fact remains, however, that firms do suffer financial difficulties and creditors are most concerned about their position should settlements or liquidation payments have to be made.

Liquidation is perhaps the most extreme solution to financial embarrassment. When accomplished under bankruptcy proceedings, the referee liquidates the assets. First, he pays himself, the government, and certain other claimants. Secured creditors are entitled to the proceeds obtained from assets against which they have claims; to the extent that their claims are not satisfied, they become general creditors. The proceeds remaining after secured creditors are paid are distributed to general creditors (on a pro rata basis if they are inadequate to satisfy claims fully). If anything is left, distribution is made to subordinated creditors, then preferred holders, and only after all other claims are satisfied is any payment made to common holders. Generally the funds are exhausted long before the common shareholders are reached.

Most creditors, having noted over the years that lawyers appear to be the only people to make money from bankruptcy proceedings, will often make great concessions to keep a debtor out of bankruptcy court. The simplest means is an extension, by which the debtor is given more time to meet his obligations. A composition involves the acceptance by the creditor of less than 100 cents on the dollar as payment in full; such a settlement may still be more than the creditor could realize from the legal proceedings. In the case of both extensions and compositions, smaller creditors must generally be paid in full lest they force the issue into the courts.

Should a company be forced into bankruptcy, it may be decided that reorganization is preferable to liquidation. In such a case, a referee is appointed who determines a new capital structure, which, among other things, should not overly burden the firm with fixed charges. It then becomes necessary to apportion the new securities among the old holders. Under the absolute priority rule, claims are settled with strict regard to their legal priority (as illustrated in the discussion of liquidation above) and all senior claims must be satisfied before anything is paid to less-senior claims. Under the rule of relative priority, all claimants participate in the reorganization, although the losses apportioned the junior claims must be greater than those experienced by senior claims. A method of distribution under the relative priority rule is to allocate new securities on the basis of the market value of the old securities.

SOLVED PROBLEM

Data for the Wagner Company are as follows:

	Current Book (in millions)	Trustee's Desired Structure (in millions)	Current Market Value (in millions)
Senior debentures	$15	$ 5	$12
Junior debentures	10	7	8
Preferred stock	5	3	4
Common stock	10	10	6
	$40	$25	$30

Determine what each holder would receive under the rules of (1) absolute priority (2) relative priority.

SOLUTION

1. The $15 million in senior debentures would command all the debentures and the preferred in the new capitalization. The holder of each $1,000 senior debenture would thus receive $333 of new senior debentures, $467 of new junior debentures, and $200 of new preferred. Each holder of a $1,000 junior debenture would get $1,000 of common stock. Common and preferred holders would get nothing.

2. Since the total market value of securities is $30 million and the securities to be distributed are valued at $25 million, each class of holder would get new securities equal to 5/6 of the market value of the securities they hold.

(a) Senior debenture holders are therefore entitled to $10 million (or 2/3 the book value of their holdings), consisting of $5 million senior debentures and $5 million junior debentures. This is equal to $333 principal amount of both debentures for each old $1,000 senior debenture held.

(b) Junior debenture holders should receive a total of $6\frac{2}{3}$ million of new securities, consisting of $2 million junior debentures, $3 million preferred, and $1\frac{2}{3}$ million common, or $200 junior debentures, $300 preferred, and $167 common for each $1,000 junior debenture held.

(c) Preferred holders will receive $3\frac{1}{3}$ million in common, or $66.70 in common for each $100 preferred share held.

(d) Common holders will receive $5 million in new common, or one new share for each two old shares.

UNSOLVED PROBLEMS

1. The Lexington Company is in the process of reorganization by a referee. He has estimated that the company is capable of $5 million E.B.I.T. per year. Senior bonds in the new capitalization should bear a coupon of 8 percent and have interest coverage of 6 times. Junior obligations should bear interest of 9 percent and have coverage of 4 times. Preferred stock should have an 8 percent yield and a coverage of 3. Common stock should be issued at a 10 price-earnings ratio. The company pays taxes of 40 percent. Construct the new capitalization.

2. Current data for the Lexington Company are given below:

	Current Book (in millions)	Current Market (in millions)
Senior debentures	$15	$12
Junior debentures	10	8
Preferred (par $100)	10	7
Common (par $15)	15	8
	$50	$35

Divide the capital structure determined in problem 1 among the old holders on the basis of (a) absolute priority, (b) relative priority.

COMPREHENSIVE CASE

The Jensen Company wishes to obtain $10 million in debt funds for 20 years. Jensen has a 10 percent after-tax cost of capital and a 50 percent tax rate. At the present time, Jensen could issue at par (1) a 7 percent, 20 year, noncallable bond; (2) a 7.5 percent, 20-year bond, callable at the end of 5 years at 105; (3) a 6.5 percent, 5-year note. The possible rates of interest at which a 15-year bond could be sold in year 6 are normally-distributed with a μ of 7 percent and σ of 2 percent.

1. If Jensen is risk-neutral, which strategy is optimal?

2. What are the probabilities that each of the other two strategies would be superior?

3. If Jensen decided to adopt the safe strategy (alternative 1) unless another alternative promised superior results 84 percent of the time, what should be done?

12 QUASI-EQUITY
INSTRUMENTS

SECTION   Preferred stock represents a curious combination of
12.1   various features of debt and common stock. It is like
common stock in that the instrument is called stock and included in the
equity section of a balance sheet, payments are called dividends and are
not deductible for tax purposes, the payment of dividends is not legally
required, and the issue has no fixed maturity. Preferred stock is like debt
in that the dividends have a fixed maximum rate, preferred holders
generally have no vote (unless a specified number of dividends are passed,
in which case they may often elect a minority of the board), holders are
entitled to no more than the amount paid into the firm in case of
liquidation, and preferred stock may contain the same call, sinking fund,
or conversion features as any debenture.[1]

Because the payment of preferred dividends is not a legal obligation as
is the payment of interest, some protection must obviously be given to the
preferred holder.[2] The right to elect a minority of the board after a
certain number (often 4 to 6 quarterly) of dividends have been passed is
hardly adequate security. Almost all preferred stock issues provide that no
dividends may be paid on common until the preferred dividend
requirement is met. In the case of cumulative preferred stocks, the
preceeding statement refers to all past and present preferred dividends
which have not been paid; in the case of noncumulative preferred, it refers
only to the preferred dividend requirement in the current year. It should
follow that most preferred stocks are cumulative, yet even in this case the

---

[1] A rare type, called participating preferred, provides that after preferred dividends have been
paid and common shareholders have received a like return, both classes may participate by some
formula in any additional dividends to be paid.

[2] Income bonds, most commonly issued in reorganizations, are somewhat like preferred stocks
in that interest must be paid by the corporation only if it is earned and thus nonpayment cannot
throw the firm into bankruptcy. Because of the interest-deductibility for taxes, some firms have
issued income bonds for new funds instead of preferred stock, but the long association of income
bonds with financially-distressed situations has made investors wary of them.

company is not required to compound the dividends in arrears. Clearly, the issuance of preferred stock with the intention of not paying dividends would be a most bizarre financial strategy. The cases of distress mentioned above invariably occur because the financial condition of the issuer deteriorates subsequent to the flotation of the stock.

The 1920s witnessed perhaps the greatest relative popularity of preferred stock. Income taxes were low and the corporate need for funds from all sources was great. As a result, major firms issued 6, 7, or even 8 percent preferred stock without any provision for retirement. As business conditions worsened and interest rates fell, companies found that they could call and refund their debt (or, at worst, wait until it matured and replace it at a lower cost), but could do nothing about their preferred stock. In addition, the increase in tax rates during the 1930s and 1940s made preferred stock a very expensive source of funds; in the 50 percent tax bracket, an 8 percent preferred stock is as costly as a 16 percent bond. As a result of this painful lesson, virtually all preferred stocks issued since World War II have a call feature. In addition, some have sinking fund requirements.

Some companies with cumulative preferred outstanding get so far behind in dividend payments that it would be virtually impossible to pay all of the arrearages. Furthermore, since no dividends may be paid on common until all of the preferred arrearages are paid, there is no advantage to the company in paying only a part of the past preferred dividends. What results is a standoff for which the best solution is a voluntary retirement of the preferred stock. The same problem is faced by companies which still have high coupon, noncallable preferred outstanding. The voluntary retirement can only be accomplished by the company purchasing the shares (through the market or by a tender offer) or by offering to exchange new securities for them.

The yield on preferred stock is simply (current dividend/current price), adjusted for call or sinking funds considerations if applicable. The "current dividend" in the above formula is generally the contractual dividend for the issue except when dividends are being passed; in such a case, the yield concept becomes essentially meaningless. An 8 percent, $100 par preferred stock would promise an $8 annual dividend. If market interest rates and the riskiness of the issue required a 4 percent yield, the stock would sell at $200 (in the absence of a call provision) because of the perpetual nature of the obligation. For this reason, voluntary retirements can be very expensive to the corporation.

The student may now be wondering why any firm would issue preferred stock instead of debt. The answer is that only certain types of firms do, most of them public utilities.[3] Such utilities are often regulated

---

[3] See Fischer and Wilt, "Non-Convertible Preferred Stock as a Financing Instrument 1950-1965," *Journal of Finance,* September, 1968, pp. 611-624.

by the government as to their capital structure, with the result that they may not issue as much debt as they could afford. Given the choices that remain, preferred stock is more desirable than common.[4] If one company purchases another by means of convertible preferred stock and meets certain other conditions, the shareholders receiving the stock may be able to defer their recognition of gain. The 85 percent intercorporate dividend exclusion (discussed in Chap. 4) often results in preferred stock having a yield equal to or less than that of debt of the same company; a firm paying a low tax rate might thus find preferred a reasonably inexpensive source of funds.

An even more vigorous defense of preferred stock is presented by Donaldson.[5] He suggests that if a firm's debt capacity is fully utilized, preferred stock may be a more desirable source of funds than retained earnings. The use of preferred stock would enable the firm to pay internally generated funds as dividends, thus increasing the well-being of the stockholder. On the other hand, the preferred dividend requirement would lower earnings and, thus, the price of the stock, which would reduce the well-being of the stockholder. The magnitude of both forces must be explored before a decision can be made. Donaldson submits the following formula as a first approximation; preferred stock, rather than retained earnings, should be used as a source of funds when

$$S\left(1 - \frac{T}{100}\right) > D \times \frac{P}{E} \times .75 \qquad (12.1)$$

Where: S = Sum required
T = Rate (percent) of personal income tax assumed to be representative of common shareholders
P = Established (and anticipated) market price of common stock
E = Established (and anticipated) earnings per share
D = Total preferred dividends required

The left side of the above equation represents the after-tax benefit to the shareholders from a dividend. The right side indicates the capital loss (after an assumed capital gains tax benefit of 25 percent) involved when the preferred stock dividend first reduces earnings, and then the price of the firm's stock. Preferred stock should be used only if the left side benefit is greater than the right side loss.

The student should consider carefully the assumptions of the above analysis, which is suboptimal from the outset (as readily conceded by Donaldson). Is it possible to estimate a marginal tax rate that will be

---

[4]This point is discussed in greater detail in Chap. 16.

[5]Gordon Donaldson, "In Defense of Preferred Stock", *Harvard Business Review,* July-August, 1962, pp. 123-36.

representative of all shareholders? How are the interests of high tax bracket vs. low bracket holders to be weighted? Is it reasonable to assume that a firm would have fully utilized its low cost, fixed income debt capacity and still be able to issue high cost fixed income preferred stock? Is the price of a firm's stock always a constant multiple of reported earnings and totally independent of dividend payments? Is a realized, after-tax dollar of dividend payments exactly comparable to an unrealized, after-tax dollar decline in stock price?

SOLVED PROBLEM

The Myron Company requires $5 million from either an 8 percent preferred stock issue or the retention of earnings. If the average shareholder has a 50 percent marginal tax rate and Myron common generally sells for 10 times earnings, what should it do?

SOLUTION

If $5,000,000 (1 - 50/100) > $400,000 × 10 × .75, issue preferred. Since $2,500,000 < $3,000,000, the firm should retain earnings.

UNSOLVED PROBLEMS

1. The Laredo Company, which has a 40 percent tax rate, is contemplating raising about $1 million. It could sell 20-year, 8 percent bonds at 98 or 6 percent preferred stock at 100.[6] What is the after-tax cost of funds from each source? Why must the tax adjustment be made?

2. The Laredo Company has discovered that it may not sell additional debt, but it would be possible to generate the $1 million internally. It is estimated that stockholders have a 50 percent marginal tax rate and that the company's stock sells at a P/E ratio of 12 times. What would the Donaldson formula suggest?

SECTION
12.2   Convertible securities, as their name implies, possess the option of being traded to the company for common stock. Both debentures and preferred stock may have a conversion

[6]Much preferred stock has a $100 par value, although $50 and $25 par is also found.

feature, the only essential differences being that the interest on the debentures should be tax-deductible to the corporation and the use of convertible preferred in a merger might be tax-free to the holder. With these exceptions, the two types of convertibles will be used interchangeably in this discussion.

The *conversion ratio* indicates the number of shares of common which may be acquired for each debenture or share of preferred. A debenture with a conversion ratio of 10 would imply that 10 common shares could be acquired from the company in exchange for each $1,000 par debenture or, viewed another way, that $100 par value of debentures was being surrendered for each share acquired (the par value divided by the conversion ratio is called the *conversion price*).[7] The rights of holders may be expressed either as a conversion ratio or as a price; the student should be able to convert one into the other.

Because the issuer of a convertible security is granting the holder an option of value, there is a *quid pro quo*. The advantage to the issuer consists of the fact that the interest or dividend rate which must be paid on a convertible security is invariably lower than the rate which would be paid on the security without the conversion feature (if indeed it could be sold at any rate). In addition, the conversion price is set at some level above the current market price of the common stock. The measure of this difference (conversion price–market price/market price) is called the *conversion premium* and may vary from a negligible amount (when the presence of the feature is required to sell the issue at any price) to 10-15 percent in normal times to 20-25 percent or more in times of great market appetite for convertible securities.[8]

The existence of convertible securities (or warrants and options, for that matter) on the books of a company implies potential dilution of earnings per share when the securities are converted.[9] Although the issuer would no longer pay interest on the securities, there would be an increase in common shares outstanding. This dilution may be illustrated by considering the following example of a company with $10 million of 6 percent debentures outstanding convertible into common at $50 a share.

---

[7]The conversion ratio or price is usually altered to reflect stock dividends and splits, although small stock dividends (3 percent or less) may not result in their alteration.

[8]Many institutional investors who are prohibited from holding common stock may purchase convertible debentures, thus increasing the demand—especially in bull markets.

[9]To prevent the deception of shareholders, the accountants require that earnings per share be computed under the assumption of conversion of all securities that are common stock equivalents (convertibles issued with a cash yield less than 2/3 of the prime rate and all options and warrants under the assumption that proceeds from their exercise are used by the firm to buy treasury stock). A fully-diluted E.P.S. figure is also presented. For more complete information, see *American Institute of Certified Public Accountants Opinion 15*, May, 1969.

	Before Conversion	*After Conversion*
E.B.I.T.	$5,000,000	$5,000,000
Interest on debentures	600,000	–
E.B.T.	4,400,000	5,000,000
Taxes (@ 50%)	2,200,000	2,500,000
E.A.T.	2,200,000	2,500,000
Number of shares	1,000,000	1,200,000
E.P.S.	$2.20	$2.08

Because a convertible security has the features of both debt and equity, it also has several different values. The *conversion value* represents the value of the bond as nothing more than the right to acquire stock and is computed by multiplying the conversion ratio by the price of the stock; thus a bond which could be converted into 10 shares of common selling at $80 a share would have a conversion value of $800 and could not sell for less or else arbitrage would drive the price back up. The *bond* (or *investment*) *value* represents the price at which the security would sell without any regard to its conversion feature or, simply, its price as straight debt. This value is also a floor on the price of the bond no matter how far the price of the stock (and the conversion value) may drop. Thus, it follows that the price of a convertible bond cannot fall below the greater of its bond value or conversion value at any point in time. On the other hand, the insurance offered by the bond value and the possible appreciation offered by the conversion value may well result in the price of the bond being greater than either of its component values.

To illustrate the above discussion, we assume the following data:[10]

1. The ABC Company will sell a 20-year, 7 percent convertible debenture; without the conversion feature, the bond would require an 8 percent yield.
2. ABC common is currently selling at $50 a share. The company is planning a 20 percent conversion premium, which implies that the conversion price will be $60 per share and the conversion ratio will be $16\frac{2}{3}$ shares per $1,000 bond.
3. ABC will call the bond issue to force conversion when the market price of the stock is 20 percent above the conversion price (to allow for any depressing effects when the conversion is effected), or at $72 per share.[11]
4. ABC has a 50 percent tax rate.

---

[10] cf. Eugene Brigham, "An Analysis of Convertible Debentures: Theory and Some Empirical Evidence," *Journal of Finances,* March, 1966, pp. 35-54. See also William Baumol, Burton Malkiel, and Richard Quant, "The Valuation of Convertible Securities," *Quarterly Journal of Economies,* February, 1966, pp. 48-59.

[11] We state this decision rule in terms of conversion price, although technically call price is more appropriate. The consideration for the firm is that the price of the stock after the bond is called not decline so far that bondholders accept redemption rather than convert their securities.

As indicated in Fig. 12.1, the conversion value of the bond will always be $16\frac{2}{3}$ (the conversion ratio) times the price of the stock, or $833 when the stock is $50, $1,000 when it is $60, and $1,200 when the stock is $72 and the bond is called. The bond value is that price at which a 7 percent, 20-year bond would sell to have a yield to maturity of 8 percent, or about $890 (this value may be determined exactly from a bond table or approximated by solving the yield to maturity formula.) The bond value will vary as the level of interest rates of the risk class of the firm varies (and, in this case, will increase as the bond approaches maturity), but it is depicted as independent of the price of the stock; it should be apparent, however, that a change in the price of the stock might well indicate a change in the risk of the firm or the level of interest rates and thus alter the bond value. The market price of the bond is shown to be greater than either of its component values when issued. It approaches the conversion value as the price of the stock rises and a call of the issue becomes more likely. There is no rule stating that the price of the stock must rise. If it does not, no conversion takes place and the company has a cheap debt issue. It is effectively prevented from issuing another convertible, however, as long as the old issue is "overhanging."

THEORETICAL PRICE BEHAVIOR OF A CONVERTIBLE SECURITY

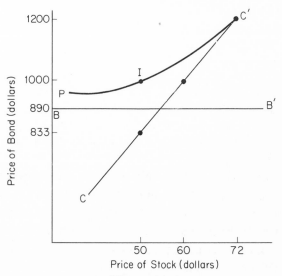

Figure 12.1

The literature in the field has not really settled the question of what the return to the holder of a convertible is, much less what constitutes the cost to the issuer. We shall take a very simple approach for our analysis.

We shall assume that the price of the stock will rise (because of earnings retention and, thus, increased future earnings) to $72 and that the issue will be called and converted. We must estimate an average rate of growth in the price of the stock. Assuming this to be 10 percent, the 44 percent increase from $50 to $72 would be accomplished in about 4 years (see Appendix A). Each convertible debenture thus represents an immediate receipt to the firm of $1,000 less flotation costs (say, 2 percent), an annual interest payment of $70 (tax-deductible) for 4 years, and the payment of $16\frac{2}{3}$ shares worth $72 (less flotation costs of, say, 6 percent) each at the end of that period. The after-tax flows are displayed below:

Year	After-Tax Flow	Present Value @ 7%	Present Value
0	+$ 980	1.0	+980
1-3	− 35	2.62	− 92
4	− 1163	.76	−884
			+ $3

Computed in this manner, the after-tax cost of the convertible would be just over 7 percent.[12] Had the net present value of the stream been zero, the after-tax cost would have been exactly 7 percent.

UNSOLVED PROBLEMS

1. The Kaplan Corporation pays a 50 percent tax rate and has 2 million shares outstanding which are currently selling for $25 each. Kaplan is planning a $10 million, 20 year, 6 percent convertible debenture issue with a 20 percent conversion premium. The price of Kaplan's common is assumed to grow at an annual rate of slightly over 6 percent and the convertible issue will be called when the price of the common is 20 percent greater than the conversion price. Kaplan could sell an ordinary debenture with an 8 percent yield.

(a) What are the conversion price and ratio for the debenture?

(b) What is the bond value of the debenture? What is the conversion value at the time of issue? Graph the theoretical price behavior of this bond.

(c) What is the after-tax cost of funds raised by the debenture issue?

(d) If Kaplan has E.B.I.T. of $10 million, illustrate the potential dilution of E.P.S. caused by this issue.

2. Rework problem 1 under the assumption that the issue will be $10 million of 6 percent, $100 par convertible preferred stock at a time when straight preferred would require an 8 percent yield.

---

[12] We ignore amortization of the bond discount.

SECTION 12.3   The use of warrants represents another means by which fixed income security holders may be given an equity participation in the firm. A warrant is nothing more than a legal instrument issued by the corporation granting the holder the right to purchase stock at some stated price. Warrants are often sold in conjunction with straight debt as an alternative to a convertible issue.[13] The exercise of a convertible bond involves trading the bond to the company for stock. In the case of a bond with warrants, exercise of the warrants involves additional money payments to the company for the stock and no change in the status of the debt. In addition, conversion of a bond means that new shares are issued for the full amount of the debt (at the conversion price); the number of warrants to be attached to a bond is completely variable. As a result, a firm which wishes to limit the dilution of the equity interest will find bonds with warrants to be more attractive than convertibles.

The balance sheet implications of convertible bonds vs. bonds with warrants may be illustrated by the following example. Assume that the Wells Corporation wishes to raise $10 million of debt funds either with a 6 percent convertible bond (at $50 per share) or by means of a 7 percent straight bond issue with warrants attached to each $1,000 bond to subscribe to 4 shares at $50 each. The balance sheets would appear as follows:

$ millions	Before Issue	CONVERTIBLE DEBENTURES		BONDS WITH WARRANTS	
		Before Conversion	After Conversion	Before Exercise	After Exercise
Debentures	–	$10.0	–	$10.0	$10.0
Common stock ($5 par)	$ 5.0	5.0	$ 6.0	5.0	5.2
Cont. in Excess of par	10.0	10.0	19.0	10.0	11.8
Retained Earnings	20.0	20.0	20.0	20.0	20.0
Total Equity	$35.0	$35.0	$45.0	$35.0	$37.0
Total Capital	$35.0	$45.0	$45.0	$45.0	$47.0

Thus, conversion of the debentures moves the entire amount of the debt down into the equity section, while exercise of the warrants leaves the debt untouched and results in a new contribution of equity funds to the firm.

The theoretical value of a warrant may be determined from the following formula:

---

[13] At the initial subscription, the warrants and bonds are sold together as a package. If the warrants are specified as "detachable", however, the purchaser of the bond may subsequently sell the warrants separately from the bond. Otherwise, "nondetachable" warrants must be exercised by the party owning the bond with which they were issued.

$$V = (P_m - P_o)N \tag{12.2}$$

Where: P_m = Market price of stock
P_o = Option price of stock
N = Number of shares which may be purchased with one warrant

This theoretical value will serve as a floor for the price of the warrant, for if the price should fall below this value there would be an arbitrage profit in selling the stock and buying and exercising the warrant to cover the sale. However, because of the speculative advantages of warrants (illustrated below), the price of a warrant may rise far above its theoretical value.

SOLVED PROBLEM

The Shaw Company has warrants outstanding that may be exercised to purchase one share of stock at $30.

1. If Shaw common is selling at $40, what is the theoretical value of the warrant?

2. If Shaw common rises by 25 percent to $50, what will happen to the theoretical value of the warrant?

SOLUTION

1. The theoretical value is ($40-$30) $\times$ 1 = $10.

2. At $50, the theoretical value would be ($50 - $30) $\times$ 1 = $20. Thus a 25 percent increase in the price of the stock would double the value of the warrant. The possibility of great gain is the reason a warrant's price may be significantly above its theoretical value.

The cost of warrants as a source of funds to the firm is virtually impossible to determine satisfactorily. In the first place the warrants usually have a long exercise period (5-10 years from issue at a minimum, and often the life of the bond issue) and there is no call provision by which the corporation can force their exercise. The approaching expiration date of warrants and a stepped-up option price over time (if provided by the indenture) would operate to force exercise. Some authorities argue that a high common dividend would encourage exercise, but such a dividend would probably be reflected in the prices of the stock and the warrant, and exercise would not be necessary to enjoy the benefits. The exercise of warrants involves an inflow of funds to the firm, thus further complicating any cost computation.

Many firms sell their securities in units, which may consist of various kinds of debt, stocks, and warrants. The securities involved are often so bizarre that no reasonable evaluation or cost computation can be made, which is one of the major reasons they are sold that way. The investor should adopt the position that the management of a firm knows more about it than anyone else, and if they have nothing good to offer, he should look elsewhere.[14]

Mention should be made of contingent interests, which is merely another way for a lender during tight money periods to get "a piece of the action". It may take the form of higher interest payments if the borrower exceeds certain performance criteria ("has a good year").

SOLVED PROBLEM

The V. O. Company pays a 50 percent tax rate and has stock outstanding which is selling for $70 a share. V. O. will sell a $10 million, 15-year, 6 percent debt issue with a 10 percent sinking fund beginning at the end of year 10. Each $1,000 par bond, will be sold with warrants having a 10-year life to purchase 3 shares at $100 each. It is assumed that the price of V.O. stock will appreciate at a compounded annual rate of 6 percent.

As best you can, determine the after-tax cost of this issue to V. O.

SOLUTION

$ millions

Years	Principal	Interest (After-tax)	Stock*	Total	Present Value Factor @ 4%	Present Value
0	+10.00	–	–	+10.00	1.00	+10.00
1-9	–	-0.30	–	- 0.30	7.44	- 2.23
10	- 1.00	-0.30	-.75	- 2.32	0.68	- 1.39
11	- 1.00	-0.27	–	- 1.27	0.65	- 0.83
12	- 1.00	-0.24	–	- 1.24	0.62	- 0.77
13	- 1.00	-0.21	–	- 1.21	0.60	- 0.73
14	- 1.00	-0.18	–	- 1.18	0.58	- 0.68
15	- 5.00	-0.15	–	- 5.15	0.56	- 2.88
						+ 0.49

*By year 10 (the expiration date of the warrants), the price of the stock would have appreciated by 79 percent to $125. Exercise at that time would be the equivalent of the company selling 30,000 shares worth $125 for $100, or a net opportunity loss of $1,020,000.

It follows that the after-tax cost of this issue is about 4%.

---

[14] Many of these techniques have been used in mergers, much to the distress of the SEC. It has not been unusual for the shareholders of an acquired company to be offered for their shares a package of new securities something like the following: 0.385 share of 5 1/2 percent convertible preferred plus 0.816 share of 6 percent straight preferred plus 1.25 shares of common plus a warrant to buy 1 share of common. A rational evaluation of such an offer is impossible as, of course, it was designed to be.

Warrants may also be created when a company sells additional shares to its own stockholdeers through a rights offering.[15] When a rights offering is held, each shareholder receives rights (the instrument is a warrant) to purchase a certain number of new shares at some subscription price for each old share held. To ensure the success of the offering, the subscription price is generally set well below market price.[16] For this reason, the rights have value and will generally be sold by those shareholders who do not plan to exercise them.

On the day of announcement, the company states that shareholders listed on its books as of the record date will receive rights to buy additional shares. These rights may be used to purchase shares anytime between the rights distribution and expiration dates. The two important periods in this chronology are the time between the announcement and the record date, when the purchaser of the stock will also receive rights (during this period the stock is said to be selling "rights on"), and the time between the record and the expiration date (when the stock is selling "rights-off").[17] Because new shares are sold at a discount, a rights offering constitutes dilution and the price of the stock should decline. During the "rights-on" period, the price of the stock thus represents the value of the rights to be acquired plus the new, lower value of the stock. The theoretical value of the right during this period may be determined as follows:

$$R_o = \frac{P_c - P_s}{N + 1} \tag{12.3}$$

Where: R_o = Theoretical value of a right when stock is selling rights-on
P_c = Price of stock "rights-on"
P_s = Subscription price
N = Number of rights to purchase one share of stock

When the stock goes "ex-rights", the price of the stock should, in theory, fall to the following value:

$$P_x = \frac{(P_c \times N) + P_s}{N + 1} \tag{12.4}$$

Where: P_x = Price of stock "ex-rights" and the rest are as above.

---

[15] New shares must be sold in this way if the stockholders have retained the preemptive right to maintain their proportionate share of ownership in the firm.

[16] To provide insurance, the issuer may engage an investment banker to do a standby underwriting. For a flat fee plus commission on all shares he actually must purchase at the subscription price, the investment banker will contract to underwrite any part of the issue not subscribed.

[17] In Wall Street parlance, the terms "cum-rights" and "ex-rights" are frequently used rather than "rights-on" and "rights-off."

The theoretical value of a right when the stock is selling "ex-rights" $(R/_x)$ is determined as follows:

$$R_x = \frac{P_x - P_s}{N} \tag{12.5}$$

SOLVED PROBLEM

The Ritter Company, whose stock is currently selling at $30 a share, has announced a rights offering by which its shareholders may subscribe for one new share for each 10 held. The subscription price will be $20/share.

1. What is the theoretical value of the right?

2. To what value should the price of the stock fall when it goes "ex-rights"?

3. If the price of the stock is $30 when it goes "ex-rights," what is the theoretical value of the right?

SOLUTION

$$1. \quad R_o = \frac{P_c - P_s}{N + 1} = \frac{\$30 - \$20}{11} = 91\cent$$

$$2. \quad P_x = \frac{(P_c \times N) + P_s}{N + 1} = \frac{\$300 + 20}{11} = \$29.09$$

$$3. \quad R_x = \frac{P_x - P_s}{N} = \frac{\$30 - 20}{10} = \$1.00$$

UNSOLVED PROBLEMS

1. The Katz Company has warrants outstanding which may be exercised to purchase one share of stock at $70.

    (a) If Katz common is selling for $100, what is the theoretical value of the warrant?

    (b) If Katz common rises in price by 50 percent, what will happen to the theoretical value of the warrant?

2. The Crown Company currently has the capitalization shown on next page. It could raise $20 million of debt funds by means of either a 7 percent convertible (@ $100 per share) debenture or an 8 percent straight debt issue with warrants to purchase 2 shares (@ $100 per share) attached to each $1,000 par bond. Show the capitalizations that would result from each alternative, both before and after conversion or exercise.

CROWN COMPANY - $ MILLION

Common Stock ($10 par)	$20
Cont. in Excess of Par	20
Retained Earnings	40
Total Equity	$80
Total Capitalization	$80

3. The Preceptor Company has a 40 percent tax rate and stock outstanding selling for $40/share. Preceptor will sell a $20 million, 7 percent, 10-year debt issue with no provision for early retirement. With each $1,000 bond will be sold warrants good for the life of the bond issue to purchase 5 shares at $50 each. If the price of Preceptor stock is assumed to grow at a 5 percent annual rate, what is the after-tax cost of this issue?

4. The Norton Company whose stock is currently selling at $50 a share has announced a rights offering by which its shareholders may subscribe for one new share for each 5 held at $40 per share.

(a) What is the theoretical value of a right?

(b) To what price should the stock fall when it goes "ex-rights"?

(c) If the price of the stock does in fact fall to $49 when it goes "ex-rights" what is the theoretical value of a right?

COMPREHENSIVE CASE

The Hutchins Company has a 50 percent tax rate and 10 percent after-tax opportunity return on funds employed. Hutchins currently has 2,000,000 common shares outstanding with a market value of $150 million, a price-earnings ratio of 12.5, and a yield of 5 percent. The company desires to raise $25 million in new funds.

1. If the new funds were raised through a stock issue, total expenses of the offering would be 8 percent of the amount raised.

(a) How many shares would be outstanding?

(b) If the funds were indeed employed at 10 percent what would be the new earnings per share?

(c) If the P/E, payout, and rate of return remained constant, how should the price of the stock grow over time?

2. If straight debt were employed, a 9 percent interest charge would be required. Continuing the assumptions of part (1), what would the new E.P.S. be and how would the price of the stock grow over time?

3. It would be possible to issue a 6 percent convertible debenture, with a 15 percent conversion premium and a call price of 106.

(a) What would be the new E.P.S.?

(b) How soon could the convertible be called if the company wished to allow for 20 percent decline in the price of the stock?

(c) Continuing our assumptions, what would be the E.P.S. and price of the stock after conversion?

4. Which plan is the best?

13 COMMON STOCK
AND RETAINED EARNINGS

SECTION 13.1   The residual owners of the firm are the common stockholders. As such, they have claim on the earnings of the firm after all creditors are paid. In case of the dissolution or liquidation of the firm, the common stockholders are entitled to the net assets remaining after the claims of creditors are satisfied. Common stockholders, as owners, are entitled to elect a board of directors to look after their interest in the firm.[1] Common shareholders also may have the right to maintain their proportional ownership in the corporation (see Chap. 12) and to examine the books of the company.

In the early stages of development of cost of capital theory it was assumed that common stock was a costless source of financing since the firm was under no legal obligation to disburse funds to stockholders. This notion was reinforced by taxation and accounting procedures which designated interest payments as an "expense" and dividend payments as "distributions." It was soon realized, however, that equity capital was supplied to firms only so long as funds were efficiently used to increase the well-being of stockholders. Far from being costless, equity funds were

---

[1]Two voting systems are possible in the election of a board of directors. Under the majority voting system, a shareholder votes for each place on the board according to the number of shares he owns. If 100 shares are owned, the holder may cast 100 votes for each director position to be filled. A candidate for director must obtain votes representing a majority of the shares outstanding to win election. Under the cumulative voting system, a stockholder has votes equal to the number of shares he owns times the number of directors to be elected. He may cast this total any way he chooses, including casting all votes for one director. Under this system, the minimum number of shares required to elect a specified number of directors is given by:

$$\frac{S \times N}{D + 1} + 1$$

Where: S is the total number of shares outstanding.

  N is the number of directors desired to elect.

  D is the number of directors to be elected.

found to be rather expensive sources of finance. Since common stockholders assume the greatest risk of all suppliers of capital, it is reasonable to expect that the anticipated rate of return to equity investors should be the largest.

It was discovered in Chap. 2 that the value of an asset is determined by discounting to the present the future stream of income which that asset is expected to generate. This valuation procedure was employed in the capital budgeting decision by the firm (Chap. 5) and in the pricing of debt securities (Chaps. 10 and 11). An investor in common stock receives dividends from his investment. Theoretically, it is this dividend stream which the stockholder discounts to determine the price of an equity. Thus, the value of a common stock is given by:

$$P_o = \frac{D_1}{(1 + k_e)^1} + \frac{D_2}{(1 + k_e)^2} + \ldots + \frac{D_\infty}{(1 + k_e)^\infty} \qquad (13.1)$$

$$P_o = \sum_{t=1}^{\infty} \frac{D_t}{(1 + k_e)^t}$$

Where: P_o is the value of a common stock.

D_1 is the dividend expected one year from now.

D_2 is the dividend expected two years from now, etc.

k_e is the appropriate rate of discount (given the risk associated with the dividend payments) applied to the stream.

Of course, different investors will have varying risk preferences and hence will employ different rates of discount. Also, the riskiness and the amount of future dividends may be variously estimated by investors. In the aggregate, it is the interaction of many investors that determines the market price of a stock. Thus, the discount rate (k_e) applied by stockholders in general is the percentage compounded annual rate of return required by them as compensation for the riskiness associated with the expected dividend stream. This rate is the opportunity rate of return anticipated by stockholders and is the rate required to persuade investors to purchase the firm's stock. As such, it is the cost of common stock to the firm.

When it assumed that D is constant and will be received for a long period of time, Eq. (13.1) reduces to:

$$P_o = \frac{D_o}{k_e} \qquad (13.2)$$

This may be rewritten to illustrate the cost of capital:

$$k_e = \frac{D_o}{P_o}$$

(13.3)

Where: k_e is the cost of common stock
D_o is the annual dividend
P_o is the market price of the firm's stock

This equation will produce the same result if aggregate or per share data are used. In determining the cost of capital, market price is clearly the pertinent price variable. Par value has no real meaning except upon the formation of a new concern. Book value is not significant since any sale of new shares would be at market, not book, value.

This simple formulation gives an adequate approximation of the cost of equity capital for nongrowth firms that distribute most of their earnings in dividends. The cost of equity for many public utility, railroad, and tobacco stocks[2] may be approached with the simple formulation. In this case, it is assumed that a constant stream of dividends is being capitalized by the stockholders to determine the price of the security.

SOLVED PROBLEMS

1. The Great American Lighting and Power Company pays a dividend of $5 per share. Although there is some slight cyclical volatility around this dividend figure, no long-term growth has been evident. The firm retains only a negligible part of annual earnings. If the price of Great American shares is $50, what is the cost of common stock to the firm?

SOLUTION

$$k_e = \frac{\$5}{\$50} = 10\%$$

2. Brown is a stockholder in the Central Railroad. Although earnings for the Central have varied considerably, Brown has determined that the long-run average dividend for the firm has been $2 per share. This is the mean dividend figure for the past twenty years. Brown expects a similar pattern to prevail in the future. Given the volatility of C.R.R. dividends, Brown has decided that a

---

[2]Diversification may well eliminate many railroad and tobacco stocks from this list in the future.

minimum rate of return of twenty per cent should be earned on the stock. What price would Brown be willing to pay for C.R.R. stock?

SOLUTION

$$P = \frac{\$2}{.20} = \$10$$

3. Assuming other investors desire the same rate of return as Brown (above) in order to compensate them for the risk associated with holding common stock in the Central Railroad (i.e., that investors are willing to pay $10 for Central stock), what is the cost of equity capital to the railroad?

SOLUTION

$$k_e = \frac{\$2}{\$10} = 20\%$$

UNSOLVED PROBLEMS

1. The Argus Tobacco Company earned $500,000 in 1969. The firm has not earned less than $400,000 in any one year since the Great Depression, although even in boom years no more than $700,000 has been earned. Long-run average earnings should approximate 1969 net income. Argus has 100,000 shares outstanding with a market price of $40 per share. The firm retains virtually none of its earnings.

(a) What is the cost of equity capital to Argus?

(b) What critical assumptions must be made about Argus' dividend policy and future earnings potential for this cost to be a reasonable approximation?

(c) What rate of return is expected by Argus stockholders? What part does earnings variability play in determining the expected rate of return?

(d) In the long-run, given that all of the above assumptions remain unchanged, what should happen to the price of Argus stock?

2. Suppose that a sudden decrease in the demand for cigarrettes reduced expected earnings for Argus (above) to $300,000. Further, assume that the risk associated with the future earnings of Argus increased such that investors required a 20 percent rate of return for holding Argus stock.

(a) Determine the new price per share of Argus' common stock.

(b) What is the new cost of equity capital to Argus?

SECTION 13.2   The simple formulation above assumed growthless conditions where earnings retention was negligible. Most firms, however, do not exemplify these characteristics, and determining the cost of equity capital for these firms is somewhat more complicated.

In Eq. (13.1), it was posited that the value of a share was determined by discounting all future dividend payments to the present. Because of limited time horizons investors rarely purchase stocks with the intention of holding the securities forever. Consequently, in order to determine the actual return to the stockholder, the holding period must be introduced as a variable. Assume that a stockholder purchases a security with the intention of holding for n years. He receives a series of dividends (D) over this period of time. At the end of the holding period, the investor also receives the prevailing market price of the stock (P_n). Thus, the investor pays a price P_o for a return $D_1 + D_2 + \ldots + D_n + P_n$ or

$$P_o = \frac{D_1}{(1 + k_e)^1} + \frac{D_2}{(1 + k_e)^2} + \ldots + \frac{D_n}{(1 + k_e)^n} + \frac{P_n}{(1 + k_e)^n} \qquad (13.4)$$

$$P_o = \sum_{t=1}^{n} \frac{D_t}{(1 + k_e)^t} + \frac{P_n}{(1 + k_e)^n}$$

The discount rate k_e is determined by the riskiness associated with the investment in the stock. This is the expected percentage rate of return to the stockholder and the cost of equity capital. The price of the stock P_n may conveniently be determined by applying an appropriate multiple to earnings in year n. P_n computed in this manner should also be the present value at n of all dividends accruing after year n. Thus, Eq. (13.4) is actually a restatement of Eq. (13.1).

SOLVED PROBLEMS

1. The Farbisher Corporation is expected to pay a dividend of $1 next year, representing one-fourth of E.P.S. It is anticipated that E.P.S. will grow by $1.00 per share for the next 5 years and that the dividend pay-out ratio will remain constant. Given the business and financial risk associated with Farbisher common, investors have been willing to pay ten times current earnings for the stock.

(a) Determine E.P.S. and dividends per share for the next 5 years.

SOLUTION

t	E.P.S.	Dividends
1	$4.00	$1.00
2	5.00	1.25
3	6.00	1.50
4	7.00	1.75
5	8.00	2.00

(b) What is the current price of Farbisher common? (assume $EPS = \$3$)

SOLUTION

$$P = (P/E.P.S.)(E.P.S.) = (10)(\$3) = \$30$$

(c) What should be the price of Farbisher common in five years? (Assume business and financial risk for the firm will not change and that interest rates will not vary).

SOLUTION

$$P = (10)\,(\$8) = \$80$$

(d) Determine k_e, the cost of equity capital (rate of return to stockholders) for Farbisher.

SOLUTION

$$P_o = \frac{D_1}{(1+k_e)^1} + \frac{D_2}{(1+k_e)^2} + \frac{D_3}{(1+k_e)^3} + \frac{D_4}{(1+k_e)^4} + \frac{D_5}{(1+k_e)^5} + \frac{P_5}{(1+k_e)^5}$$

$$\$30 = \frac{1.00}{(1+k_e)^1} + \frac{1.25}{(1+k_e)^2} + \frac{1.50}{(1+k_e)^3} + \frac{1.75}{(1+k_e)^4} + \frac{2.00}{(1+k_e)^5} + \frac{80.00}{(1+k_e)^5}$$

	$k_e = .26$		$k_e = .24$	
$t = 1$	$(1.00) \times (.794) =$	.794	$(1.00) \times (.806) =$	.806
$t = 2$	$(1.25) \times (.630) =$	.788	$(1.25) \times (.650) =$	.813
$t = 3$	$(1.50) \times (.500) =$	.750	$(1.50) \times (.524) =$	.786
$t = 4$	$(1.75) \times (.397) =$	.695	$(1.75) \times (.423) =$	.740
$t = 5$	$(82.00) \times (.315) =$	25.830	$(82.00) \times (.341) =$	27.962
		$28.857		$31.107

$$k_e \simeq 25\%$$

2. Rework solved problem number one in Sec. 13.1 Assume a 5-year time horizon. Let $D = E.P.S.$ Use the steps outlined above in solution.

SOLUTION

(a)

t	E.P.S.	Div.
1	$5	$5
2	5	5
3	5	5
4	5	5
5	5	5

(b) $\$50 = (P/E.P.S.)(\$5); P/E.P.S. = 10$

(c) $P = (10)(\$5) = \$50$

(d) $P_o = \dfrac{\$5}{(1+k_e)^1} \div \dfrac{\$5}{(1+k_e)^2} + \dfrac{\$5}{(1+k_e)^3} + \dfrac{\$5}{(1+k_e)^4} + \dfrac{\$5}{(1+k_e)^5} + \dfrac{\$50}{(1+k_e)^5}$

$k_e = .10$

$$
\begin{array}{lll}
t = 1 \ldots 5 & (5.00) \times (3.791) = & 18.90 \\
t = 5 & (50.00) \times (.621) = & \underline{31.10} \\
& & \$50.00
\end{array}
$$

$k_e = 10\%$

UNSOLVED PROBLEMS

1. The Beame Company has increased its dividend by $0.10 per year for the past ten years. A similar pattern is expected in the next few years. The firm pays out roughly one-half of current earnings in dividends as a matter of policy. In the past, the firm's $P/E.P.S.$ multiple has ranged from 12-16, depending on the general level of interest rates. The firm's business and financial risk has not changed over the past ten years and is not expected to change in the future.

(a) Determine E.P.S. and dividends per share for the Beame Company over the next four years. Dividends this year ($n = 0$) were $2.00 per share.

(b) What is the current price of Beame stock? High interest rates have forced the $P/E.P.S.$ multiple to the low end of the range (i.e., 12x).

(c) Assuming continued high rates of interest, what should be the price of Beame in four years?

(d) Determine k_e for the Beame Company.

2. Prudence N. Vestor, a wealthy widow, is considering the purchase of

common stock in the Security National Bank. After examining many details about the past and future of Security National Bank, Mrs. Vestor has estimated that the bank will pay a dividend of $1.00 for the next three years and $1.50 for the following four years. After seven years, she plans to retire and sell her stock in order to purchase corporate bonds. The current market price of Security National Bank stock is $20. The price is expected to rise proportionately to the increase in dividends.

(a) What is the cost of equity capital to Security National Bank (assuming Mrs. Vestor's projections are an adequate depiction of the future)?

(b) If Mrs. Vestor believes that she should get a return of a least 12 percent from SNB stock given risk considerations, should she buy the stock?

(c) What price would Mrs. Vestor be willing to pay for the stock?

(d) Why do you suppose the market price of the stock is different from your answer to question (c)?

SECTION 13.3

When dividends are expected to grow at a constant percentage rate, Eq. (13.1) becomes:

$$P_o = \frac{D_o\,(1+g)^1}{(1+k_e)^1} + \frac{D_o\,(1+g)^2}{(1+k_e)^2} + \ldots + \frac{D_o\,(1+g)^\infty}{(1+k_e)^\infty} \qquad (13.5)$$

The investor pays a price P_o for a stream of payments expected to grow by g percent for infinity. Such growth expectations may be unwarranted for most firms. Nevertheless, if growth can continue for a relatively long period of time, a similar result obtains. This follows because the present value of payments received in the distant future approaches zero.

In the continuous case (continuous rather than discrete compoundings), Eq. (13.5) becomes:

$$P_o = \int_o^\infty D_o e^{gt} e^{-k_e t} d_t = \int_o^\infty D_o e^{-t(k_e - g)} d_t \qquad (13.6)$$

Integrating, we find:[3]

$$P_o = \frac{D_o}{k_e - g} \qquad (13.7)$$

---

[3]If g exceeds k_e the market price of the stock would be infinite. This is known as the Petersburg Paradox. See David Durant, "Growth Stocks and the Petersburg Paradox," *Journal of Finance*, September, 1957, pp. 348-63.

Solving for the cost of equity capital:

$$k_e = \frac{D_o}{P_o} + g \qquad\qquad (13.8)$$

SOLVED PROBLEMS

1. Windsong International paid $2 in dividends per share this year. Dividends are expected to grow by 10 percent well into the future. Windsong stock sells for $20 per share. Determine the cost of equity capital to Windsong.

SOLUTION

$$k_e = \frac{\$2}{\$20} + .10 = 20\%$$

2. James Bell is a potential stockholder in the Bering Corporation. Bering pays a dividend of $.50 per share and is expected to increase this amount by 20 percent annually for quite some time in the future. If Bell believes he should earn 25 percent on his investment, how much should he be willing to pay for Bering shares?

SOLUTION

$$P_o = \frac{\$.50}{.25 - .20} = \frac{\$.50}{.05} = \$10$$

UNSOLVED PROBLEMS

1. Alameda Mines earned $2 per share this year. Earnings are expected to grow by 10 percent annually for the next thirty years due to important ore discoveries. The firm retains 50 percent of net income for the reinvestment in mining exploration. This retention policy will continue in the future.

(a) Determine k_e assuming a current market price per share of $20.

(b) What price would a potential stockholder be willing to pay for Alameda stock if he desired a 20 percent rate of return?

2. Alameda Mines (above) has just discovered a new mineral deposit. Upon announcement of the discovery, the firm's stock advanced to $50 per share. Earnings are now expected to increase by 13 percent per year in the future. If

the firm continues its past retention policy, what is the new cost of equity capital to Alameda? How do you explain this result, given the cost of capital before the new discovery?

SECTION 13.4

Many companies which anticipate rather large increases in earnings in the future pay little or no dividends preferring to reinvest in lucrative projects. In such cases the cost of equity may be approached by considering the price appreciation of the common stock. Given unchanged P/E.P.S. multiples, the rate of increase in earnings will equal the price increases of the common stock. Changes in the general level of interest rates, in the business and financial risk of the firm, and in expectations about future earnings may alter the P/E.P.S. multiples which investors are willing to pay for stocks, however.

Two variations on Eq. (13.8) may be employed to determine the cost of equity for growth firms which pay only negligible dividends. The first of these considers some mean value of future earnings (E_A) as compared to the current price of the common stock, or

$$k_e = \frac{E_A}{P_o} \tag{13.9}$$

This formulation assumes that the firm retains earnings to reinvest at profitable rates of return. Increased future earnings, resulting from reinvestment of current earnings, produce higher stock prices, which constitute the return to investors. The second variation more specifically includes the growth rate expected for future earnings (g):[4]

$$k_e = \frac{E_o}{P_o} + g \tag{13.10}$$

SOLVED PROBLEMS

The Norris Company is a growth firm that pays no dividends. The firm earned $1,000,000 this year. Future anticipated earnings are expected to be $2,5000,000. This is equivalent to a 6 percent compounded annual increase

---

[4]The g in Eq. (13.10) is a growth rate for earnings, but the g in Eq. (13.8) relates to dividends. The two will be the same only if the dividend payout ratio remains constant in the future.

in earnings. The total value of the firm's common stock (market) is $25,000,000. Determine the cost of common stock financing.

SOLUTION

$$k_e = \frac{E_A}{P_o} = \frac{\$2,500,000}{\$25,000,000} = 10\%$$

$$k_e = \frac{E_o}{P_o} + g = \frac{\$1,000,000}{\$25,000,000} + 6\% = 10\%$$

UNSOLVED PROBLEMS

1. Determine the compounded annual growth rate anticipated for a firm whose stock sells for $10 per share if current E.P.S. is $2 and expected future E.P.S. is $2.50.

2. The Ace Bullet and Bomb Company has increased E.P.S. by 10 percent for the past thirty years. It appears that a similar growth rate may be expected in the future. If stockholders believe that the risk associated with purchasing Ace stock requires a 12 percent rate of return, and the firm now earns $2 per share, what is the price of Ace stock?

SECTION 13.5   An additional refinement must be made for an adequate reflection of the cost of equity capital. A firm may raise equity funds either through the sale of common stock or through the retention of earnings. The effect of both is to increase the stockholders' investment in the firm. Nevertheless, if common stock is sold to the public, investment banker fees and other underwriting costs are incurred. The cost of common stock should be adjusted to reflect the flotation expense.

SOLVED PROBLEM

The Barnard Company paid a dividend of $.60 per share this year. Dividends are expected to grow by 5 percent per year in the future. The price of Barnard stock is $12 per share. If the firm sold additional stock, the net proceeds to the company would be $10 per share. What is the cost of common stock financing to Barnard?

SOLUTION

$$k_e = \frac{D_o}{P_o{'}} + g$$

$$k_e = \frac{\$.60}{\$10.00} + .05 = 11\%$$

Where: $P_o{'}$ is the adjusted (to reflect flotation costs) price of the common stock.

SECTION
13.6
The retention of earnings as a source of funds differs from the sale of common stock in that the double taxation of dividends is avoided (see Chap 4). Assume that investors expect an equity return of k_e. If a cash dividend were paid, taxes equal to the marginal tax bracket (t) of stockholders would be paid. Thus, (t) (k_e) would accrue to the government, and investors would be left $(1 - t)$ (k_e).[5] If earnings were retained, on the other hand, the full return would accrue to stockholders and double taxation would be avoided. Similarly, if dividends were paid to stockholders and then additional shares were sold to stockholders, personal taxes would be paid on dividends before new shares could be purchased. This would reduce the volume of funds available for investment and thus the income which could be earned. Some authorities contend that when earnings are retained the cost of equity should be adjusted to reflect the avoidance of double taxation. These authorities would compute the cost of retained earnings as follows:

$$k_{re} = (k_e)(1 - t) \qquad\qquad (13.11)$$

where t is the marginal tax bracket of stockholders.

If a firm had a cost of equity of 10 percent and stockholders were in the 25 percent marginal bracket, only 75 percent of funds distributed as dividends could be used to purchase additional shares, providing a (.10) $(1 - .25)$ = 7.5% return on the gross amount distributed. The cost of retaining earnings would thus be 7.5 percent.

Other authorities disagree with this adjustment. It is suggested that t may vary from 0 to 70 percent among the different stockholders of a given firm and that no equitable weighting system may be constructed to determine t. More significantly, it is argued that the real cost of retained earnings is the opportunity cost to the firm of not investing in projects of risk equal to the overall riskiness of the firm. Since the firm may purchase

---

[5] $(t)(k_e) + (1 - t)(k_e) = k_e$

its own common stock (which is of equal risk to the overall riskiness of the firm), the minimum opportunity cost of retained earnings is simply k_e the rate of return available from investing in the firm's stock. Under this view, the cost of retained earnings equals the cost of common stock financing.

Regardless of the merits of the above argument, retaining earnings does circumvent the flotation process, hence saving the firm flotation costs. Thus, the cost of retained earnings must be lower than the cost of common stock financing by at least this amount.

SOLVED PROBLEM

The Xavier Corporation, a dynamic growth firm which pays no dividends, anticipates a long-run level of future earnings of $7 per share. The current price of Xavier shares is $54\frac{1}{2}$, although flotation costs for the sale of new shares would average about 10 percent of the price of the stock.

1. What is the cost of equity capital to Xavier?

SOLUTION

$$P_o = \$54.50$$
$$P_o' = (.9)(54.50) = \$49$$

$$k_e = \frac{E_A}{P_o'} = \frac{\$7}{\$49} = 14.3\%$$

2. What is the cost of retained earnings to Xavier?

SOLUTION

$$k_{re} = \frac{E_A}{P_o} = \frac{\$7.00}{\$54.50} = 12.8\%$$

UNSOLVED PROBLEM

The Czar Metals Corporation paid a dividend of $1 per share this year. Dividends are expected to grow by 4 percent per year for the next twenty years. The current price of Czar shares is $10, and the weighted average marginal tax bracket of Czar shareholders is 30 percent. If Czar sold additional shares, the gross spread (flotation cost) would be about twenty percent of the value of the shares.

1. Determine the cost of common stock to Czar.

2. Determine both possible costs of retained earnings to Czar. Which cost do you think is more valid? Why?

3. Czar is a closely held corporation with ten stockholders all of whom are in the same marginal tax bracket. Would these data influence your decision?

COMPREHENSIVE PROBLEM

Security analysts have made the following probabilistic estimates about future dividends and share prices of the Xerses Corporation for the next five years.

Dividends:	Amount	Probability	Dividends:	Amount	Probability
Year X_1	$0.80	0.1	Year X_3	$1.00	0.3
	1.00	0.8		1.50	0.4
	1.20	0.1		2.00	0.3
Year X_2	$0.90	0.2	Year X_4	$1.25	0.2
	1.20	0.6		1.75	0.5
	1.50	0.2		2.25	0.3

Dividends:	Amount	Probability	Share Price:	Price	Probability
Year X_5	$1.50	0.3	Year X_5	$100	0.12
	2.00	0.5		95	0.14
	2.50	0.2		90	0.24
				85	0.18
				80	0.14
				75	0.10
				70	0.08

The current price of Xerses shares is $65. If new shares were sold, the firm would net $60.

1. Determine the cost of common stock to Xerses.

2. Determine the cost of retained earnings to Xerses.

14 DIVIDEND
POLICY

Much of the discussion in the previous chapter assumed a given dividend policy for the firm. Indeed, determining the cost of equity capital depends upon some knowledge of the future dividend paying potential of the firm. Since retention policy is the mirror-image of dividend policy, no analysis of the cost of equity capital is complete without detailed consideration of the variables significant to the dividend decision.

There are two forms of dividends: stock dividends and cash dividends. The payment of stock dividends does not fundamentally affect the value of the firm or influence the volume of financing available to the firm. In fact, stock dividends are actually very much like stock splits. Cash distributions, on the other hand, may very well affect the value of the firm and clearly influence the volume of funds available to the firm.

Several legal constraints bear upon the cash dividend policy decision. A firm may not pay a dividend which will impair capital. Dividends must be paid out of the firm's earnings. Some states even require that corporations chartered in those states pay dividends only out of current (annual) earnings. Dividend payments may also be constrained by contract restrictions placed upon the firm. A bond indenture, for example, may limit (or prohibit) the payment of cash dividends until a specified times-interest-earned multiple is reached. By law also, a firm may not pay a dividend which would cause it to become insolvent.

Assuming that the legal constraints to the payment of cash dividends are satisfied, there are two remaining variables to consider. The first is a financial constraint: a firm can pay a dividend only to the extent that it has cash to disburse. A firm with a substantial net income cannot pay cash dividends, for example, if these earnings are still in the form of accounts receivable. (The cash constraint as a variable was discussed in detail in Chap. 7.) The second variable is an economic one. The question is raised: Does the volume of dividends paid affect the value of the firm? If the answer to this question is yes, then there must be some optimum level of dividends which maximizes the market price of the firm's stock.

A näive approach to the dividend policy decision would be to assume that the payment of a cash dividend is inherently a favorable activity. Indeed, Wall Street typically greets the increase in cash dividends by a firm bullishly. Nevertheless, it must be remembered that the payment of a cash dividend necessarily reduces the amount of funds that the firm may reinvest, and this, in turn, may reduce the future earning capacity of the firm.

Several models have been designed to illustrate optimizing variables. The Walter formula is perhaps the most extensively cited:[1]

$$P = \frac{D + \frac{r}{k_e}(E - D)}{k_e} \tag{14.1}$$

Where: P = market price per share
  D = dividend per share
  E = earnings per share
  r = investment rate of return
  k_e = the equity capitalization rate (cost of equity capital)

According to the Walter model, the firm should retain earnings if $r > k_e$ but should distribute dividends if $r < k_e$.

A valuation model applicable to below-average shares (nongrowth, non-blue chip) to test the significance of dividend payments is described by Graham and Dodd:[2]

$$P = M\left(\frac{E}{3} + D\right) \tag{14.2}$$

Where: P, E, D are as in Eq. (14.1)
  M is the price-earnings multiple

According to this formulation, investors in below-average securities place considerable emphasis on the value of dividends. The denominator implies that dividends are four times as valuable to the investor as earnings retained. This constant postulates that the normalized price will be

---

[1] James E. Walter, "Dividend Policies and Common Stock Prices," *Journal of Finance,* March, 1956, pp. 29-41.

[2] B. Graham, D. Dood and S. Cottle, *Security Analysis,* 4th ed. (New York: McGraw-Hill Book Company, 1962), p. 518.

achieved at a payout of 2/3. A higher payout is considered favorable for below-average securities and will produce a market price higher than the normalized value. A payout of less than 2/3 will have the opposite effect.

SOLVED PROBLEMS

1. The Karnes Realty Company earns $4 per share, is capitalized at a rate of 10 percent, and has a rate of return on investment of 12 percent.

(a) According to the Walter formulation, what would be the price of the stock if the firm had a payout of 25 percent?

SOLUTION

$$P = \frac{1 + \frac{.12}{.10}\,(4-1)}{.10}$$

$$P = \frac{1 + (1.2)(3)}{.10} = \frac{4.6}{.10} = \$46$$

(b) Is this the optimum payout ratio according to Walter?

SOLUTION

$$r > k_e, \text{ thus share price is maximized if } \frac{D}{E} = 0$$

$$P = \frac{0 + \frac{.12}{.10}\,(4)}{.10} = \frac{4.8}{.10} = \$48$$

2. The Thol Corporation has grown by a negligible rate over the past several years. Stockholders in the firm have a decided preference for dividends, although it is felt that about 1/3 of annual earnings should be reinvested in the firm. The historical price-earnings multiple assigned to Thol has been 12:1. Assume that this multiple adequately reflects the riskiness of the firm and is in line with the general level of interest rates.

(a) Determine the price of Thol shares if the E.P.S. is $3. Use the Graham and Dodd formulation.

SOLUTION

$$P = 12 \left(\frac{3}{3} + 2\right) = \$36$$

(b) What should happen to the price of Thol shares if a nonoptimum payout of 1/2 were employed?

SOLUTION

$$P = 12 \left(\frac{3}{3} + 1.50 \right) = \$30$$

UNSOLVED PROBLEMS

1. Rework solved problem number 1 above (Karnes Realty) assuming $k_e = 12$ percent and $r = 10$ percent.

2. The Karnes Realty Company (above) will increase annual earnings per share at a rate of 10 percent. Let $k_e = 12$ percent and $r = 10$ percent. Can you defend the position that "capitalization rates and rates of return on investment tend to become equal in equilibrium"? Assume that the perpetual growth model $[k_e = (D_o/P_o) + g]$ applies to Karnes. Use the Walter formulation in your valuation of Karnes shares.

3. In what respect may the Walter model be criticized as providing an "either-or" decision? Without modification, would the Walter model be useful to most firms? What modifications might you suggest?

4. The Katz Corporation earns $1,000,000 and has 1,000,000 shares outstanding. The firm can reinvest in projects yielding the following rate of return:

Project	Amount	Return
A	$100,000	9%
B	200,000	12
C	300,000	4
D	300,000	11
E	100,000	6

The firm has a cost of equity capital of 10 percent. Using a variation of the Walter model, where r_n is the *marginal* investment rate of return, determine the optimal payout for Katz. The following revised equation may be helpful:

$$P = \frac{D + \sum_{n=1}^{m} \frac{r_n}{k_e} \left(\frac{A}{S} \right)_n}{k_e}$$

$$\sum_{n=1}^{m} \left(\frac{A}{S} \right)_n = E - D$$

Where: A is the dollar investment amount per project
         S is the number of shares outstanding

5. The Gemini Cement Company earned $1.50 this year. The firm paid no dividends and can reinvest earnings to yield 4 percent. The P/E.P.S. multiple assigned to Gemini is 9:1.

(a) Price Gemini shares using the Graham and Dodd formulation.

(b) Compare this price with the actual market price of the stock $[P = (E.P.S.) (P/E.P.S.]$.

(c) Do you think the Graham and Dodd valuation is appropriate for this stock? Why or why not?

(d) Do you think the dividend policy of Gemini is optimal? Why or why not?

(e) Would you anticipate a higher price for Gemini if another payout were employed?

SECTION 14.2   The previous section discussed the impact of dividend policy on the value of the firm. Both models assumed that the dividend decision would affect the price of the firm's stock. Given certain assumptions, however, dividend policy may not influence the worth of the firm.

In a famous article, Merton Miller and Franco Modigliani (M-M) argue that the value of a share of stock is independent of the dividend policy of the firm.[3] Assuming perfect capital markets, investor rationality, certainty about future events, the absence of transaction and flotation costs, no preferential capital gains taxation, and a given, unchanged investment policy for the firm, they postulate that the market price of a share of stock at the beginning of any period, say t_o, will be given by:

$$P_o = \frac{1}{1 + k_e} (D_1 + P_1) \tag{14.3}$$

Where: P_o is market price per share at t_o
   P_1 is market price per share at t_1
   k_e is the equity capitalization rate appropriate for a firm in a given risk class
   D_1 is the dividend paid at the end of t_o (beginning of t_1)

If a stock is expected to sell at $100 one year from now, and is to pay a dividend of $5 one year from now, the current value of the stock is $105

[3]Merton Miller and Franco Modigliani, "Dividend Policy, Growth, and the Valuation of Shares," *Journal of Business*, October, 1961, pp.411-33.

discounted by the appropriate rate, i.e., k_e. A firm committed to equity financing may retain earnings and forego selling additional shares, or it may pay a dividend and sell shares. According to M-M, the discounted value per share before and after a dividend payment (with an accompanying sale of shares) will be the same as if earnings had been retained (with no accompanying sale of shares). Let n shares be outstanding at t_o and let Δn be the number of new shares sold at t_1. Rewriting Eq. (14.3) to consider the total value of the enterprise at t_o we obtain:

$$nP_o = \frac{1}{(1 + k_e)} \ [nD_1 + (n + \Delta n)P_1 - \Delta nP_1] \qquad (14.4)$$

The total value of new shares to be sold (ΔnP_1) will depend on the volume of new investment (I), the net income earned during the period (Y), and the dividends paid on outstanding shares (nD_1), or

$$\Delta nP_1 = I - (Y - nD_1) \qquad (14.5)$$

Substituting Eq. (14.5) into Eq. (14.4), we obtain:

$$nP_o = \frac{1}{(1 + k_e)} \ [(n + \Delta n)P_1 - I + Y] \qquad (14.6)$$

Since D_1 does not appear in Eq. (14.6), M-M conclude that P_o is not a function of D_1. The other variables, $n, \Delta n, P_1, I$, and Y, are assumed to be independent of D_1.

SOLVED PROBLEM

The John Company is in a risk class which has been assigned a capitalization rate of 12 percent by investors. The firm's stock is selling at $10 per share, with 500,000 shares outstanding. The firm is considering the possibility of paying a dividend of $.40 per share one year from now.

1. What will be the price of the firm's stock in one year if a dividend is paid?

SOLUTION

$$P_o = \frac{1}{1 + k_e} \ (D_1 + P_1)$$
$$P_o (1 + k_e) - D_1 = P_1$$
$$\$10 \ (1.12) - \$.40 = \$10.80$$

2. What will be the price of the firm's stock if no dividend is paid?

SOLUTION

$$\$10\,(1.12) - \$0.00 = \$11.20$$

3. The firm will earn $1.00 per share next year. New investments of $1,000,000 are expected. If the firm pays a dividend, how many new shares must be issued?

SOLUTION

$$\Delta n P_1 = I - (Y - n D_1)$$
$$\Delta n\,(10.80) = 1,000,000 - (500,000 - 200,000)$$
$$\Delta n = \frac{700,000}{10.80} = 64,815 \text{ shares}$$

4. If the firm does not pay a dividend, how many new shares must be issued?

SOLUTION

$$\Delta n\,(11.20) = 1,000,000 - 500,000$$
$$\Delta n = \frac{500,000}{11.20} = 44,643 \text{ shares}$$

5. What is the value of the firm at P_o?

SOLUTION

$$V = n P_o$$
$$V = 500,000 \times \$10 = \$5,000,000$$

6. Compute the present value of the firm under the assumption that a dividend is paid.

SOLUTION

$$V = \frac{1}{(1 + k_e)}\,[(n + \Delta n)P_1 - I + Y]$$

$$V = \frac{1}{1.12}\,[(564,815)(10.80) - 1,000,000 + 500,000]$$

$$V = (.893)[6,100,000 - 500,000]$$

$$V = (.893)(5,600,000) = \$5,000,000$$

7. Compute the present value of the firm under the assumption that a dividend is not paid.

SOLUTION

$$V = \frac{1}{1.12} \; [(544{,}643)(\$11.20) - 1{,}000{,}000 + 500{,}000]$$

$$V = (.893)[6{,}100{,}000 - 500{,}000]$$

$$V = (.893)(5{,}600{,}000) = \$5{,}000{,}000$$

Given the M-M assumptions, it appears that the value of the firm is not affected by dividend policy.

UNSOLVED PROBLEMS

1. The Perfecto Economic Programming Company has a cost of equity capital of 10 percent. The current market value of the firm is $2,000,000 (@ $20 per share).

(a) Assume values for I, Y, and D_1. Show that, under the M-M assumptions, the payment of D_1 does not affect the value of the firm.

(b) What objections may be raised to the M-M analysis of dividend policy?

2. Re-compute the seven items (a-g) in the solved problem. Assume the following values:

$$k_e = 8\%$$
$$P_o = \$25$$
$$D_1 = \$1$$
$$n = 100{,}000$$
$$I = \$650{,}000$$
$$Y = \$100{,}000$$

SECTION 14.3   Although most authorities agree that the M-M logic is unimpeachable, the unrealistic assumptions which they posit seem to render their model of little use to the decision-making financial manager. In particular, the presence of flotation costs and preferential capital gains tax treatment make many managers believe that an extra dollar of dividends is not worth an extra dollar of retained earnings to the stockholder, especially if the extra dollar of retained earnings can be reinvested by the firm at a lucrative rate. Also, such factors as the cash needs of the firm and the dividend predilections of the firm's shareholders must be considered in the dividend decision.

A firm which is temporarily short of cash may wish to defer dividend payments even if the profits of the firm are quite high. Similarly, a firm whose stockholders are in high marginal income tax brackets may do the stockholders a service by retaining earnings. If these earnings can be reinvested at high rates of return, the price of the firm's common stock should advance. Thus, shareholders would be able to enjoy a capital gain which is taxable at one-half the regular rate, or a maximum of 25 percent. On the other hand, if dividends were paid, these distributions would be taxed at the regular marginal rate.

A firm which has few opportunities for reinvestment at lucrative rates should pay out most of its earnings. Similarly, a firm held by stockholders who depend upon dividend income for a livelihood (the proverbial widows and orphans) and who are in low marginal tax brackets should have a relatively high dividend payout. Clearly, a railroad possessing little growth potential, whose stock is held in large part by eleemosynary institutions (that pay no taxes), should have a low rate of earnings retention.

The dividend policy for growth companies, for growthless companies, for firms held almost entirely by dividend oriented stockholders, and for concerns owned primarily by capital gains oriented investors is rather easy to set. Complications arise when a firm's reinvestment opportunities are erratic, or when the various stockholders of a firm have disparate goals. Fortunately, there is a strong tendency for capital gain oriented stockholders to purchase shares of firms with profitable reinvestment opportunities that distribute little or no dividends. A similar tendency exists for dividend-oriented investors to buy the stocks of companies that evidence rather stable and predictable earnings and that distribute large dividends. Under this theory of dividend payment, a firm maintains its basic policy until conditions change. A growth company continues to retain most of its earnings until it is no longer able to reinvest in projects that have high yields. A stable, nongrowth concern changes its policy only if especially attractive projects that would enhance the firm's growth potential become available. In each case, it is assumed that the stockholder mix will adjust to reflect the change in policy. This contrasts with other theories of dividend payment where it is assumed that policy should be set to reflect the stockholder mix (see above).

A policy of altering the dividend payout to conform with the growth potential of the firm articulates with the decision-making convention of investing in all projects which yield more than the cost of capital (see Chap. 5). Such a passive role for the dividend decision may not be possible for many widely held corporations, however. Because of faulty market perception (and other imperfections), the investment community may well expect a firm to pay a certain minimum dividend even though lucrative reinvestment possibilities abound and the firm cannot sell additional shares. Although such expections may be economically unjustifiable, many corporate managers feel that they must satisfy investor expectations. Thus, dividend policy becomes an active rather than a passive consideration. The operational effect of such a suboptimal policy is to impose funds constraint on reinvestment (see Chap. 18).

In addition to the basic policy of high payout vs. low payout, the financial manager must decide whether a target dollar payout or a target percentage payout is optimal. A firm which pays a target dollar amount is illustrated below:

Year	E.P.S.	D.P.S.
1	$2.50	$.625
2	0.50	.625
3	2.00	.625
4	0.00	.625

Such a policy reduces the volatility of the dividend stream paid to stockholders. Of course, as earnings indicate an upward (downward) trend, dividends may be adjusted accordingly. Nevertheless, changes in the dollar distribution are not abrupt and are made only after a trend is evident. For example,

Year	E.P.S.	D.P.S.
5	(.50)	.25
6	(.75)	.25
7	(.25)	nil
8	(.50)	nil

A policy of paying out a target percentage of earnings may be illustrated by considering the previous E. P. S. pattern:

Year	E.P.S.	D.P.S. (50% of E.P.S.)
1	$2.50	$1.25
2	0.50	0.25
3	2.00	1.00
4	0.00	0.00

Although the total distribution in both cases is identical, i.e., $2.50 (ignoring the time value of money), investors tend to prefer the less erratic stream produced by the constant dollar payout strategy. The less volatile stream is usually capitalized at a lower rate. Hence, the cost of equity capital to the firm is usually lower if the firm pays a constant dollar dividend than if the firm paid a constant percentage of earnings.

UNSOLVED PROBLEM

The Windsor Steel Company has produced the following earnings and dividends per share over the past nine years:

Year	E.P.S.	D.P.S.	Market Price Per Share
19x1	$2.00	$1.00	$16
19x2	2.20	1.10	17
19x3	2.40	1.20	18
19x4	2.10	1.05	17
19x5	1.90	.95	15
19x6	1.60	.80	12
19x7	1.80	.90	12
19x8	2.00	1.00	14
19x9	2.10	1.05	16

1. What kind of stockholder do you think owns Windsor shares?

2. What is the average dividend yield per share over the nine-year period?

3. Would you describe Windsor as a growth stock?

4. Do you think the dividend policy for Windsor is optimal? What suggestions for change would you make? What impact might these changes have on the firm's cost of equity capital? On the price of the firm's stock?

5. Can you suggest any reasons to justify (or explain) the current retention policy of Windsor?

SECTION 14.4   Stock dividends are a method by which the firm "capitalizes" retained earnings into the permanent capital accounts. Consider this example:

Common Stock ($1 Par, 100,000 shares)	$100,000
Common Stock, Excess over Par	50,000
Retained Earnings	250,000
	$400,000

Now assume the firm declares a 5 percent stock dividend. Shareholders receive 5 additional shares for every 100 they own. If the market price of the firm's stock is $10 per share, the new balance sheet would appear as follows:[4]

Common Stock ($1 Par, 105,000 shares)	$105,000
Common Stock, Excess over Par	95,000
Retained Earnings	200,000
	$400,000

The effect of the the stock dividend is to transfer $50,000 from retained earnings into permanent capital (Common Stock and Common Stock, Excess over Par). Stock dividends are most useful to firms such as commercial banks which must by law maintain certain balances in permanent capital accounts.[5]

The economic effect of the stock dividend is subject to disagreement. Theoretically, the net worth of the company is no larger (or smaller) as a result of a stock dividend, and the stockholder has no greater percentage ownership in the firm than he had before the stock dividend. In fact, the only thing stockholders have that they did not have before is a larger number of pieces of paper (stock certificates). The price of the firm's stock should decline in proportion to the additional number of shares outstanding. Consider the example above.

Before Dividend:

Value of firm = 100,000 shares $\times$ $10 @ = $1,000,000

After Dividend:

Value of firm = 105,000 shares $\times$ $9.52 @ = $1,000,000

Although there is no economic reason for the stock dividend to possess value, market imperfections and imperfect knowledge may lend a certain usefulness to the stock dividend. It is contended that many investors in high tax brackets prefer stock dividends to cash dividends, since the extra stock accruing from a stock dividend may be sold if funds are needed.

---

[4]When stock dividends are greater than 20-25 percent, book rather than market price may be used in the recapitalization.

[5]The Common Stock and Common Stock, Excess over Par Accounts are permanent in that cash dividends may be charged only against retained earnings and may not be charged against these accounts.

Whereas the cash dividend would be taxed at regular rates, only the profit resulting from the sale of the additional stock would be taxed, and then only at the capital gains rate (assuming, of course, that the stock were held for longer than six months). Assume an investor bought 100 shares of ABC Consolidated at $9 per share one year ago. Assume further that the firm's stock had advanced to $10. If the firm paid $1 in cash dividends, the ex-dividend price of the stock(the day after dividend payment) would be $9. The income to the stockholder would be 100 shares $\times$ $1 = $100. He would still have his original $900 investment intact. Assuming the investor is in the 60 percent marginal tax bracket, his after tax return would be

$$100 \text{ shares @ } \$1 = 100 \times (1 - .6) = \$40.$$

On the other hand, if the firm paid an 11 percent stock dividend, the price of the stock would fall to $9.01 but the stockholder would have 111 shares. He could obtain almost $100 and maintain his original $900 investment (as he did with the cash dividend above) by selling his extra shares: 11 shares $\times$ $9.01 = $99.11. The profit from this sale would be:

Proceeds	$9.01 $\times$ 11 =	$99.11
Basis $\dfrac{\$900}{111}$	= $8.11 $\times$ 11 =	89.21
Taxable gain		$ 9.90

Capital gains taxes would be: (.25) ($9.90) = $2.48. The investor would have $96.63, whereas only $40 would remain if a cash dividend were paid. It should be pointed out, of course, that a similar effect would obtain if no dividend at all were paid and ten of the original one hundred shares were sold.

Proceeds	$10 $\times$ 10 = $100	$100.00
Basis	$ 9 $\times$ 10 = 90	
Taxable gain	$ 10	
Capital gains rate	25%	
Tax	$2.50	2.50
Net retention		$ 97.50

Other reasons frequently given for paying stock dividends include the following: (1) the payment of a stock dividend may indicate that the firm is growing, and (2) the payment of a stock dividend may keep the price of the stock in some "optimum" range. The first assumes that investors could not perceive such growth otherwise, although, of course, they could since the price of the stock would be advancing. The second assumes that investors are irrational. Indeed, is there a difference between owning 100 shares @ $20 or 10 shares @ $200?[6]

If a firm believes that the price of its stock is out of the "optimum range," a more efficacious method of adjustment is the stock split. The stock split has the following impact on the capital accounts:

Common Stock ($1 Par, 100,000 shares)	$100,000
Common Stock, Excess over Par	50,000
Retained Earnings	250,000
	$400,000

Assume a 2 for 1 split:

Common Stock ($0.50 Par, 200,000 shares)	$100,000
Common Stock, Excess over Par	50,000
Retained Earnings	250,000
	$400,000

The major effects are to reduce the par value of the stock and to increase the number of shares outstanding. The price of the firm's stock should fall in proportion to the size of the split. Some analysts believe that the public greets stock splits enthusiastically. As an omen of future growth, a split may be considered bullish. Of course, earnings growth would follow regardless of the split. Since cash dividends are frequently increased after a split, some writers have argued that this factor renders a split bullish. Again, the dividend increase and not the split is the moving force. It might be suggested, furthermore, that a growing firm which splits its stock should *not* increase the cash dividend payout if the firm can continue to reinvest in projects yielding lucrative rates of return (see discussion above).

---

[6]The assumption that investers prefer stocks priced in the $20-$80 range has often been made. Nevertheless, such popular growth stocks as IBM and Xerox have sold beyond this range. Furthermore, the brokerage commission on 10 shares of a $200 stock is *below* that for 100 shares of a $20 stock!

UNSOLVED PROBLEMS

ACE CORPORATION
CAPITAL STRUCTURE
DECEMBER 31, 19x1

Common Stock ($10 Par, 100,000 shares)	$1,000,000
Excess over Par	500,000
Retained Earnings	3,500,000
Net Worth	$5,000,000

1. The firm earned $2,272,000 net after taxes in 19x1. The firm pays no cash dividend. The stock of Ace Corporation is selling for $125.

(a) The firm declared a 10 percent stock dividend on January 1, 19x2. Reformulate the capital structure.

(b) Determine E.P.S. before and after the stock dividend.

(c) What should the price of the stock be after the stock dividend?

2. James Brown bought 100 shares of Ace (above) one year ago at $113\frac{5}{8}$. He is in the 40 percent marginal tax bracket.

(a) Suppose Brown sold the extra shares he received from the declaration of the stock dividend. What would be his after-tax return?

(b) Suppose Ace paid a cash dividend of 50 percent of net income and did not pay the stock dividend. What would be the price of the stock the day before the dividend? The day after the dividend?

(c) Assume Ace paid the cash and not the stock dividend. Compute Brown's after-tax return.

(d) Assume Ace paid neither a cash nor a stock dividend, and that Brown decide to sell 10 percent of his holdings. Determine his after-tax return.

3. The Ace Corporation (above) has decided to pay a 50 percent stock dividend on January 1, 19x2 rather than a 10 percent stock dividend. Reformulate the capital structure. How would this declaration differ from declaring a 3:2 stock split?

15 THE
COST OF CAPITAL

SECTION 15.1
In the previous six chapers, the specific costs of the various sources of funds have been discussed. It remains for this chapter to unify these computations into an overall measure of the firm's cost of capital.

In general, the cost of capital to the firm will be a function of two variables: the pure rate of interest and the riskiness associated with the firm. The pure or riskless rate of interest will vary according to the supply of and demand for credit within the economy. Keynesian economists would argue that, indeed, it is monetary supply and demand that determine the pure rate of interest. In any case, equilibrium conditions in the credit markets will be influenced by the availability of profitable investment projects and by the policies established by the monetary and fiscal authorities.

Beyond the pure rate of interest, the firm must compensate capital suppliers for the riskiness associated with their investment. A firm that undertakes highly risky projects and which manifests great variability in anticipated revenues will pay a rather large risk premium to the suppliers of funds. On the other hand, a conservative firm that invests in projects of moderate riskiness and that has only slight variability associated with future revenues will be required to pay only a small risk premium to suppliers.

Both the pure rate of interest and the applicable risk premium will determine the costs of all of the sources of funds. Short-term creditors will receive the smallest premium for assuming risk, since their obligations are most likely to be paid. This condition obtains because of the short time period over which risks are assumed and the fact that short-term obligations are typically the first satisfied by the firm. Bondholders and other long-term creditors receive a larger risk premium in proportion to the extra risks assumed. Thus, the longer the maturity of a note or bond issue, in general, the larger the yield.[1] Additionally, the more "junior" the

---

[1] This may not be altogether correct in every case, since interest rate expectations also influence the term structure of yields. See Chap. 11.

obligation (that is, the larger the volume and number of obligations which have a prior claim to earnings and assets), the greater must be the expected return to the supplier. Since common stockholders incur the greatest risk both from the standpoint of maturity (the life of common stock is generally infinite) and priority of earnings and asset claims, the anticipated yield to common stockholders should be the largest of all suppliers of funds. This does not mean to imply, of course, that the *realized* return to stockholders is necessarily the largest. It is indeed the possibility that shareholders may receive little, no, or even a negative return that justifies the size of the risk premium, and hence the amount of the *anticipated* return.

Bearing in mind that changes in the pure rate of interest and changes in the risk complexion of the various sources of finance will alter the cost of capital, we may approach a computation of the average cost of funds to the firm. In our analysis, we shall adopt the view that the costs of *all* sources of funds determine the average cost. Some authorities would confine consideration to long-term sources, arguing that the investment in assets is financed by long-term debt, preferred stock, and equity sources. In this volume, however, it is maintained that the total asset mix (including current and fixed assets) is financed by the total of all sources of funds.[2]

Given the cost calculations of each source, a weighted average cost may be computed.[3] For the weighted average to be consistent, the individual sources must be adjusted to reflect disparate taxation treatments.[4] Since the investment decision is typically made on an after-tax basis (see Chap. 5), it is logical to compute the weighted average cost of capital on the same basis. Debt sources (i.e., short-term sources, term debt, leases, bonds, etc.) give rise to payment such as interest or lease payments which are tax deductible. Thus, the real cost to the firm is less than the stated cost. For example, assume that a firm earns $1,000,000, and pays 40 percent in

[2]Cf. Douglas Vickers, *The Theory of the Firm: Production, Capital and Finance* (New York: McGraw-Hill, 1968) pp. 81-82. Vickers (among others) particularly objects to tying specific assets to specific sources of financing, such as current assets to current liabilities and fixed assets to long-term sources.

[3]Many authorities contend that depreciation is a source of funds and as such has a specific cost. This position is adopted here. Funds generated from depreciation have an opportunity cost associated with them, since the firm could choose not to replace plant and equipment as assets depreciated. If such a decision were made, the cash generated from depreciation could be used to reduce all of the sources of financing. Assuming that the firm was financed optimally (i.e., using the cheapest possible mix of sources), each source would be reduced proportionally. The weighted average cost of all sources would, consequently, be the opportunity cost of depreciation. Since depreciation has a cost equal to the weighted average cost of capital, it need not be included in the weighted average determination.

[4]Interest expenses and leasing payments are tax deductible, but preferred and common stock dividends are not.

taxes. The after-tax net income is $600,000. Now, assume that the firm also pays 7 percent interest on a $10,000,000 bond issue. Interest expense is $700,000. Net income before taxes becomes $1,000,000 − $700,000 = $300,000. Taxes are now (.40) ($300,000) = $120,000, and net income after taxes is $180,000. Thus, although the firm pays $700,000 in interest, net income after taxes is reduced by only $600,000 − $180,000 = $420,000. The difference is explained by the fact that the interest expense of $700,000 reduces taxes by $280,000 (i.e., .40 × $700,000). Since taxes are reduced by the marginal tax rate times the cost of the source of funds, it may be said that the after-tax cost of debt funds (including leases) is the pre-tax cost less the tax saving, or

$$k_i\!*\!D = k_iD - k_iDt \qquad (15.1)$$

Where: $k_i\!*$ is the after-tax percentage cost of debt.
D is the volume of debt financing.
k_i is the pre-tax percentage cost of debt.
t is the marginal tax bracket of the firm.

In our example above,

$$k_i\!* (10,000,000) = (.07)(10,000,000) - (.07)(10,000,000)(.40)$$

$$k_i\!* = \frac{700,000 - 280,000}{10,000,000} = 4.2\%$$

Dividing both sides of Eq. (15.1) by D, and factoring out k_i on the right-hand side, we obtain:

$$k_i\!* = k_i(1 - t) \qquad (15.2)$$

Thus, the after-tax cost of debt may be computed immediately by adjusting the pre-tax cost by $(1 - t)$. This adjustment does not apply to preferred and common stock dividends, since these payments are not tax deductible. Dividends are considered to be distributions and not expenses by the Internal Revenue Service.

The after-tax weighted average cost of capital is computed by multiplying the cost of each source (after-tax) by the proportion of total financing represented by that source. Assume the following simplified capital structure:

Source	After-Tax Cost	Amount	
Short-Term Debt	4%	$ 200,000 =	20%
Bonds	5	300,000 =	30
Preferred Stock	8	100,000 =	10
Common Stock	12	200,000 =	20
Retained Earnings	10	200,000 =	20
		$1,000,000 =	100%

The after-tax weighted average cost of capital would be:

$$
\begin{array}{l}
(4\%)\,(.2) = 0.8\% \\
(5\ )\,(.3) = 1.5 \\
(8\ )\,(.1) = 0.8 \\
(12\ )\,(.2) = 2.4 \\
(10\ )\,(.2) = 2.0 \\
\hline
\qquad\quad\ 7.5\%
\end{array}
$$

The same computation may be made employing dollar costs:

$$
\begin{array}{l}
(4\%)\,(\$200,000) = \$\ 8,000 \\
(5\ )\,(\ 300,000) = \quad 15,000 \\
(8\ )\,(\ 100,000) = \quad\ \ 8,000 \\
(12\ )\,(\ 200,000) = \quad 24,000 \\
(10\ )\,(\ 200,000) = \quad 20,000 \\
\hline
\qquad\qquad\qquad\quad \$75,000
\end{array}
$$

$$
\frac{\$75,000}{\$1,000,000} = 7.5\%
$$

SOLVED PROBLEM

The Empleado Corporation has the following capital structure:

Trade Credit	$ 200,000
Short-term note	200,000
Bonds	300,000
Preferred Stock (Par $100)	300,000
Common stock (Par $10)	500,000
Retained Earnings	500,000
	$2,000,000

The firm has credit terms 2/10 net 30 and does not take advantage of discounts. The pre-tax cost of the short-term note is 6 percent. The pre-tax cost of bonds is 7.6 percent. Preferred stock costs the firm 8 percent. Common stock costs 10 percent and retained earnings 9.8 percent. If the firm is in the 30 percent marginal tax bracket, compute the weighted average cost of capital to Empleado.

SOLUTION

Trade credit costs $2/98 \times 360/20 = 36.7\%$ since discounts are not taken. Failure to take discounts increases the cost of materials purchased by Empleado. Since this extra cost is tax deductible, the after-tax cost of trade credit is $(36.7\%)(.7) = 25.69\%$. The after-tax cost of the note is $(6\%)(.7) = 4.20\%$. The after tax cost of bonds is $(7.6\%)(.7) = 5.32\%$. The weighted average cost of capital is:

Source	After-Tax Cost	Weight	
Trade Credit	25.69%	.10	= 2.569%
Short-Term Note	4.20	.10	= 0.420
Bonds	5.32	.15	= 0.798
Preferred Stock	8.00	.15	= 1.200
Common Stock	10.00	.25	= 2.500
Retained Earnings	9.80	.25	= 2.450
			9.937%

UNSOLVED PROBLEMS

1.

ROHRBACK CORPORATION
CAPITAL STRUCTURE

Accounts Payable	$ 500,000
Short-Term Note (8%)	250,000
Bonds (9s of 1998)	1,000,000
Common Stock ($1 par)	1,250,000
Retained Earnings	2,000,000
	$5,000,000

The firm takes advantage of trade discounts. The yield to maturity on the bonds is 8.6 percent. The cost of equity capital is 10 percent (ignore flotation costs). The firm is in the 50 percent marginal tax bracket. Compute the weighted average cost of capital to Rohrback.

2. The Sharpe Co. has the following capital structure:

Trade Credit	$ 300,000
Bonds (8s of 1976)	200,000
Preferred Stock (Par $10)	100,000
Common Stock (Par $1)	300,000
Retained Earnings	100,000
	$1,000,000

The firm has credit terms 1/10 net 70 and does not take advantage of discounts. The pre-tax cost of bonds is 8%. Preferred stock costs the firm 10%. Common stock and retained earnings cost 15%. If Sharpe is in the 22% marginal tax bracket, what is its weighted average cost of capital?

SECTION 15.2   In the previous section, the weighting system was implicitly assumed to be at book (balance sheet) values. Although the use of book values in weighting has considerable appeal because of the simplicity of determination, market value weights may be computed that are more consistent with the cost calculations (where market values were employed). When market value weights are used, the cost of capital may be considerably different from the book weight computation. This is particularly so if the price of the firm's stock is substantially greater than (or less than) its book value. Unfortunately, market prices (particulary for equities) may be quite volatile, and the use of market weights may produce considerably different average costs over time unless market prices are normalized. Moreover, most bankers and financial analysts employ book value data in determining the financial riskiness of the firm (see Chap. 8.) If the firm used market weights in choosing future sources of financing, the book value proportions of financing would tend to change. Such a change could produce an unfavorable reaction if the book proportions of debt increased relative to the book value of equity (resulting in an increase in *perceived* financial risk).

For the average cost of capital computation to have any meaning, future financing must correspond to the current mix of funds. If another mix were employed in the future, the weights assigned to each cost would change, and there would be a new average cost of capital. Presumably, the firm seeks to achieve an optimal mix of financing.[5] Once such a mix is obtained, future financing should correspond to that mix. Of course, in

---

[5]Optimal financing is discussed in detail in the next chapter.

the short run funds are generally not obtained proportionally to the optimal structure (a bond issue may be floated in one year, and a stock issue the next). Nevertheless, in the long run firms can maintain the desired mix.

SOLVED PROBLEMS

Rework solved problem number 1 in the previous section using market value weights. Assume that all short-term sources have a market value equal to their book values.[6] Assume the following market value for the other sources:

Bonds	90 (percent of par, usually $1,000)
Preferred Stock	$75 per share
Common	$50 per share

SOLUTION

The reformulated capital structure becomes:

Trade Credit	$ 200,000	=	5.9%
Short-Term Note	200,000	=	5.9
Bonds	270,000	=	8.0
Pfd. Stock	225,000	=	6.6
Equity[7]	2,500,000	=	73.6
	$3,395,000		100.0%

The weighted average cost at market value weights becomes:

Source	After-Tax Cost	Weight		
Trade Credit	25.69	.059	=	1.516%
Short-Term Note	4.20	.059	=	0.248
Bonds	5.32	.080	=	0.426
Preferred Stock	8.00	.066	=	0.528
Equity[7]	10.00	.736	=	7.360
				10.078%

---

[6]This assumption may be made in almost every case since short-term obligations must be paid within one year at face value.

[7]50,000 shares X $50 share. In the case of market weights, the common stock par, common stock excess over par, and the retained earnings accounts are combined because the market price per share encompasses the total equity of the firm. If separate common stock and retained earnings costs have been computed (due to flotation expenses), the cost of common stock is generally used.

UNSOLVED PROBLEM

1. Rework problem number 1 in Sec. 15.1 (Rohrback Corporation) using market value weights. Assume the following market values:

Bonds	105
Common Stock	$5 per share

2. Rework problem number 2 in Sec. 15.1 (Sharpe Co.), using market value weights. Assume the following market values:

Bonds	90
Preferred Stock	$7 per share
Common Stock	$2 per share

SECTION 15.3   Although the major determinants of the cost of capital are the pure rate of interest and the riskiness of the firm, the volume of financing sought may also influence the cost, at least in the short run. Assuming that capital markets are imperfect, the firm might not be able to obtain all of the financing desired at a point in time at the "going" rate, i.e., the pure rate plus a risk premium. If the demand for finance by the firm were large, it might be expected that the short-run cost would rise.[8]

There are two analytical approaches to the phenomena of short-run increasing capital costs. The marginal sequential costing of funds approach considers the impact of each marginal increase in financing on the average cost of capital to the firm.[9] For example, a firm may incur some debt financing at 6 percent, followed by retained earnings financing at 10 percent, again followed by debt at 7 percent, followed by retained earnings at 11 percent, followed by debt at 9 percent, followed by common stock financing at 14 percent. The marginal sequential cost of debt funds includes costs of nonequity sources. Implicit costs are present, since the increased use of debt financing not only increases the cost of debt but

[8]It is possible, of course, that large firms may be able to discriminate against suppliers, thereby preventing the cost of capital from rising. See Douglas Vickers, "Elasticity of Capital Supply, Monopsonistic Discrimination and Optimum Capital Structure," *Journal of Finance,* March, 1967, pp. 1-9.

[9]See Robert Lindsay and Arnold Sametz, *Financial Management: An Analytical Approach* (Homewood, Ill.: Richard D. Irwin, Inc., 1967), Chaps. 19-20

also increases the cost of equity. This results because increased debt financing augments the financial riskiness of the firm and affects debt and equity suppliers (see Chap. 16). For the financial risk of the firm to remain constant, the financial mix must be maintained at the optimum. Thus, any increase in debt financing, which may have a rather low explicit cost, must be accompanied by an eventual increase in equity financing. The higher cost associated with the increased equity financing becomes the implicit cost of increased debt financing.

The second approach to analyze short-run increasing capital costs simply traces the impact of additional financing on the average cost of capital. Assume the after-tax weighted average cost of capital is 7.5 percent. Extra debt financing of $1,000,000 will cost 6 percent and will increase the cost of equity by $\frac{1}{2}$ percent. If the optimal financing mix of the firm is half debt and half equity, if the firm is in the 50 percent marginal tax bracket, and if the current cost of equity is 12 percent, the marginal cost of funds is:

Source	After-tax Cost	Weighted		
Debt	3%	.5	=	1.50
Equity	12.5%	.5	=	6.25
				7.75%

SOLVED PROBLEM.

The Ajax Corporation has an after-tax weighted average cost of capital of 7 percent. The firm is in the 50 percent marginal tax bracket, and has an optimum debt/equity mix of 1:2. The current cost of debt is 6 percent. The current cost of equity is 9 percent. Additional short-run financing will cost the following:

Marginal Volume of Finance	Source	Cost of Debt	Cost of Equity
(a) $100,000	Debt	7.0%	10.0%
(b) 100,000	Equity	7.5	10.5
(c) 100,000	Equity	8.0	11.0
(d) 100,000	Debt	9.0	12.0

Determine the marginal cost of each $100,000 of added finance.

SOLUTION

	Source	After-tax Cost	Weight	
(a)	Debt	3.50%	1/3 =	1.17
	Equity	10.00	2/3 =	6.67
				7.84%
(b)	Debt	3.75	1/3 =	1.25
	Equity	10.50	2/3 =	7.00
				8.25%
(c)	Debt	4.00	1/3 =	1.33
	Equity	11.00	2/3 =	7.33
				8.66%
(d)	Debt	4.50	1/3 =	1.60
	Equity	12.00	2/3 =	8.00
				9.50%

UNSOLVED PROBLEM

The Simpleton Company has determined its optimum capital structure to be .25 debt and .75 equity. The firm has a cost of debt capital of 6 percent and a cost of equity of 10 percent. The firm is in the 50 percent tax bracket. Marginal financing will cost the firm:

	Marginal Volume	Source	Cost of Debt	Cost of Equity
(a)	$250,000	Debt	6.5%	10.5%
(b)	250,000	Equity	7.0	11.5
(c)	250,000	Equity	8.0	13.0
(d)	250,000	Equity	10.0	15.0

1. Determine the initial weighted average cost of capital.

2. Compute the marginal cost for each marginal volume of financing.

3. If the firm can earn 10 percent on its investment in assets, how much extra financing should be secured?

COMPREHENSIVE PROBLEM

The Shiboleth Corporation has the following capital structure:

SHIBOLETH CORPORATION
CAPITAL STRUCTURE
DECEMBER 31, 1970

Accounts Payable	$ 1,000,000
Notes Payable (7%)	2,000,000
Bonds (6s of 1980)	5,000,000
Preferred Stock	2,000,000
Common Stock ($10 par)	5,000,000
Retained Earnings	5,000,000
	$20,000,000

Current Liabilities: The firm purchases on terms 3/10 net 60 and does take advantage of discounts. Notes are not discounted or amortized but do require a 20 percent compensating balance which would not otherwise be maintained.

Bonds: Were sold at par five years ago. Current price is 90. The issue has no sinking fund provisions.

Preferred Stock: Par value, $100. Dividend, $5. Current price is $80 per share.

Equity: Dividends are $1 per share and are growing by 10 percent annually. The price of the stock is $20 per share. Flotation costs of new shares would be $2 per share.

Compute the after-tax weighted average cost of capital to Shiboleth using book value weights and market weights. The firm's marginal tax bracket is 50 percent.

16 OPTIMUM
CAPITAL STRUCTURE

Although a variety of sources of funds are available to the firm, there are essentially two major forms of financing: debt financing and equity financing. In this chapter, we wish to investigate the impact on the average cost of capital of using each of these major sources. Much of the explication in the earlier chapters of this book has been based upon the assumption that there exists for each firm an optimal asset and financing mix. Now we shall examine in detail the financial structure of the firm. Our objective shall be to specify that mix of sources which will produce the lowest possible after-tax weighted average cost of capital. This mix is called the optimum capital structure.

We found in Chap. 3 that the asset mix of the firm may increase the variability of the firm's net income, *given a pattern of sales variability*. This phenomenon, called operating leverage, occurred because of the presence of operating fixed costs. It was discovered that the larger the volume of operating fixed costs relative to total costs experienced by any firm, the greater the net income variability evidenced by that firm. A firm with a volatile pattern of revenues will have an even more volatile pattern of net income if the firm must meet fixed costs. The variations in revenues associated with and the fixed costs experienced by the firm determine its business risk characteristics. It was indicated in the previous chapter that the cost of capital to the firm was a function of this business risk.

Depreciation, overhead, permanent salaries, etc. are all fixed expenses which influence the riskiness of the firm. As we observed in Chap. 3, however, the use of debt financing by the firm gives rise to fixed interest costs. The increased volatility in net income resulting from the use of debt sources of funds is termed financial leverage. Thus, another risk, called financial risk, ensues from the use of fixed payment (debt) financing.

Although the overall variability of net income experienced by the firm determines the average cost of capital, it is useful to delineate the factors contributing to this variability. For this reason, we discussed operating and financial leverage separately in Chap. 3. We illustrate an income statement to iterate:

APEX CORPORATION
INCOME STATEMENTS

	19x2	*19x3*	
Sales	$100,000	$110,000	(Δ 10%)
Variable Costs	50,000	55,000	
Operating Fixed Costs	30,000	30,000	
E.B.I.T.	$ 20,000	$ 25,000	(Δ 25%)
Interest	10,000	10,000	
Net Before Taxes	$ 10,000	$ 15,000	
Taxes (50%)	5,000	7,500	
Net Income	$ 5,000	$ 7,500	(Δ 50%)

Thus, the riskiness of the firm ensues from the variability of revenues (Δ10 percent in the example). If there is no variability here, there will be no variability in net income, regardless of other factors. Assuming that revenue variability does exist, however, the riskiness associated with E.B.I.T. (Δ 25 percent in the example) will increase as operating fixed costs emanating from the asset investment are larger. This variability is again magnified when the fixed costs resulting from the use of debt sources of funds are considered. Thus, the 50 percent change in net income in the example is produced by business risk (variations in E.B.I.T. resulting from volatile revenues and fixed operating costs) and financial risk (variations in net income resulting from volatile E.B.I.T. and fixed financial costs).

Since the increased use of debt sources of finance augments the riskiness of the firm, we should expect, *ceteris paribus,* that the cost of funds from various sources would rise as increasing amounts of debt were employed. The cost of equity capital would clearly rise as additional debt funds were used, since additional financial leverage increases the variability of earnings available to pay dividends. The possibility of loss or even insolvency is also enhanced as the firm increases its debt commitments. The cost of debt capital might also rise as the firm employed added debt sources. This follows since greater financial leverage may mean reduced safety (times-interest-earned coverage) for debt holders.[1]

---

[1] If it is assumed that the size of the firm does not change (i.e. total assets are constant) as financial leverage increases, the firm must be substituting debt sources for equity sources. In this case, expected revenues would not change, and interest coverage would clearly be reduced. On the other hand, if the increased debt is used to expand the asset base, two outcomes are possible. Given a specific MEC schedule for the firm, increased investment (movement down the MEC curve) can only reduce the rate of return and thus lower the interest coverage of the debt. If, however, new lucrative opportunities appear (an outshift in the MEC curve), it is entirely conceivable that the increased asset investment could generate sufficient revenues to increase the times-interest-earned coverage (which, by virtue of the MEC curve shift, would increase even more if the additional debt were not sold). In any case, however, increased financial leverage does increase the overall riskiness of the firm. As the firm incurs additional debt, the ability of the firm to service that debt (interest

If the use of debt funds increases the cost of debt and equity to the firm, the question may be raised: Why does the firm employ debt sources in the first place? The answer to this question is twofold. First, if the firm can invest the funds secured by using debt at a larger return than their cost, the difference may accrue to the stockholders. Secondly, even though both the costs of debt and equity may rise as additional funds are borrowed, the weighted average cost may actually *fall*. This apparent paradox requires illustration. Assume that the Wotan Company is financed entirely by equity which costs the firm 10 percent. The after-tax weighted average cost of capital to Wotan is obviously 10 percent. Now, let us assume that Wotan secures 1/4 of its funds from debt sources at an after-tax cost of 3 percent, and that the use of financial leverage increases the cost of equity to 11.5 percent. The new average cost is:

Structure	Weight	Cost		
Debt	.25	3%	=	.750
Equity	.75	11.5%	=	8.625
				9.375%

Thus, the weighted average cost of capital has *fallen* from 10 percent to 9.375 percent. The "mystery" of this phenomena is obviously explained by the fact that a cheaper source (debt) is being substituted for a more expensive source (equity). The change in weights within the structure (equity declines from 100 percent of the structure to 75 percent) produces the lower cost.[2]

Let us continue with our Wotan example to try to discover the optimum structure for the firm. For sake of convenience, the following notation will be employed:

---

and principal payments) must eventually be reduced. Thus, even for the firm with an expanding asset base, the cost of debt should not fall with increased financial leverage and should indeed rise at some point. Institutional rules of thumb as to the "appropriate" debt/equity ratios and times-interest-earned multiples almost guarantee an eventual increase in the cost of debt as financial leverage is increased.

[2] The real cost of debt financing includes not only the explicit cost associated with debt but also the increased return demanded by equity holders to compensate them for the greater risk they must bear. The distinction between the *nominal* costs of debt and equity and the *real* costs is explained by William Baumol and Burton Malkiel, "The Firm's Optimal Debt-Equity Combination and the Cost of Capital," *Quarterly Journal of Economics,* November, 1967, pp. 547-71. The solution which obtains when nominal costs are employed is identical to that which follows from equating the marginal real costs of debt and equity, since the nominal cost calculation seeks to minimize average costs.

k_i = the cost of debt capital
k_e = the cost of equity capital
k_o = the weighted average cost of capital
$D/D + E$ = the percentage of debt in the capital structure
$E/D + E$ = the percentage of equity in the capital structure

These symbols may be used to produce the following equation which simplifies our calculations:

$$k_o = (k_i)(D/D{+}E) + (k_e)(E/D{+}E) \qquad (16.1)$$

Thus, in the previous example, k_o = (.03)(.25) + (.115)(.75) = .09375 or 9.375%. Assume now that Wotan increases its use of debt sources so that $D/D{+}E$ = .5. Assume that k_i rises to 4 percent and k_e to 14 percent. The k_o is (.04)(.5) + (.14)(.5) = .09 or 9%. The weighted average cost of capital has again fallen with the increased use of debt. Let us once more increase $D/D{+}E$. Assume $D/D{+}E$ = .67, k_i = 6%, and k_e = 18%. k_o = (.06)(.67) + (.18)(.33) = .10 or 10%. This time, the increased use of debt *increases* the weighted average cost of capital. The reverse in the movement of k_o may be explained by the fact that increases in k_i and k_e are no longer out-weighted by the substitution of the cheaper for the more expensive source. We should expect that any further increase in $D/D{+}E$ would increase k_o even more.[3]

Summarizing, we have found:

$D/D + E$	k_o
.00	10.000%
.25	9.375
.50	9.000
.67	10.000

The optimum structure is somewhere between $D/D{+}E$ = .25 and $D/D{+}E$ = .67. These results are graphed in Fig. 16.1. The heavy lined k_o function assumes the weighted average is at its lowest point at $D/D{+}E$ = .50, although it is entirely reasonable that another value, not computed in the example, is the optimum. Two such possible values are indicated by points A and B (along the two broken lines) in Fig. 16.1.

In practice it may be rather difficult to determine the specific financing mix which is optimal. It is not so difficult to identify nonoptimal mixes, however. In the above example, values of $D/D{+}E<.25$ and $D/D{+}E>.67$ are

---

[3] In the previous analysis we obtained the optimum structure by minimizing average costs. The same solution ensues where the marginal real cost of debt equals the marginal real cost of equity. See footnote on previous page.

clearly nonoptimal. It should not be an especially complicated problem for the financial manager of Wotan to determine that only a negligible amount of debt financing is nonoptimal. Similarly, it should be easy to determine that extreme levels of debt financing are not optimal. Because of the difficulties associated with pinpointing exactly the optimal $D/D+E$, an optimal range of $D/D+E$'s is frequently sought. Some authorities even argue that there is not one specific optimum $D/D+E$, but rather that the k_o function is saucer shaped, providing a range of structures where k_o does not vary appreciably.[4]

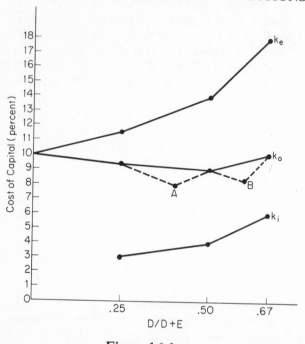

OPTIMUM CAPITAL STRUCTURE, IMPERFECT CAPITAL MARKET CONDITIONS

Figure 16.1

UNSOLVED PROBLEMS

1. The Mercouri Mattress Company has estimated that the following after-tax costs of capital would prevail at various capital structures:

[4] Ezra Solomon, *The Theory of Financial Management* (New York: Columbia University Press, 1963), pp. 91-98.

$D/D+E$	k_i	k_e
.00	–	8.0%
.20	3.5%	9.0
.40	4.0	10.5
.60	5.0	13.0
.80	7.0	16.0

(a) Determine the approximate optimum structure.

(b) Graph your results, indicating the k_e, k_i, and k_o functions.

2. The Centrox Corporation now has a $D/D+E$ of 0.8. The firm has an average cost of capital of 14 percent. The cost of equity capital is two times the cost of debt capital. Determine k_e and k_i.

3. Centrox (above) believes it is overly levered. It has been estimated that the cost of debt capital would fall by 1 percent and that the cost of equity would decline by 2 percent if $D/D+E$ were reduced to 0.5.

(a) Determine the new k_e, k_i, and k_o if $D/D+E$ is reduced to 0.5.

(b) Should the reduction in leverage be effected? Explain your results.

SECTION 16.2   The optimum capital structure for any firm will depend upon the degree of business risk characteristic of that firm. Companies that experience rather stable (or predictable) revenue patterns, such as public utilities, may incur heavy nonfinancial fixed costs and still have an optimal structure where $D/D+E$ is high. Many public utility companies, in fact, are able to support larger amounts of debt than they are allowed to have by the regulatory authorities. These firms are able to approach an optimal structure by using another form of fixed payment security which operates in a fashion very similar to that of debt in increasing the financial leverage of the firm. This form of financing is, of course, preferred stock (see Chap. 12).

Firms which experience highly unstable (or unpredictable) patterns of revenue, on the other hand, may engage in only nominal debt financing if they are also characterized by high operating fixed costs. Companies such as railroads, which have rather volatile revenues and which have high operating fixed costs, clearly should *not* engage in much debt financing. Indeed, one of the reasons many of the railroads in the United States have evidenced meager long-run profitability and have been frequently in receivership is their debt-laden (nonoptimal) financial structures. The fallacy of the proposition that a firm's debt capacity is a function of its volume of mortgagable assets is well illustrated by this example.

A firm's optimal capital structure may change over time. For example, any long-run trend toward higher interest rates would, *ceteris paribus,* increase the riskiness of the firm, increase the costs of debt and equity, reduce the level of investment, and might alter the optimal $D/D+E$. Similarly, any change in the volatility of expected revenues or the volume of operating fixed costs should alter the optimal $D/D+E$.

UNSOLVED PROBLEM

Discuss the impact of the following on the firm's choice of capital structure:

1. The firm expects a less volatile pattern for the business cycle.

2. The firm is becoming more capital intensive (substituting capital inputs for labor).

3. The firm has negotiated a guaranteed annual wage with its employees.

4. Interest rates have advanced sharply.

SECTION 16.3

There exists a school of thought which maintains that there is no optimal financing mix for the firm, i.e., that the weighted average cost of capital is independent of the capital structure. The original impetus for this position came from an early article published, not surprisingly, by Modigliani and Miller.[5] In this article, M-M make these explicit assumptions:

1. Firms can be grouped into homogeneous business risk classes.
2. Investors are perfectly rational.
3. Securities markets operate under conditions of perfect competition where there are no transactions costs.
4. There are no corporate income taxes. (This assumption is later dropped).

Given two firms with the same business risk and the same operating income, M-M argue that the value (V) of these firms must be identical regardless of the method of financing. Consider two firms, A and B, evidencing the following pattern of E.B.I.T., interest payments and net income:

	A	B
E.B.I.T.	$1,000	$1,000
Interest	–	200
Net Income	$1,000	$ 800

[5] Franco Modigliani and Merton Miller, "The Cost of Capital, Corporation Finance and the Theory of Investment," *American Economic Review,* June, 1958, pp. 261-97.

A is financed entirely by equity, where k_e = .08. The value of firm A is: V_A = \$1,000/.08 = \$12,500. B is financed by bonds, where k_i = .04, and equity, where k_e = .10. The value of B is: V_B = \$200/.04 + \$800/.10 = \$5,000 + \$8,000 = \$13,000. Now, according to M-M, the reason $V_A < V_B$ is that the price of B's stock is too high. They argue that B stock is worth only \$7,500, that k_e for B should be .1067 (i.e., $10\frac{2}{3}$ percent) rather than .10, and that in equilibrium shareholders will sell B stock, thus driving down its price.

M-M's argument may be illustrated with an example. Assume that Schwartz owns 1 percent of the stock of firm B. It would pay Schwartz to sell his stock and buy A stock. If Schwartz sold B, the proceeds would be $(1/100) \times (\$8,000)$ = \$80. Now, Schwartz could assume the same riskiness associated with his investment in B by engaging in what M-M call "homemade leverage." Thus, firm B was financed 5/13 by debt, whereas firm A has no debt. For Schwartz to have the same risk with his purchase of A as he had when he owned B, he should borrow \$50. Schwartz' personal capital structure mix (\$50 debt, \$80 personal equity) would be the same as firm B's. With the proceeds from the sale of B plus the \$50 loan, Schwartz could now buy \$130/\$12,500 or 1.04 percent of A. The question may be raised: Why would Schwartz sell B, borrow, and buy A? The answer is easily found. If Schwartz held B, his return would be (.01) (\$800) = \$8. If he sells, borrows, and buys A, however, his gross return is (.0104) (\$1,000) = \$10.40. From this gross return, he must pay interest of (.04) (\$50) = \$2.[6] Nevertheless, his net return from holding A is \$8.40, which is larger than the return would be if he held B. Thus, he would sell A and buy B.

The impact of many stockholders selling B and buying A would reduce the price of B until returns were equalized. Since the appropriate return for an unlevered equity in this example was assumed to be 8 percent, the price of A would not rise. When the value of the stock of B declined to \$7,500, equilibrium would be reached. To see why this is true, let us return to our example. If Schwartz sold B, his proceeds would be (.01) (\$7,500) = \$75. He would borrow \$50, since 5/12.5 is the same debt/equity (risk) mix evidenced by firm B. His total of \$125 would buy \$125/\$12,500 or 1 percent of A. His return if he held B would be (.01) (\$800) = \$8. If he bought A, his net return would be (.01) (\$1,000) − (.04) (\$50) = \$10 − \$2 = \$8. There would be no advantage in selling B and buying A. Thus, in equilibrium the value of A (\$12,500) equals the value of B (\$7,500 + \$5,000 = \$12,500).

A number of criticisms have been raised about the M-M explication and its applicability to the real world. It is observed that markets are not

---

[6] An implicit assumption made by Modigliani and Miller is that the rate of interest paid by the investor is the same as that paid by the firm, e.g. 4 percent in this example.

perfect and investors are not necessarily rational. There is no guarantee that investors would engage in the arbitrage-homemade leverage process so crucial to the M-M argument. Furthermore, even if investors wished to behave as M-M suggest, there are institutionally imposed restrictions to prevent such behavior. Federal Reserve margin restrictions, for example, limit the degree of homemade leverage which the investor may assume. Also, there is every reason to believe that the borrowing rate paid by the investor would be greater than the rate incurred by the corporation. As such, there would be a clear preference for corporate rather than personal borrowing. Moreover, it seems likely that the presence of transactions costs (brokerage fees, etc.) which M-M assume away, would tend to reduce the practicability of the arbitrage process. Additional criticism has stemmed from the observation that the personal risk assumed by the investor in homemade leverage is really greater than the indirect risk he assumes by owning the common stock of a levered company. Whereas the corporation is protected by limited liability, the investor is not.

When one considers the specific cost functions implicit in the M-M analysis, it is not difficult to find further objections to it (see Fig. 16.2). As leverage $(D/D+E)$ increases, M-M agree that k_i and k_e will rise. In the early stages of increased leverage, because of the weighting rearrangements, k_o may remain constant even though k_i and k_e both rise. Nevertheless, a point is eventually reached where k_e must fall if k_i continues to rise. (Consider the case where $k_i > k_o$ then it must be that $k_e < k_o$!) It seems unreasonable to expect that stockholders would capitalize riskier earnings at a lower k_e, and this factor alone would tend to cause k_o to rise at extreme levels of $D/D+E$.[7] When M-M relax their assumption of no corporate taxation, it clearly pays to have all interest payments assumed by the corporation (and none by investors) in order to minimize the effects of double taxation. The result is an optimum capital structure where $D/D+E$ approaches unity. In Fig. 16.2, this is illustrated by a downshift in k_i to k_i' and the resulting negatively sloped k_o' function. The conclusion that $D/D+E$ should approach unity (and that k_o' will continually *fall* as financial risk is increased) is immediately suspect.

Although M-M have produced a logical system, given their assumptions and constraints, it should not be surprising that few academics and virtually no financial practitioners accept the M-M hypothesis as an explanation of any real world phenomena. Most do believe that the firm may employ a judicious amount of debt (what is judicious for one firm may be niggardly or extravagant for another) to reduce the average cost of capital but that extreme leverage must raise k_0.

---

[7] Miller and Modigliani argue that some investors will become risk seekers at high levels of $D/D + E$ and that k_e will fall for this reason. It seems a bit contrived that some investors would suddenly become assumers of risk, whereas before all were rational avoiders.

CAPITAL STRUCTURE UNDER PERFECT CAPITAL MARKET CONDITIONS (MODIGLIANI AND MILLER VERSION)

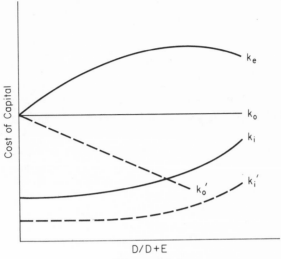

Figure 16.2

COMPREHENSIVE PROBLEMS

1. Sieg Fried is organizing a new franchising concern. Fried believes that he will need $1,000,000 to organize his firm. The Valhalla Corporation, a Small Business Investment Company, has offered to lend Fried any capital he might need either through purchasing bonds in the firm or making a personal loan to Fried. Fried has determined four possible financing plans:

A. Form the corporation with 100,000 shares of $10 par stock, borrowing the entire $1,000,000 from Valhalla on a personal basis (paying 8 percent interest).

B. Form the corporation with 50,000 shares of $10 par stock, borrowing $500,000 on a personal basis, and selling $500,000 worth of bonds (@ 8 percent) to Valhalla.

C. Form the corporation with 25,000 shares of $10 par stock, borrowing $250,000 on a personal basis, and selling $750,000 worth of bonds (@ 8 percent) to Valhalla.

D. Form the corporation with 1 share of $1 par stock, borrowing $1 on a personal basis, and selling $999,999 worth of bonds (@ 8 percent) to Valhalla.

(1) Ignoring corporate and personal taxes, which of the four alternatives is optimal to Fried? Let E.B.I.T. = $100,000, and let all

earnings be paid out in dividends.

(2) Assuming a 50 percent marginal tax rate for the firm and a 20 percent rate for Fried, which alternative is optimal?

(3) Analyze your results.

(4) Comment on the astuteness of the management of Valhalla.

2. Answer number 1 (above) letting E.B.I.T. be $200,000. What conclusions can you draw? Why do these results obtain?

3. Let E.B.I.T. be $50,000. Do you arrive at the same conclusions?

4. Graph the results you obtain in items A. through C. above. Prepare three graphs. On the first graph, plot the personal profit to Fried against E.B.I.T. under the assumptions of part 1 (no taxes). Four functions should be included, one for each financing alternative. On the second graph, plot the personal profit to Fried under the assumptions of part 2 (with taxes). On the third graph, plot E.P.S. against E.B.I.T. under the assumptions of part 2. In what sense may these graphs be described as indifference curves?

III INTEGRATED SYSTEMS CONCEPTS

17 INTEGRATION OF THE INVESTMENT AND FINANCING SUBSYSTEMS

SECTION 17.1   The investment opportunities faced by a firm at a specific point in time were described as a project investment return schedule in Chap. 5. Called the firm's marginal efficiency of capital function, this schedule was constructed as an aid to determining the volume of investment to be undertaken by the firm. It was suggested that all projects yielding more than the firm's average cost of capital (k_o) should be accepted, and that projects yielding less than this amount should be rejected. The firm's average cost of capital was assumed to be a constant amount. These relationships are depicted in Fig. 17.1.

INVESTMENT EQUILIBRIUM FOR THE FIRM
WHERE THE COST OF CAPITAL IS INDEPENDENT
OF THE VOLUME OF FINANCING SECURED

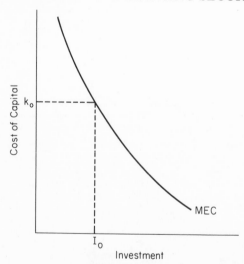

Figure 17.1

The simple model developed early in Chap. 5 implicitly assumed that all projects along the *MEC* schedule were of equal risk; otherwise, they could not be compared. It was also assumed that these projects were of equal riskiness to the previous projects accepted by the firm, since the cost of capital (k_o) is a function of the risk associated with the firm's previous investments. Although several techniques were described which enable the financial manager to deal with projects of unequal risk (such as varying the cutoff rate, or adjusting returns to reflect a certainty equivalent), the precise impact of risk on the *MEC* and on k_o was not outlined.

When projects are undertaken that alter the risk characteristics of the firm, the cost of capital may be expected to change. If projects are accepted that increase the riskiness of the firm, k_o should rise. If lower risk projects are accepted, k_o should fall. This change in k_o is the rationale for altering the cutoff rate when projects of varying degrees of risk are considered. A more appropriate portfolio selection decision model will be constructed in Sec. 17.5.

The simple model encompassed in Fig. 17.1 also assumed that k_o was independent of I; that is, the firm could secure any volume of financing desired without altering the cost of funds. We found in Chap. 15, however, that only under conditions of perfect capital markets can the firm secure all the financing desired without influencing the cost of funds.

INVESTMENT EQUILIBRIUM FOR THE FIRM
WHERE THE COST OF CAPITAL IS A FUNCTION
OF THE VOLUME OF FINANCING SECURED

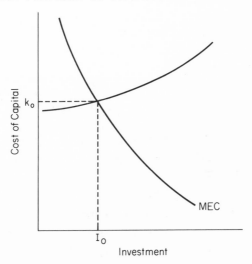

Figure 17.2

It seems reasonable to expect that at some point k_o should rise as the volume of financing demanded becomes large. This is depicted in Fig. 17.2. The firm still invests down to the point where the internal rate of return equals k_o.

The exact shape of k_o will depend on the size and nature of the firm under consideration. Small firms may well have a k_o which is linear and horizontal. It is possible that the monopsonistic character of very large firms could also produce a linear-horizontal or even a negatively sloped k_o function. Reduced investment banking spreads (lower flotation costs) as the issue size of securities increases could also result in a negatively sloped k_o, at least for small values of I.

The shape of k_o as a function of I should not be confused with the shape of k_o as a function of $D/D+E$. It was found in Chap. 16 that k_o was most likely saucer shaped when capital structure was the independent variable. An integration of the capital structure—investment size models is indicated in Fig. 17.3. In this diagram, k_o is illustrated as being independent of the volume of financing by function $k_o \neq f(I)$. The case where $k_o = f(D/D+E,I)$ is illustrated by function $k_o = f(I)$.

UNSOLVED PROBLEMS

1. The Wingate Company has determined that the following projects are equal in risk to each other and to the previously accepted projects of the firm:

Project	Amount	Return
A	$1,000	8%
B	1,000	7
C	2,000	6
D	600	9
E	1,400	10
F	2,000	5

The firm has an optimal $D/D+E$ which produces a k_o of 6 percent. Each $1,000 of added financing will cost the firm an extra 1 percent. The first $1,000 costs 6 percent.

(a.) Construct an MEC and a $k_o = f(I)$ curve.

(b.) Determine the optimal level of investment.

(c.) Determine the marginal and average rates of return at optimal I.

(d.) What is the cost of capital at optimal I?

2. Answer number 1 (above) assuming a perfectly elastic k_o function (i.e., where $k_o \neq f(I)$).

CAPITAL STRUCTURE AND
INVESTMENT EQUILIBRIUM

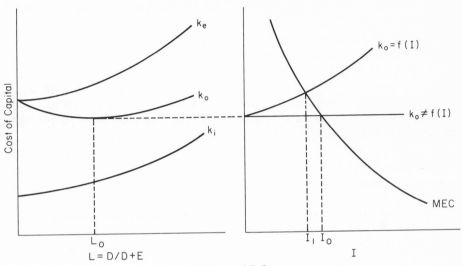

Figure 17.3

SECTION 17.2   A complete integration of the investment and financing subsystems requires a more adequate method for dealing with risk. We need, in fact, a comprehensive measure of the overall riskiness of each project under consideration for investment. The most promising technique for determining a measure of overall riskiness is simulation, which is merely a means of combining specified probability distributions.[1]

There are a number of variables that contribute to the riskiness of a project. Such factors as the volume of sales, selling price, production costs, project life, required investment, and the salvage value associated with any project are individually subject to risk. In order to assess the total riskiness of the project, the riskiness of each component variable must be determined. Simulation makes it possible to unify these separate risky variables into a general risk measure for the project. Let us consider an example.

The financial manager for the Central Manufacturing Company is attempting to measure the riskiness of a new project. The project is a new product which should increase the total sales of Central. The financial manager has obtained from the marketing department probability distributions of future sales expected from this project. From the

[1]Cf. David B. Hertz, "Risk Analysis in Capital Investment," *Harvard Business Review,* January-February, 1964, pp. 95-106; and Hertz, "Investment Policies that Pay Off," *Harvard Business Review,* January-February, 1968, pp. 96-108.

production and accounting departments, the financial manager has received distributions of production costs, required investment, and the salvage value anticipated for the project. The manager's task now is to arrange these data into a meaningful simulation of the future performance of the project. Since many of the data are not independent, it would seem logical for the manager to prepare appropriate tables of conditional probabilities. Thus, it may be that future sales would depend on the level of expected sales in period t_1. If sales were high in t_1, it may be that the new product has "caught on" and future sales levels will also be high. On the other hand, if sales were low in t_1, it could be that the new product has been poorly received and future sales will also be low. It is also likely that cost data will depend on future sales projections, unless all costs are fixed. Thus, a high volume of sales would most likely produce higher costs than a low volume of expected sales. Let us suppose that the following data for period t_1 have been determined:

Sales	Cash Expenses (Including Income Taxes)	Net Cash Flows
100 (.3)	70 (.2)	30 (.06)
	80 (.6)	20 (.18)
	90 (.2)	10 (.06)
90 (.5)	65 (.1)	25 (.05)
	75 (.7)	15 (.35)
	85 (.2)	5 (.10)
80 (.2)	60 (.2)	20 (.04)
	70 (.5)	10 (.10)
	80 (.3)	0 (.06)

The data may be grouped into the following net cash flow distribution for t_1:

Net Cash Flow	Probability
30	.06
25	.05
20	.22
15	.35
10	.16
5	.10
0	.06
	1.00

The same process may be repeated to determine net flows for future periods, although sales in t_2 would depend on sales in t_1, etc. A more complicated conditional probability distribution would prevail in each period.

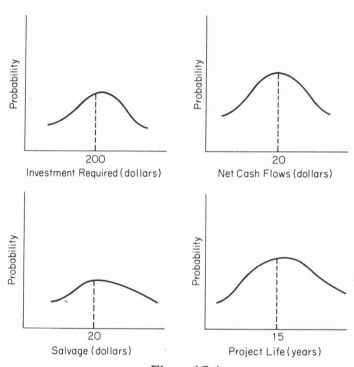

Figure 17.4

Now, let us suppose that the manager has determined the probability distributions diagramed in Fig. 17.4. Given this information, the financial manager may employ a computer to combine all possible values (and probabilities) of the four independent variables. Each combination will produce an internal rate of return. After all possible combinations of the independent variables are calculated, they are arrayed in a frequency distribution (see Fig. 17.5). This distribution relates the relative probability that any one internal rate of return will occur. Since there may be several thousand or even several million combinations (depending upon the number and variability of the independent variables), it is obvious that the help of a computer is required in simulation.

SIMULATED FREQUENCY DISTRIBUTION OF INTERNAL RATES OF RETURN

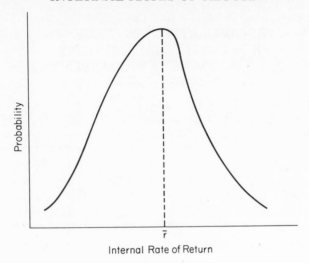

Figure 17.5

SECTION
17.3
The dispersion (variability) around the mean value of the internal rates of return determined by simulation indicates the riskiness of the project. An appropriate measure for this dispersion is the standard deviation. This measure was discussed in Chap. 2. The standard deviation of internal rates of return (σ_r) is given by:

$$\sigma_r = \sqrt{\sum_{t=1}^{n} (r_t - \bar{r})^2 \, p_t} \qquad (17.1)$$

Thus, if the following distribution of internal rates of return were determined:

I.R.R.	Probability
4%	.1
5	.2
6	.5
8	.2

the mean rate of return ($\bar{r}$) would be $(.1)(.04) + (.2)(.05) + (.5)(.06) + (.2)(.08) = .06$ or 6%. The standard deviation of internal rates of return would be:

$r_t - \bar{r}$	$(r_t - \bar{r})^2$	p_t
4% – 6% = –2%	$(-2\%)^2 = 4\%$	4% × .1 = .4%
5 – 6 = –1	$(-1)^2 = 1$	1 × .2 = .2
6 – 6 = 0	$(0)^2 = 0$	0 × .5 = .0
8 – 6 = 2	$(2)^2 = 4$	4 × .2 = .8
		$\sigma_r^2 = 1.4\%$

$$\sigma_r = \sqrt{\sigma_r^2} = \sqrt{1.4\%} \simeq 1.2\%$$

Given values for $\bar{r}$ and σ_r, it is possible to assess the impact on the overall riskiness of the firm of accepting the project. It is clear that some projects that by themselves would be quite risky would not appreciably affect the riskiness of the firm. Projects with low degrees of correlation with existing projects may complement the revenue patterns resulting from previous investments and through diversification could even lower overall business risk. A classic example is the snowsuit company that assumes as a capital project the development of swimwear products. Taken alone, the σ_r for the project might be quite high. Nevertheless, the impact on the total σ_r might be to reduce risk for the firm.

Since the real risk of accepting a project is the effect the project has on the overall riskiness of the firm, we should examine the impact of acceptance on the existing $\bar{r}$ and σ_r for the firm. Assume that the Mikado Company earns an average return ($\bar{r}$) of 8 percent on its investment in assets and that the aggregate σ_r is 2 percent. Assume further that Mikado is contemplating investing in the project considered above ($\bar{r} = 6$ percent, $\sigma_r = 1.2$ percent). It has been estimated that the project would have a correlation coefficient of .6 with the present asset investment of Mikado. The project would increase total assets by 10 percent. We may construct the following correlation table.[2]

	Amount*	$\bar{r}$	σ_r	Correlation Coefficient
Present Asset Investment (P_{11})	$1,000,000	8.0% = $80,000	2.0% = $20,000	1.00
New Project Alone (P_{22})	100,000	6.0 = 6,000	1.2 = 1,200	1.00
New Project Added to the Present Investment (P_{12})				.60

*The projects are assumed to have infinite lives.

If the new project were accepted, the new investment would be $1,100,000. The new $\bar{r}$ would be: $86,000/$1,100,000 = 7.8 percent. The standard derivation for the combined new investment in assets is given by:

[2] Adapted from James C. Van Horne, *Financial Management and Policy*, pp. 92-93.

$$\sigma_{12} = \sqrt{(C_{11})(\sigma_{11}^2) + (2)(C_{12})(\sigma_{11})(\sigma_{22}) + (C_{22})(\sigma_{22}^2)} \qquad (17.2)$$

$$\sigma_{12} = \sqrt{(1.00)(20,000)^2 + (2)(.60)(20,000)(1,200) + (1.00)(1,200)^2}$$

$$\sigma_{12} = \$20,750.$$

The coefficient of variation $(\sigma_{11}/\bar{r}_{11})$ of the present asset investment is $\$20,000/\$80,000 = .25$. With the new project, the coefficient of variation becomes $\$20,750/\$86,000 = .24$. If the firm accepted the project, the rate of return on assets would be reduced from 8.0 percent, to $\$86,000/\$1,100,000 = 7.8$ percent. Nevertheless, the riskiness of the firm would also be reduced. Whether or not the project were selected would depend on the risk preferences of the owners (or managers) of the firm. Risk preference will be discussed in the next section.

UNSOLVED PROBLEMS

1. The Ruler Corporation uses computer simulation to determine the frequency distribution of internal rates of return of prospective projects. The following distributions have been computed:

A		B		C	
I.R.R.	Probability	I.R.R.	Probability	I.R.R.	Probability
6%	.3	7%	.2	8%	.1
8	.4	10	.5	11	.8
10	.3	12	.3	14	.1

Determine $\bar{r}$ and σ_r for each project.

2. The Ruler Corporation (above) earns an average return of 10 percent on its investment in assets with an aggregate σ_r of 4 percent. The firm has estimated correlation coefficients for each project A–C:

Amount		$\bar{r}$	σ_r	Correlation Coefficient
Present Investment	$100,000	10%	4%	1.00
A alone	20,000			1.00
B alone	15,000			1.00
C alone	10,000			1.00
A with Present Investment				0.80
B with Present Investment				0.20
C with Present Investment				0.50

Determine the present coefficient of variation. Compute the combined coefficients of variation of the present investment and project A, of the present investment and project B, and of the present investment and project C.

SECTION 17.4

Once the firm has computed the mean rates of return and coefficients of variation for various combinations of projects and the existing asset investment, an investment decision may be made. Let us assume the following combined rates of return and coefficients of variation:

	$\bar{r}$	$\sigma/\bar{r}$
Present Investment (PI)	8%	.25
PI and Project M	6	.20
PI and Project N	5	.28
PI and Project O	10	.36
PI and Project P	7	.20
PI and Project Q	8	.30
PI and Project R	12	.30
PI and Project S	4	.25
PI and Project T	9	.15

These projects are plotted in Fig. 17.6. We may observe immediately from this risk-return map that all projects in quadrant IV should be accepted, since assuming these projects increases the firm's rate of return on investment and decreases the riskiness of the firm. Similarly, all projects in quadrant II should be rejected, since assuming these projects would decrease the firm's rate of return and would increase the riskiness of the firm. Thus, project T would be accepted and project N would be rejected immediately. By inspection it may be seen that project S is as risky as the present investment, but yields a smaller return; this project should be rejected. Project Q yields the same return as the present investment but is riskier. Project Q should be rejected. We are left with projects M, P, O, and R. Project M may be eliminated, since it is of equal risk to project P, but its yield is lower. Project O is riskier and yields less than R. It should be rejected.

The decision to invest in P and/or R depends upon three variables: (1) the nature of the projects, (2) the availability of funds, and (3) the firm's attitude toward risk. In any case, project T would be accepted. If P and R are not mutually exclusive with one another, and if there is no funds constraint, all three could be accepted.[3] Assuming projects are not

[3]Capital budgeting under a funds constraint is discussed in Chap. 18.

AN ARRAY OF INVESTMENT PROJECTS
UNDER CONDITIONS OF RISK

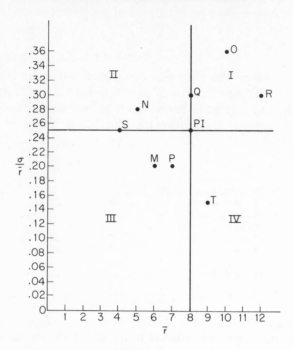

Figure 17.6

mutually exclusive and that there is no funds constraint, the risk preferences of the firm would determine the acceptability of projects P and R.[4] Acceptance of project P would reduce the riskiness of the firm and would also reduce the firm's rate of return on assets. If the firm wished to move into a lower risk class, this project could be accepted. Contrariwise, acceptance of project R would increase the riskiness of the firm and would also increase the rate of return on assets. If the firm wished to enter a higher risk class, this project could be accepted.[5]

The impact on k_o of investing in P, R, and T should be considered. If k_o is upward sloping as a function of the volume of investment, k_o would initially increase, given any additional investment. Nevertheless, acceptance of T

---

[4]There is an implicit assumption made here that the returns from projects M-T are statistically independent. Thus, although the present investment and, say, project P may have a positive correlation coefficient, the coefficient for projects P and O, for example, is assumed to be zero.

[5]If more than one project is selected, correlations among projects must be considered. The significant risk variable would be the impact on the firm's coefficient of variation of accepting the package of projects.

and/or P would reduce the riskiness of the firm and should tend to reduce k_o. Acceptance of R would increase the riskiness of the firm and should further increase k_o. Let us assume that all projects (M-T) are mutually exclusive, i.e., only one of the eight projects may be accepted. T is clearly the superior investment. We trace the acceptance process in Fig. 17.7. Originally, the cost of capital is k_o. Given the upward sloping $k_o = f(I)$ function, k_o is greater than the internal rate of return on T. Nevertheless, the reduced risk accruing to the firm as a result of accepting T will shift down the $k_o = f(D/D+E)$ function such that the new average cost of capital becomes k_o'. Even considering the upward sloping $k_o' = f(I)$ function, the cost of capital is less than the internal rate of return on T. Thus, the project should be accepted.

THE INVESTMENT AND FINANCING PROCESS UNDER CONDITIONS OF RISK

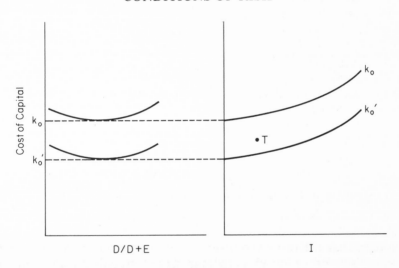

Figure 17.7

UNSOLVED PROBLEMS

1. Plot a risk-return map for the projects being considered by the Ruler Corporation (unsolved problem above).

2. Assume that the projects under consideration by Ruler are not mutually exclusive and that the firm does not wish to enter a new risk class. Which project(s) would be accepted?

3. Trace the acceptance process in terms of the average cost of capital for Ruler. Assume that $k_o \neq f(I)$. Let $k_o = 8\%$

SECTION 17.5   To complete our discussion of integrated concepts, we shall adapt a portfolio theory to the investment decision of the firm.[6] As we have indicated previously, the firm is able to reduce risk through diversification (assuming that all projects under consideration are not perfectly positively correlated, in which case all combinations would be equally risky). On the other hand, it is not possible to increase expected return through diversification (i.e., a portfolio composed of equal investment in a 7 percent project and a 9 percent project would have an expected return of 8 percent no matter what the risk might be.) Combining these two concepts, we may describe a method of asset selection.

PORTFOLIO SELECTION

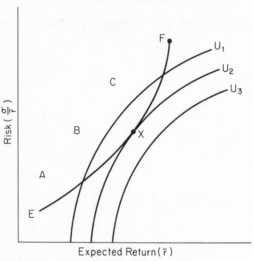

Figure 17.8

Suppose that the firm is confronted with numerous possible investment projects, each of which may be represented graphically in terms of its expected return and risk (a few such possibilities are shown as points A,B,C, and F in Fig. 17.8). Assume further that the correlation coefficient of each project with every other project is known. The firm then may simulate a very large number of possible portfolios (by varying the level of investment in projects and the combination of projects) and compute the expected return and risk of each. Every portfolio that offered the highest return for a given level of risk could be graphed. The curve formed by

---

[6]The mathematics of diversification, risk reduction, and the obtaining of an efficient portfolio are discussed by Harry Markowitz, "Portfolio Selection," *The Journal of Finance,* March, 1952, pp. 77-91. See also Markowitz, *Portfolio Selection* (New York: John Wiley and Sons, Inc. 1959); and Paul Samuelson, "General Proof that Diversification Pays," *Journal of Financial and Quantitative Analysis,* March, 1967, pp 1-13.

these points would be the firm's efficiency frontier (shown as *EF* on Fig. 17.8). This curve would depict the highest return that the firm could achieve at whatever level of risk it chose to adopt.

A few additional observations may be made about a firm's efficiency frontier. It is impossible for any point on the curve to indicate a higher expected return than that of the most lucrative individual project (because diversification cannot increase the expected return). Given the projects available to the firm, it is impossible to achieve a higher return at any specified level of risk than indicated by *EF* (i.e., to operate in the area to the right of *EF*). It is inefficient for the firm to invest in portfolios represented to the left of *EF* because an increase in return and/or reduction in risk could be effected by selecting one of the portfolios on the efficiency frontier. We have thus determined that the firm should invest in one of the combinations of projects represented as points along the curve *EF*.

The determination of which portfolio to select involves the consideration of whose risk-return preferences are controlling and how they are to be measured. This problem was considered in Chap. 5 and no better resolution can be offered here. At any rate, assuming that such a measurement can be made, a family of indifferences curves may be drawn.[7] ($U_1 U_2$, and U_3 in Fig. 17.8). It should follow that the point of tangency of the efficiency frontier with the highest indifference curve would represent the highest level of utility attainable and would be the optimal solution (point x on Fig. 17.8). It would then be necessary to return to the data used to construct *EF* in order to determine which combination of projects was depicted by point x.

The less risk averse (defined as demanding a smaller $\Delta \bar{r}$ for a given $\Delta \sigma / \bar{r}$) the decision maker is, the more vertical will be his indifference curves and the higher will be the risk and return of the portfolio at the point of tangency. At the point of complete risk neutrality the indifference curves would be vertical lines and the optimal portfolio would consist solely of the single most lucrative project. On the other hand, a high degree of risk-averseness would imply a smaller slope for the indifference curves and a portfolio of lower risk and return.

COMPREHENSIVE PROBLEMS

1. As the new financial manager of the Fly-by-Night Oil and Gas Exploration Company, it is your responsibility to decide among the many

---

[7]Indifference curves merely depict all points having the same utility. Thus, all points on U_1 provide identical utility to all other points on U_1. Similarly, all points on U_2 yield the same utility as all other points on U_2. Furthermore, all points on U_2 have a constant amount of greater utility than all points on U_1.

lucrative investment alternatives available to F-B-N. In the past, the firm has employed a rather unsophisticated approach to most of its managerial problems. Now, with an infusion of young managers, the entire philosphy of the firm has changed. The president of the company, to whom you report, has given you complete freedom of choice in determining the capital budget for the firm. The only constraint imposed is that projects selected be similar in nature to the projects previously accepted by the firm. Previous projects were usually quite risky, but the returns well justified the risk. Although F-B-N did not hesitate to assume risk, the firm considered itself a rational risk avoider. That is, great risks were accepted only if very great returns were anticipated.

In order to begin your capital budgeting program, you have decided to compute the cost of capital for F-B-N. For the past two years, the firm has been in a cash bind. The capital supply sources employed by F-B-N have been strained as a consequence. You have before you the most recent balance sheet capital structure of the firm (at book values). You have decided to compute the weighted average cost of capital of F-B-N from these data.

F-B-N OIL AND GAS
CAPITAL STRUCTURE
JAN. 1, 1969

Accounts Payable	$1,000,000
Notes Payable (8%)	600,000
Bonds (7s of 1979)	3,000,000
Common Stock	2,000,000
Retained Earnings	3,000,000
	$9,600,000

Accounts Payable: The firm purchases on account with terms 2/10, net 30. The firm does not take advantage of discounts.

Bonds: Were sold at par five years ago. Current price is $80. The issue has no sinking fund provisions.

Common Stock: Par value, $20 per share. Book value, $50. Current earnings are $6 per share and are growing at a rate of 10 percent annually. Anticipated earnings (long-run) are expected to be $12 per share. Market price of the stock is $60 per share.

(a.) Calculate the after-tax weighted average cost of capital for F-B-N. The firm's marginal tax bracket is 25 percent. Use market value weights.

(b.) What recommendations would you make regarding changing the firm's capital structure? Do you think F-B-N has an "optimum" structure?

2. Given your computations above, you are now considering investing in two projects. Both of these projects are equal in risk to each other and approximate the riskiness of previous projects accepted by the firm. Project A requires an initial cash outlay of $8,400, while project B requires a $6,000 outlay. Both projects would be depreciated on a straight-line basis with no expected salvage value. Each project is assumed to have a life of 6 years. Net cash benefits before depreciation and taxes have been projected as follows:

Year	A	B
X_1	$2,600	$1,600
X_2	2,600	1,600
X_3	2,600	1,600
X_4	2,000	1,600
X_5	2,000	1,600
X_6	2,000	1,600

(a.) Determine the payback, the average rate of return, the internal rate of return, and the net present value for each project.

(b.) Which project(s) would you select? Why?

3.   (a) What would be the impact on the firm's weighted average cost of capital if the Federal Reserve System reduced the money supply? Trace the separate impacts on each category of financing.

(b) What impact would a reduction in the money supply have on the firm's investment choice? What effect might an increase in the supply of money have on the decision?

(c) Assume that projects A and B are *less* risky than the previous projects accepted by the firm. Would this change in assumptions affect your decision? What would happen to the weighted average cost of capital if either A or B were accepted given this changed assumption?

18 DYNAMIC PROBLEMS
IN MULTI-PERIOD PLANNING

SECTION
18.1
Throughout the first unit of this book, we were fairly consistent in our assumption that funds were available to the firm at a known and constant cost. We began to relax these assumptions in Chap. 8, but even by Chap. 17 we continued to assume that funds were available, even if the cost could only be approximated and probably was increasing with the amount demanded. If, however, we assume that the curve depicting the availability of funds to the firm either becomes discontinuous at some point or else begins to move upward so abruptly that the cost of funds becomes prohibitive, the result is a funds constraint upon the firm. This condition necessitates the rationing of available funds and is often analyzed with linear programming techniques.[1] For purposes of explication, we will attempt a less rigorous approach.

The profitability index (PI), or discounted benefit-cost ratio, was briefly introduced in Chap. 5 and defined as:

$$\text{PI} = \frac{\text{Discounted Present Value of Cash Inflows}}{\text{Discounted Present Value of Cash Outflows}} \qquad (18.1)$$

It should follow that the PI $\times$ PV of Outflows = PV of Inflows and that (PI $-$ 1.0) $\times$ PV of Outflows = Net PV of Project.

SOLVED PROBLEM

The Hanke Company has no more than $500,000 to invest this year. Given the following possible projects, what selection is optimal subject to the constraint of a funds limitation?

---

[1] Cf. Weingartner, H. Martin, *Mathematical Programming and the Analysis of Capital Budgeting Problems* (Chicago: Markham Publishing Company, 1967); G. David Quirin, *The Capital Expenditure Decision* (Homewood, Ill.: Richard D. Irvin, Inc., 1967); and James C. T. Mao, *Quantitative Analysis of Financial Decisions* (Toronto: Collier-Macmillan Canada, Ltd., 1969).

Project	Outlay (all in t_o)	PI	NPV = (PI - 1) $\times$ Outlay
1	$300,000	1.50	$150,000
2	100,000	1.40	40,000
3	150,000	1.30	45,000
4	200,000	1.20	40,000
5	50,000	1.10	5,000
6	400,000	1.05	20,000

SOLUTION

1. It will be observed that, with a $500,000 budgetary limitation, some profitable projects (defined as PI>1.0) cannot be undertaken. Our answer, therefore, can only be optimal subject to this constraint.

2. The analyst must satisfy himself that a rationing situation exists because of discontinuities in the supply of funds function, and not because the cost of capital has merely been underestimated.

3. The normal approach to a rationing problem involves accepting projects in descending order of their profitability indices. The PI is the appropriate measure for operations under a funds constraint because it does indicate which projects give the "most bang for the buck."

4. The above example, however, also illustrates the consideration of full funds utilization. Under the criteria listed in number 3, we would select projects 1, 2, and 5, utilizing $450,000 and adding $195,000 to the present value of the firm. On the other hand, the selection of projects 1, 3, and 5 would utilize the entire $500,000 and add $200,000 to the present value of the firm.

Capital shortages may extend over several periods, further complicating the planning process. Because it may no longer be assumed that funds will always be available for profitable projects, a multi-period planning horizon becomes essential. In sum, the planner must be careful not to commit funds for this period that could be employed much more profitably next period.

SOLVED PROBLEM

The Muscat Company has a 50 percent tax rate and a 10 percent after-tax cost of capital. Capital expenditures are planned on a 2-year basis, for which Muscat has a total of $2,000,000 available now. The possible projects are listed below. None will generate any cash flow during the initial 2-year period. In each case, the total cash outlay will occur in the initial year of the life of the investment. Treasury bills are yielding 6 percent.

PROJECTS AVAILABLE IMMEDIATELY			PROJECTS AVAILABLE NEXT YEAR		
Project	Amount	PI	Project	Amount	PI
1	200,000	1.10	6	$400,000	1.30
2	1,000,000	0.90	7	500,000	1.20
3	600,000	1.20	8	600,000	1.10
4	500,000	1.15			
5	300,000	1.30			

SOLUTION

1. The first step involves putting the computations for projects not available until next year on a comparable basis with those available immediately. For example, project 6 involves an outlay next year of $400,000 and a PI of 1.30. It must follow that the present value of the inflows next year is $520,000. The present value this year, at a 10 percent cost of capital, would be ($520,000) $\times$ (.909) = $472,680. On the other hand, part of the cost could be avoided by investing in Treasury bills at a 3 percent after-tax return. The present value of the outlay is thus ($400,000) $\times$ (0.97) = $388,000 and the adjusted PI is ($472,680/$388,000) = 1.22.

2. Performing similar operations and ordering the result, we obtain the following:

Project	Amount	PI	NPV
5	$ 300,000	1.30	$ 90,000
6	388,000	1.22	84,000
3	600,000	1.20	120,000
4	500,000	1.15	75,000
7	485,000	1.12	60,000
1	200,000	1.10	20,000
8	582,000	1.03	18,000
2	1,000,000	0.90	(100,000)

Projects 5, 6, 3, 4, and 1, costing a total of $1,988,000, will add $389,000 to the net present value of the firm.

UNSOLVED PROBLEMS

1. The Cohen Company has a 50 percent tax rate and an 8 percent after-tax cost of capital. The firm has a 3-year capital expenditures plan, for which a

total of $5,000,000 has been budgeted and is now available. None of the projects will generate any cash during the 3-year period and all of them are assumed to have the entire cash outlay take place in the first year of their life. Treasury securities are available in 1-year maturities at 4 percent and in 2-year maturities at 6 percent. Which projects should be undertaken?

PROJECTS AVAILABLE THIS YEAR			PROJECTS AVAILABLE NEXT YEAR		
Project	Amount	PI	Project	Amount	PI
1	$ 300,000	1.40	6	$1,000,000	1.10
2	1,000,000	1.10	7	800,000	1.15
3	500,000	1.15	8	500,000	1.20
4	200,000	1.50	9	200,000	1.40
5	100,000	1.05	10	100,000	1.70

PROJECTS AVAILABLE YEAR AFTER NEXT		
Project	Amount	PI
11	$300,000	2.00
12	400,000	1.20
13	100,000	1.60
14	500,000	1.50
15	800,000	1.10

2. Rework unsolved problem number 1 (above) by switching Projects Available Year after Next with Projects Available this Year.

SECTION 18.2   Throughout this book, we have used the standard deviation of cash flows within a given period as the appropriate measure of dispersion. This measurement, first introduced in Chap. 2, may be redefined as:

$$\sigma_t = \sqrt{\sum_{x=1}^{n} (F_{xt} - \overline{F}_t)^2 \, P_{xt}} \qquad (18.2)$$

Where: σ_t = Standard deviation of cash flow in t^{th} period
$\overline{F}_t$ = Expected value of cash flow in t^{th} period
F_{xt} = X^{th} net cash flow in t^{th} period
P_{xt} = Probability of Xth net cash flow in t^{th} period.

If we wish to isolate the time value of money, then it is possible to express the expected value of a probability distribution of net present values for a proposal as follows:

$$EPV = \sum_{t=0}^{\infty} \frac{\overline{F}_t}{(1+r)^t} \tag{18.3}$$

Where: r = Pure (risk-free) rate of interest and the rest are as above.

Finally, if we are able to assume that the cash flows in various time periods are independent of each other, it is possible to compute the standard deviation for the entire probability distribution of net persent values:

$$\sigma_{\overline{x}} = \sqrt{\sum_{t=0}^{\infty} \frac{(\sigma_t)^2}{(1+r)^{2t}}} \tag{18.4}$$

SOLVED PROBLEMS

1. The March Company is analyzing a project which will cost $6,000. The expected inflows are given below. What are the *EPV* and σ if r = 4 percent?

YEAR 1		YEAR 2		YEAR 3	
Probability	*NCF*	*Probability*	*NCF*	*Probability*	*NCF*
.125	$2,000	.125	$2,000	.125	$2,000
.750	3,000	.750	3,000	.750	3,000
.125	4,000	.125	4,000	.125	4,000

SOLUTION

$$EPV = (\$3,000 \times 2.78) - \$6,000 = \$2,340$$

$$\sigma_1 = \sigma_2 = \sigma_3 = \sqrt{(-1000)^2 \times .125 + 0 + (1000)^2 \times .125}$$

$$= \sqrt{250,000}$$

$$= \$500$$

$$\sigma_{\bar{x}} = \sqrt{\frac{(500)^2}{(1.04)^2} + \frac{(500)^2}{(1.04)^4} + \frac{(500)^2}{(1.04)^6}}$$

$$= \sqrt{(231,250) + (213,750) + (197,500)}$$

$$= \sqrt{642,500}$$

$$\sigma_{\bar{x}} = \$802$$

2. What is the probability that the present value of this project will be negative?

SOLUTION

$$\frac{\mu}{\sigma_{\bar{x}}} = \frac{2340}{802} = 2.92$$

$$P(X < \mu - 2.92 \ \sigma_{\bar{x}}) = .0018$$

UNSOLVED PROBLEMS

1. The Purcell Company is considering a project which will cost $5,000. The expected cash flows, which are independent of each other, are given below. Determine the *EPV* and $\sigma_{\bar{x}}$ if $r = 6$ percent.

YEAR 1		YEAR 2		YEAR 3	
Probability	*NCF*	*Probability*	*NCF*	*Probability*	*NCF*
.1	−1000	.1	0		
.1	0	.2	+1000		
.2	+500	.4	+2000	.1	+1500
.3	+2000	.2	+3000	.8	+2000
.2	+4000	.1	+4000	.1	+2500
.1	+6000				

2. What is the probability that $EPV \leqslant 0$?

3. Recompute the answers to numbers 1 and 2 by switching the data for years 1 and 3.

SECTION 18.3   A major problem in financial analysis to which we have given little attention thus far is the interdependence of cash flows over time. Although it is simpler from a computational standpoint to assume that flows are independent, the fact remains that projects which begin poorly tend to get worse, and those which begin well often build momentum. Consider the following joint probability distribution:

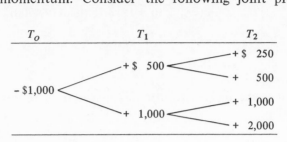

T_o	T_1	T_2
- $1,000	+ $ 500	+ $ 250
		+ 500
	+ 1,000	+ 1,000
		+ 2,000

If 10 percent is the appropriate rate of discount, a tabular present value display may be constructed.

PERIOD 0		PERIOD 1		PERIOD 2			TOTAL	
$P(O)$	$PV of F_o$	$P(1/0)$	$PV of F_1$	$P(2/1)$	$PV of F_2$	P_x	PV_x	EPV
				.5	207	.25	-$ 338	-$ 84.50
		.5	$455	.5	413	.25	- 132	- 33.00
1.00	-$1,000							
		.5	$909	.5	826	.25	+ 735	+ 183.75
				.5	1,652	.25	+ 1,561	+ 390.25
								+$456.50

The expected present value of this project is thus $456.50. The standard deviation may be determined from the following formula:

$$\sigma = \sqrt{\sum_{x=1}^{n} (PV_x - EPV)^2 \, P_x}$$

$$= \sqrt{(-794.50)^2(.25) + (-588.50)^2(.25) + (278.50)^2(.25) + (1104.50)^2(.25)}$$

$$= \sqrt{157,808 + 86,583 + 19,391 + 304,980}$$

$$= \sqrt{568,762}$$

$$\sigma \simeq \$754$$

Thus,

$$\frac{\mu}{\sigma} = \frac{\$456.50}{\$754} = .605$$

Therefore,

$$P(X \leqslant \mu - .605\sigma) = 27\%$$

The project has an expected net present value of $456.50 with a standard deviation of $754. There is a probability of .27 that the project will have a negative net present value.

Suppose, however, that the project has an abandonment value of $500 at the end of period 1.[2] The tree diagram indicates that the success or failure of the project should be apparent by the end of period 1 and the abandonment value would be very attractive if the less successful earnings projections were being realized. Let us, then, adopt the decision rule that the project will be abandoned if the $500 earnings are realized in period 1. The tableau would now appear as follows:

PERIOD 0		PERIOD 1		PERIOD 2		TOTAL		
$P(0)$	$PV\,of\,F_0$	$P(1/0)$	$PV\,of\,F_1$	$P(2/1)$	$PV\,of\,F_2$	P_x	PV_x	EPV
		.5	455 +455*		(abandoned)	.5	-$ 90	-$ 45
1.0	-1000		910	1.0	0			
		.5	$909	.5	$ 826	.25	+ 735	+ 183.75
				.5	1,652	.25	+ 1,561	+ 390.25
								$529.00

*Abandonment value.

$$\sigma = \sqrt{(-619)^2(.5) + (206)^2(.25) + (1032)^2(.25)}$$
$$= \sqrt{191,580 + 10,609 + 266,256} = \sqrt{468,445} \simeq \$684$$

Thus,

$$\frac{\mu}{\sigma} = \frac{\$529}{\$684} = .773$$

and

$$P(X \leqslant \mu - .773\sigma) = 22\%$$

As we suggested many chapters ago, a project should be abandoned whenever the net present value of doing so is greater than the net present value of continuing operations. As shown above, abandonment may also enter the planning process. The existence of an abandonment value increased the expected present worth and reduced the risk of the project illustrated. The possibility of abandonment does present the firm with a means to limit its risk exposure.

[2] Cf. Alexander Robichek and James Van Horne, "Abandonment Value and Capital Budgeting," *Journal of Finance,* December, 1967, pp. 577-89. Also see Edward Dyl and Hugh W. Long, "Abandonment Value and Capital Budgeting: Comment," *Journal of Finance,* March, 1969.

UNSOLVED PROBLEMS

1. The Mendey Company, which has a 12 percent after-tax cost of capital, is analyzing a project for which expected cash flows are given below. The project itself would have a cost of $10,000. Determine EPV and σ.

T_1		T_2		T_3	
P (1)	F_1	P (2/1)	F_2	P (3/2)	F_2
		.5	+ 2,000	.4	+ 1,000
				.6	+ 2,000
.4	+$3,000				
		.5	+ 3,000	.6	+ 3,000
				.4	+ 4,000
		.4	+ 3,000	.2	+ 1,000
				.8	+ 3,000
.6	+$5,000				
		.6	+ 7,000	.2	+ 7,000
				.8	+20,000

2. If the project could be abandoned at the end of T_2 for $3,000, (a) what decision rule would you adopt and (b) how would this rule affect EPV and σ?

3. Rework unsolved problems 1 and 2 by assuming P(1) of $3,000 = 0.7 and P(1) of $5,000 = 0.3.

SECTION 18.4

In many cases, it is possible for a company to grow and acquire assets over time by the acquisition of other firms.[3] The attractiveness of such an acquisition is a function of the assets (both tangible and intangible) to be acquired and the form and amount of payment to be made. The merger decision thus combines the investment and financing decisions in a multi-period plan.[4]

Mergers may occur for any number of reasons. Perhaps the oldest and strongest motivation is the simple desire to increase power over the

---

[3]Cf. William W. Alberts, and Joel E. Segall, eds., *The Corporate Merger* (Chicago: University of Chicago Press, 1966).

[4]Technically speaking, a combination of two or more companies in which one is the survivor is called a merger; if a totally new company absorbs the old companies, a consolidation has been effected. A combination of firms involved in different stages of the production of the same product is a vertical merger; and the combination of firms in totally unrelated lines of business is called a conglomerate merger. A combination of companies in the same business is called a horizontal merger.

market. In the latter part of the last century, this market power was used by the early monopolists (of whom John D. Rockefeller is perhaps the best example) to destroy competitors and then raise prices to whatever level the market would bear. In more recent times, public opinion and the anti-trust laws have required that greater subtlety be employed. The increased market power resulting from a merger may raise profits through "operating economies," such as bulk purchases, reciprocal purchases, advertising discounts, better channels of distribution (everything from more freight cars when needed to more shelf space), and better access to and bargaining position for external funds.[5] Merger also allows a firm to acquire large numbers of talented management and research personnel and at the same time to gain increased market power to sell whatever they produce. Galbraith goes so far as to suggest that modern corporations are willing to undertake risky research ventures because their control of the market will enable them to sell whatever results from the project.[6]

In other cases, merger may occur because the acquired company is a bargain; poor management, inadequate capital, stock market disfavor, a poor year, or other factors may reduce the price of the stock to the point that the firm is worth a great deal more than the cost of acquiring it. The acquired firm may have vast sums in the form of liquid assets, such that the acquiring firm could raise more money by merging with it than by selling securities on the market. It is further possible that the acquired firm would have tax-loss-carry-forwards which could be used to reduce future tax liabilities of the merged company.

There are two remaining arguments for merger which must be examined rather closely. The first is diversification. If a firm is able to acquire other firms whose earnings do not correlate very closely with its own (coefficient of correlation less than +1, and the closer to -1 the better), the probability distribution for earnings of the new firm should show less dispersion (be less risky) than for the old firm. If $1 of earnings for the merged firm is less risky, it should be discounted at a lower rate. This would result in an increase in the price of the stock and shareholder well-being. The merger would thus serve a valid economic function.[7] It should be pointed out, however, that such diversification could also be achieved by shareholders in their own portfolios.

Much is written about the growth resulting from mergers. To the extent that the merged firms are able to interact and combine their talents to do things that neither could do before (the synergism or "2+2=5" effect), a

---

[5]The eventual goal of many large firms is complete autonomy from the requirements of the capital markets.

[6] J.K.Galbraith, *The New Industrial State* (Boston: Houghton Mifflin Company, 1967).

[7]This analysis is merely an extension of the examination of correlation of flows undertaken in Chap. 17.

valid justification for the merger and, perhaps, an increase in stock price may exist. On the other hand, the merger of firms in totally different lines of business with no subsequent interaction can create value through diversification but not through real growth, although growth may appear to occur. Consider the following problem:

SOLVED PROBLEM

The Great Lakes and Eastern Company (G+E) has 1,000,000 shares outstanding and earns $2 per share. Because of G+E's risk and growth possibilities, its stock sells for $40 per share. The Moribund Cement Company has 500,000 shares outstanding and earns $1 per share; because of its risk and lack of growth possibilities, the market is only willing to pay $10 per share for its stock. G+E plans to merge with Moribund as a strictly financial transaction, with no integration of the business. The merger will be effected by offering G+E stock for Moribund stock in the ratio of their market prices.

1. What is the ratio of exchange of G+E shares for Moribund shares? How many G+E shares will be outstanding after the merger?

2. What will be the new G+E earnings per share? What apparent growth has taken place?

3. Ignoring possible diversification effects, what should the price and P/E ratio for new G+E stock be if the market were rational?

4. What would be the price of G+E stock if the market retained the P/E ratio of 20? What would happen to new G+E if it merged with another company identical to Moribund?

SOLUTION

1. .25 G + E for 1 Moribund
   1,125,000 shares

2. $2.00 × 1,000,000 shares = $2,000,000
   $1.00 ×   500,000 shares =   500,000

   $2,500,000 ÷ 1,125,000 shares
   = $2.22/share

$$\frac{\$2.22 - 2.00}{\$2.00} = 11\% \text{ "growth"}$$

3. $40 × 1,000,000 shares = 40,000,000
   $10 ×   500,000 shares = 5,000,000

$$45,000,000 ÷ 1,125,000 \text{ shares } = \$40/\text{share}$$

$$\frac{\$40}{\$2.22} \simeq 18 \text{ times}$$

If the market were rational and both G+E and Moribund were appropriately valued there is no reason that G+E's price should change. Its *P/E* ratio would decline because of the increased risk and lack of growth associated with the Moribund portion of the new company.

4. ($2.22)(20) = $44.40 new price

A new Moribund would receive an exchange ratio of $(10) ÷ (44.40) = .225$ shares of G+E per share. This would increase the number of G+E shares outstanding by $(500,000)(.225) = 112,500$ to 1,237,500 shares. Earnings per share would be:

Old G + E	2,000,000
Moribund	500,000
Identical Moribund	500,000

$$3,000,000 ÷ 1,237,500 = \$2.42$$

$$\text{"Growth"} = \frac{\$2.42 - 2.22}{2.22} = 9\%$$

Retaining the 20 multiple the price of G+E would go to $48.40. The only reason the growth rate declined was that Identical Moribund was smaller relative to new G+E than was Moribund relative to old G+E.

	Year 0	*Year 1*	*Year 2*
Identical Moribund – Net Income	$ 500,000	$ 500,000	$ 500,000
Moribund – Net Income	500,000	500,000	500,000
Old G + E – Net Income	2,000,000	2,000,000	2,000,000
Merged G + E – Net Income	$2,000,000	$2,500,000	$3,000,000
Merged G + E – E.P.S.	$ 2.00	$ 2.22	$ 2.42
Merged G + E – Market Price	$40.00	$44.40	$48.40
"Growth" Rate		11%	9%

We see in this example how it is possible to combine companies without growth in order to acquire a "growth" company. As indicated in the discussion of Identical Moribund, a company must find ever-larger merger partners if the apparent growth rate is not to decline. In addition the market must be willing to assign a constant P/E ratio to earnings of ever-declining quality. On the other hand, if companies can be bought with convertible securities, warrants, or other kinds of "funny money," the apparent growth rate can be made even more spectacular. The student of finance should find encouragement in the above discussion; there is still a sucker born every minute.

A merger may be effected either by the purchase of a firm's assets or its stock. A purchase of assets generally requires only the approval of the board of directors of the purchasing company; in both cases, some form of approval by the stockholders of the selling company is required. A purchase of stock also generally involves the acquisition of the liabilities and assets of the firm. If the purchase is made in the form of cash or debt securities, any gain is taxable immediately either to the firm or to the shareholders (if distributed under a plan as a dividend in total or partial liquidation); the acquiring company, however, is often able to write up the assets for additional depreciation if a cash purchase is made. A purchase for stock will usually defer taxation to the holder until the stock is disposed of, but the purchasing company will only acquire the assets at their book value. In any case, the purchase may result from negotiations with the company or a direct tender offer to the stockholders for their shares. Dissenting stockholders may go to court to have a fair market value of their shares determined and demand payment in cash.

The determination of merger terms is, at best, a rather inexact art. The success of the proposal is generally dependent upon not only the value of the offer but also its form. The first parameter is generally market value. The stockholder of the acquired company will certainly not accept securities with a market value less than those he is surrendering; as a rule, the offer must have a greater market value in order to overcome his inertia. There may also be an income constraint, in that the shareholder does not wish to suffer a decline in his dividend income. Earnings per share and even book value may also be considerations, and certainly tax treatment is important. The acquiring company, on the other hand, generally wishes to minimize cash outlays and equity dilution.

There are several ways to resolve these conflicts. As we indicated in the solved problem above, the acquiring company in a merger generally sells at a higher P/E ratio than the acquired company; as long as this ratio is maintained, it is possible to offer stock worth more than the market price of the acquired company and still raise the earnings per share (and thus the price) of the stock of the acquiring company.[8] The shares of acquired

---

[8]In addition, no flotation costs are incurred for stock issued in this manner.

companies often have rather poor markets so that a cash offer is attractive even though it has unfavorable tax consequences. The interest deduction for taxes and the fact that no equity is surrendered may make debt so attractive to the acquiring company that it would be willing to offer a sufficiently large premium over market to overcome the tax disadvantages to the shareholders of the acquired company. Convertible debt would have the advantage of a lower coupon and the disadvantage of equity dilution.

Consider the unique properties of convertible preferred stock in mergers. If properly constructed, the exchange would be tax-free. In addition many acquired companies pay larger dividends than the acquiring company, so that a simple exchange of stock would reduce the income of the acquired company shareholders and cause them to disapprove the merger. The preferred, however, could be constructed with a yield to maintain their level of income (keeping them happy) and yet allow the company to pay a low (or no) dividend on its common stock (thus conserving cash). Finally, the conversion premium could be set so that the company would not issue as many new shares of common as it would on a simple exchange of stock.

SOLVED PROBLEMS

1. Assume that G+E (see solved problem number 1 above) has a book value of $20 per share and a 25 percent payout and that Moribund has a book value of $10 per share and a 75 percent payout. Evaluate the position of a Moribund shareholder before and immediately after the merger (ignore any price changes).

SOLUTION

	BEFORE	AFTER
	1 share Moribund	*.25 shares G + E*
Market Value	$10.00	$10.00
Earnings	1.00	0.56
Dividends	0.75	0.14
Book Value	10.00	5.66

This analysis merely confirms our earlier conclusions. As indicated, there is reason to doubt that the market value can be maintained.

2. Assume that the Moribund shareholders have become somewhat less excited about the G+E offer. G+E then offers to pay a 25 percent premium

over market for Moribund shares in the form of a $100 par, 6 percent convertible preferred (with a 20 percent conversion premium). Evaluate the new proposal.

SOLUTION

Notice first of all that the market premium and the conversion premium offset. The Moribund shareholder is still offered 1 share of G+E for each 4 Moribund, only now at $12.50 vs. $50 instead of $10 vs. $40. Upon conversion, therefore, the Moribund shareholder will get no more of G+E than was indicated in problem number 1 above. Until conversion, he will receive a $6 dividend for each 8 shares held, or the same $0.75 dividend per Moribund share he is currently receiving. Assuming, however, that the market is willing to pay $100 a share for the preferred, the Moribund shareholder has received a premium, in that he can always sell the stock to some unsuspecting person.

From the standpoint of the acquiring firm, the merger decision is essentially a rather complicated capital budgeting decision. If the company to be acquired will not alter the risk of the total firm, the matter is greatly simplified. Even the problem of which securities to offer can be approached with the knowledge that additional securities can be sold to return the firm to its optimal capital structure. If, on the other hand, the acquisition will result in an alteration of the risk class of the firm, then the cost of capital and optimal capital structure may well change. In such a case, the total effect of the merger must be analyzed before its desirability may be determined. At the least, any merger which requires the firm to raise new funds in the market may well invoke the up-sloping supply of funds function $[k_o = f(I)]$ as well as any unsettling effects caused by alterations of the capital structure $[k_o = f(D/D + E)]$.

SOLVED PROBLEM

The Jumbo Company has a 10 percent after-tax cost of capital. Acquisition of the Major Company would result in the following average cash flows. What is the maximum price that Jumbo should pay for Major?

	YEARS			
	1-4	*5-8*	*9-12*	*13-16*
Net Flow from Major	$1,000,000	$2,000,000	$3,000,000	$1,000,000
Additional Investment Required	500,000	1,000,000	1,000,000	–
Net	$ 500,000	$1,000,000	$2,000,000	$1,000,000

SOLUTION

Years	*Net Cash Flows*	*Present Value Factor @ 10%*	*Present Value*
1-4	$ 500,000	3.17	$1,585,000
5-8	1,000,000	2.16	2,160,000
9-12	2,000,000	1.48	2,960,000
13-16	1,000,000	1.01	1,010,000
			$7,715,000

UNSOLVED PROBLEMS

1. Rework solved problem number 1 under the assumption that G+E has earnings of $3 per share and a *P/E* of 15 and that Moribund has a *P/E* of 8.

2. The Punch Company has a 12 percent after-tax cost of capital. Acquisition of the Judy Company would result in the following average cash flows. What is the maximum price that Punch should pay for Judy?

	YEARS ($ MILLION)			
	1-3	*4-6*	*7-9*	*10-12*
Net Flow from Judy	$10	$12	$15	$10
Additional Investment Required	$ 2	$ 4	$ 6	$ 0

COMPREHENSIVE PROBLEM

The Axle Conglomerate has 10 million shares outstanding, earns $5 per share, and sells at a 16 *P/E* ratio. The Small Steel Company has 2 million shares outstanding, earnings per share of $2, and a *P/E* ratio of 10. Axle common has a 3 percent yield, while Small yields 6 percent; both firms have a 50 percent tax rate. It is felt that Small holders would require a 30 percent premium over the current market price of their stock to induce them to sell their shares.

1. The merger could be effected with common stock.

   (a) What is the ratio of exchange?

   (b) How many shares would be outstanding?

   (c) What would be the new earnings per share?

   (d) If the P/E remained constant, what would be the new price of the stock?

2. The merger might be effected with $100 par, 7 percent convertible preferred with a 20 percent conversion premium.

   (a) What is the ratio of exchange in terms of Axle preferred? In terms of Axle common?

   (b) What would be the earnings per share before conversion? After conversion?

   (c) What happens to the dividend income of the holder of one share of Small as he obtains first Axle preferred and then Axle common?

   (d) Axle preferred is callable at 105 and allowance for a 15 percent decline in price of the common must be made on any call. If Axle net income after taxes grows at a compound rate of 10 percent and the P/E remains constant at 16, when will the preferred be called? If the after-tax cost of funds to Axle is 12 percent, what is the cost of Small Steel under the assumptions in this section?

3. The merger could also be effected by means of $1,000 par, 7 percent convertible debenture with a 20 percent conversion premium.

   (a) If Small shareholders have a 50 percent marginal tax bracket and an average tax basis of $10 per share, what exchange ratio must be offered to be as attractive as the premium for the common or preferred stock plans (if the stockholders do not plan to sell the stock)?

   (b) What would be the earnings per share before and after conversion?

   (c) Under the assumptions of 2(d), when will the debenture issue be converted? What is the cost of Small Steel under this means of financing?

COMPREHENSIVE REVIEW CASE

1. Below you will find the following financial information about the Amalgamated Iron and Steel Company: Balance Sheets for 1968-69, Income Statement for 1969, and Financial ratios for the firm for 1967-68 and for the

BALANCE SHEET, DECEMBER 31, 1968, 1969

ASSETS

	1968	1969
Cash	$ 500,000	$ 200,000
Accounts Receivable	2,500,000	3,200,000
Inventory	2,700,000	4,000,000
Fixed Assets, Net	8,300,000	10,600,000
Goodwill	1,000,000	1,000,000
Total Assets	$15,000,000	$19,000,000

LIABILITIES

	1968	1969
Notes Payable	$ 2,000,000	$ 2,600,000
Accounts Payable	1,000,000	3,200,000
Accrued Wages and Taxes	1,000,000	1,000,000
Long-Term Debt*	5,000,000	6,000,000
Preferred Stock	2,000,000	2,000,000
Common Stock (100,000 shares)	1,000,000	1,000,000
Retained Earnings	3,000,000	3,200,000
Total Liabilities & Equity	$15,000,000	$19,000,000

*Long-term debt: $1 million 8% of 1988 (issued in 1969)
 $2 million 6% of 1986 (issued in 1966)
 $3 million 3% of 1973 (issued in 1953)

STATEMENT OF INCOME AND RETAINED EARNINGS
YEAR ENDED DECEMBER 31, 1969

Net Sales:		
Credit		$ 8,000,000
Cash		2,000,000
Total		$10,000,000
Costs and Expenses:		
Cost of Goods Sold	$6,000,000	
Selling, General & Admin. Expense	1,000,000	
Depreciation	710,000	
Interest on Long-term Debt	290,000	
		8,000,000
Net Income Before Taxes		2,000,000
Taxes on Income		1,000,000
Net Income After Taxes		1,000,000
Less: Dividends on Preferred Stock		120,000
Net Income Available to Common		880,000
Add: Retained Earnings at 1/1/68		3,000,000
Less: Dividends Paid on Common		680,000*
Retained Earnings at 12/31/69		$ 3,200,000

*Dividends of $6.80 were paid in 1969, up from $5.60 in 1968 and 1967.

Financial Ratios	1967	1968	Industry 1969
a. Current Ratio	1.60x	1.43x	1.75x
b. Acid Test Ratio	.86x	.75x	1.00x
c. Receivables Turnover	3.10x	3.00x	4.00x
d. Inventory Turnover	2.06x	2.00x	2.50x
e. Total Debt to Total Liability & Equity	.56	.60	.50
f. Gross Profit Margin	40%	40%	40%
g. Net Profit Margin	14%	14%	15%
h. Rate of Return on Equity	25%	26%	24%
i. After-Tax Rate of Return on Tangible (net operating) Assets (EAT + I/Tangible Assets)	9.2%	9.0%	10.5%
j. Tangible Asset Turnover	66.0%	64.0%	70.0%
k. Interest Earned (Long-Term Debt)	10.2x	10.0x	11.0x
l. Price Earnings Ratio (1968 average daily price of $100 per share)	12.5	12.5	13.5

industry for 1969. You are asked to evaluate the position of the company. Be certain to cite specific ratio levels and trends as evidence. As president of Amalgamated, what particular areas would receive your greatest attention and what policies would you change or implement? (Note: Computation of 1970 financial ratios for Amalgamated would appear to be an excellent initial step in your evaluation.)

2. Given the data above, what would be your decision in each of the following situations? Be specific in your reasoning.

(a) You are the credit manager of the Bituminous Coal Company, a major supplier to the steel industry. One of the salesmen in your firm has indicated that Amalgamated wishes to buy $500,000 worth of materials on terms 2/30, net 90 as of January 1, 1970. Would you grant these terms? (Your usual policy is terms net 30. Nevertheless, the purchasing agent at Amalgamated has stated that your competition will get the order if you cannot meet their payment request.)

(b) You are the investment manager of a large insurance company. Amalgamated has approached you with a proposal for a privately placed note for $1,000,000 at an effective rate of 7 percent. Should you make the loan?

(c) The stock of Amalgamated is selling at $90 per share. The company offers you, a wealthy tycoon, the opportunity to buy 50,000 additional shares of $88. Will you buy? (Does the firm's present capital structure influence your decision? If so, why?)

3. The Bach Brake Company (see Comprehensive Case, Chap. 8) wishes to merge with Amalgamated by an exchange of stock. It is felt that a 20 percent premium over market would be required by Amalgamated shareholders. The

Amalgamated debt and preferred stock would be assumed by the new company.

(a) If the merger were effected with common stock (Bach selling at $12 a share) what would be the ratio of exchange, the reformulated financial statements for 1968 and 1969 (the income statement in 1969 only), and the new ratios for the combined company?

(b) If the merger were effected with $100 par, 6 percent preferred convertible at 15 percent above the market and callable at 106, what would be the new earnings per share for 1969 before and after conversion for the combined company? If the price of Bach common were to rise at a 9 percent compounded rate and a 20 percent price decline were to be allowed for, when could the preferred be called? If Bach has a 10 percent after-tax cost of capital, what is the effective cost of purchasing Amalgamated in this way?

APPENDICES

APPENDIX A: COMPOUND SUM OF $1

Year	1%	2%	3%	4%	5%	6%	7%	8%	9%	10%	12%	14%	15%	16%
1	1.010	1.020	1.030	1.040	1.050	1.060	1.070	1.080	1.090	1.100	1.120	1.140	1.150	1.160
2	1.020	1.040	1.061	1.082	1.102	1.124	1.145	1.166	1.188	1.210	1.254	1.300	1.322	1.346
3	1.030	1.061	1.093	1.125	1.158	1.191	1.225	1.260	1.295	1.331	1.405	1.482	1.521	1.561
4	1.041	1.082	1.126	1.170	1.216	1.262	1.311	1.360	1.412	1.464	1.574	1.689	1.749	1.811
5	1.051	1.104	1.159	1.217	1.276	1.338	1.403	1.469	1.539	1.611	1.762	1.925	2.011	2.100
6	1.062	1.126	1.194	1.265	1.340	1.419	1.501	1.587	1.677	1.772	1.974	2.195	2.313	2.436
7	1.072	1.149	1.230	1.316	1.407	1.504	1.606	1.714	1.828	1.949	2.211	2.502	2.660	2.826
8	1.088	1.172	1.267	1.369	1.477	1.594	1.718	1.851	1.993	2.144	2.476	2.853	3.059	3.278
9	1.094	1.195	1.305	1.423	1.551	1.689	1.838	1.999	2.172	2.358	2.773	3.252	3.518	3.803
10	1.105	1.219	1.344	1.480	1.629	1.791	1.967	2.159	2.367	2.594	3.106	3.707	4.046	4.411
11	1.116	1.243	1.384	1.539	1.710	1.898	2.105	2.332	2.580	2.853	3.479	4.226	4.652	5.117
12	1.127	1.268	1.426	1.601	1.796	2.012	2.252	2.518	2.813	3.138	3.896	4.818	5.350	5.936
13	1.138	1.294	1.469	1.665	1.886	2.133	2.410	2.720	3.066	3.452	4.363	5.492	6.153	6.886
14	1.149	1.319	1.513	1.732	1.980	2.261	2.579	2.937	3.342	3.797	4.887	6.261	7.076	7.988
15	1.161	1.346	1.558	1.801	2.079	2.397	2.759	3.172	3.642	4.177	5.474	7.138	8.137	9.266
16	1.173	1.373	1.605	1.873	2.183	2.540	2.952	3.426	3.970	4.595	6.130	8.137	9.358	10.748
17	1.184	1.400	1.653	1.948	2.292	2.693	3.159	3.700	4.328	5.054	6.866	9.276	10.761	12.468
18	1.196	1.428	1.702	2.026	2.407	2.854	3.380	3.996	4.717	5.560	7.690	10.575	12.375	14.463
19	1.208	1.457	1.754	2.107	2.527	3.026	3.617	4.316	5.142	6.116	8.613	12.056	14.232	16.777
20	1.220	1.486	1.806	2.191	2.653	3.207	3.870	4.661	5.604	6.728	9.646	13.743	16.367	19.461
25	1.282	1.641	2.094	2.666	3.386	4.292	5.427	6.848	8.623	10.835	17.000	26.462	32.919	40.874
30	1.348	1.811	2.427	3.243	4.322	5.743	7.612	10.063	13.268	17.449	29.960	50.950	66.212	85.850

Appendices A-D are from MANAGERIAL FINANCE, Third Edition, by J. Fred Weston and Eugene F. Brigham. Copyright © 1962, 1966, 1969 by Holt, Rinehart and Winston, Inc. Reprinted by permission of Holt, Rinehart and Winston, Inc.

Year	18%	20%	24%	28%	32%	36%
1	1.180	1.200	1.240	1.280	1.320	1.360
2	1.392	1.440	1.538	1.638	1.742	1.850
3	1.643	1.728	1.907	2.067	2.300	2.515
4	1.939	2.074	2.364	2.684	3.036	3.421
5	2.288	2.488	2.932	3.436	4.007	4.653
6	2.700	2.986	3.635	4.398	5.290	6.328
7	3.185	3.583	4.508	5.629	6.983	8.605
8	3.759	4.300	5.590	7.206	9.217	11.703
9	4.435	5.160	6.931	9.223	12.166	15.917
10	5.234	6.192	8.594	11.806	16.060	21.647
11	6.176	7.430	10.657	15.112	21.199	29.439
12	7.288	8.916	13.215	19.343	27.983	40.037
13	8.599	10.699	16.386	24.759	36.937	54.451
14	10.147	12.839	20.319	31.691	48.757	74.053
15	11.974	15.407	25.196	40.565	64.359	100.712
16	14.129	18.488	31.243	51.923	84.954	136.970
17	16.672	22.186	38.741	66.461	112.140	186.280
18	19.673	26.623	48.039	85.071	148.020	253.340
19	23.214	31.948	59.568	108.890	195.390	344.540
20	27.393	38.338	73.864	139.380	257.920	468.570
25	62.669	95.396	216.542	478.900	1033.600	2180.100
30	143.371	237.376	634.820	1645.500	4142.100	10143.000

Year	40%	50%	60%	70%	80%	90%
1	1.400	1.500	1.600	1.700	1.800	1.900
2	1.960	2.250	2.560	2.890	3.240	3.610
3	2.744	3.375	4.096	4.913	5.832	6.859
4	3.842	5.062	6.544	8.352	10.498	13.032
5	5.378	7.594	10.486	14.199	18.896	24.761
6	7.530	11.391	16.777	24.138	34.012	47.046
7	10.541	17.086	26.844	41.034	61.222	89.387
8	14.758	25.629	42.950	69.758	110.200	169.836
9	20.661	38.443	68.720	118.588	198.359	322.688
10	28.925	57.665	109.951	201.599	357.047	613.107
11	40.496	86.498	175.922	342.719	642.684	1164.902
12	56.694	129.746	281.475	582.622	1158.831	2213.314
13	79.372	194.619	450.360	990.457	2082.295	4205.297
14	111.120	291.929	720.576	1683.777	3748.131	7990.065
15	155.568	437.894	1152.921	2862.421	6746.636	15181.122
16	217.795	656.840	1844.700	4866.100	12144.000	28844.000
17	304.914	985.260	2951.500	8272.400	21859.000	54804.000
18	426.879	1477.900	4722.400	14063.000	39346.000	104130.000
19	597.630	2216.800	7555.800	23907.000	70824.000	197840.000
20	836.683	3325.300	12089.000	40642.000	127480.000	375900.000
25	4499.880	25251.000	126780.000	577060.000	2408900.000	9307600.000
30	24201.432	191750.000	1329200.000	8193500.000	45517000.000	230470000.000

APPENDIX B: SUM OF AN ANNUITY OF $1 FOR n YEARS

Year	1%	2%	3%	4%	5%	6%
1	1.010	1.020	1.030	1.040	1.050	1.060
2	2.030	2.060	2.091	2.122	2.152	2.184
3	3.060	3.122	3.184	3.246	3.310	3.375
4	4.101	4.204	4.309	4.416	4.526	4.637
5	5.152	5.308	5.468	5.633	5.802	5.975
6	6.214	6.434	6.662	6.898	7.142	7.394
7	7.286	7.583	7.892	8.214	8.549	8.897
8	8.369	8.755	9.159	9.583	10.027	10.491
9	9.462	9.950	10.464	11.006	11.578	12.181
10	10.567	11.169	11.808	12.486	13.207	13.972
11	11.683	12.412	13.192	14.026	14.917	15.870
12	12.809	13.680	14.618	15.627	16.713	17.882
13	13.947	14.974	16.086	17.292	17.599	20.051
14	15.097	16.293	17.599	19.024	20.579	22.276
15	16.258	17.639	19.157	20.825	22.657	24.673
16	17.430	19.012	20.762	22.698	24.840	27.213
17	18.615	20.412	22.414	24.645	27.132	29.906
18	19.811	21.841	24.117	26.671	29.539	32.760
19	21.019	23.297	25.870	28.778	32.066	35.786
20	22.239	24.783	27.676	30.969	34.719	38.993
25	28.525	32.670	37.553	43.312	50.113	58.157
30	35.133	41.379	49.002	58.328	69.761	83.801

Year	7%	8%	9%	10%	12%	14%
1	1.070	1.080	1.090	1.100	1.120	1.140
2	2.215	2.246	2.278	2.310	2.374	2.440
3	3.440	3.506	3.573	3.641	3.770	3.921
4	4.751	4.867	4.985	5.105	5.353	5.610
5	6.153	6.336	6.523	6.716	7.115	7.536
6	7.654	7.923	8.200	8.487	9.089	9.730
7	9.260	9.637	10.028	10.436	11.300	12.233
8	10.978	11.488	12.021	12.579	13.776	15.085
9	12.816	13.487	14.193	14.937	16.549	18.337
10	14.784	15.645	16.560	17.531	19.655	22.044
11	16.888	17.977	19.141	20.384	23.133	26.271
12	19.141	20.495	21.953	23.523	27.029	31.089
13	21.550	23.215	25.019	26.975	31.393	36.581
14	24.129	26.152	28.361	30.772	36.280	42.842
15	26.888	29.324	32.003	34.950	41.753	49.980
16	29.840	32.750	35.974	39.545	47.884	58.118
17	32.999	36.450	40.301	44.599	54.750	67.394
18	36.379	40.446	45.018	50.159	62.440	77.969
19	39.995	44.762	50.160	56.275	71.052	90.025
20	43.865	49.423	55.764	63.003	80.698	103.769
25	67.676	78.954	92.324	108.182	149.334	207.332
30	101.073	122.346	148.576	180.943	270.293	406.737

Year	16%	18%	20%	24%	28%	32%
1	1.160	1.180	1.200	1.240	1.280	1.320
2	2.506	2.572	2.640	2.778	2.918	3.062
3	4.066	4.215	4.368	4.684	5.016	5.362
4	5.877	6.154	6.442	7.048	7.700	8.398
5	7.977	8.442	8.930	9.980	11.136	12.406
6	10.414	11.142	11.916	13.615	15.534	17.696
7	13.240	14.327	15.499	18.123	21.163	24.678
8	16.518	18.086	19.799	23.712	28.369	33.895
9	20.321	22.521	24.959	30.643	37.592	46.062
10	24.733	27.755	31.150	39.238	49.399	62.122
11	29.850	33.931	38.580	49.985	64.510	83.320
12	35.786	41.219	47.497	63.110	83.853	111.303
13	42.672	49.818	58.196	79.496	108.612	148.240
14	50.660	59.965	71.035	99.815	140.303	196.997
15	59.925	71.939	86.442	125.011	180.870	261.360
16	70.673	86.068	104.931	156.253	232.790	346.310
17	83.141	102.740	127.117	194.994	299.250	458.450
18	97.603	122.414	153.740	243.033	384.320	606.470
19	114.380	145.628	185.688	302.601	493.210	801.860
20	133.841	173.021	224.026	376.465	632.589	1059.780
25	289.088	404.272	566.377	1113.634	2184.704	4259.376
30	615.162	933.319	1418.259	3274.736	7517.696	17082.120

Year	36%	40%	50%	60%	70%	80%
1	1.360	1.400	1.500	1.600	1.700	1.800
2	3.210	3.360	3.750	4.160	4.590	5.040
3	5.725	6.104	7.125	8.256	9.503	10.872
4	9.146	9.846	12.188	14.810	17.855	21.370
5	13.799	15.324	19.781	25.295	32.054	40.265
6	20.126	22.853	31.172	42.073	56.191	74.278
7	28.732	33.395	48.258	68.916	97.225	135.500
8	40.435	48.153	73.887	111.866	166.983	245.699
9	56.352	68.814	112.330	180.585	285.570	444.058
10	77.998	97.739	169.995	290.536	487.170	801.105
11	107.437	138.235	256.493	466.458	829.888	1443.788
12	147.475	194.929	386.239	747.933	1412.510	2600.619
13	201.926	274.300	580.859	1198.293	2402.968	4682.914
14	275.979	385.420	872.788	1918.869	4086.745	8431.045
15	376.690	540.990	1310.700	3071.800	6949.200	15178.000
16	513.660	758.780	1967.500	4916.500	11815.000	27322.000
17	699.940	1063.700	2952.800	7867.900	20088.000	49181.000
18	953.280	1490.600	4430.700	12590.000	34151.000	88527.000
19	1297.800	2088.200	6647.500	20146.000	58058.000	159349.000
20	1766.368	2924.880	9972.750	32235.200	98700.300	286830.000
25	8232.080	15745.800	75750.000	338032.000	1401429.000	5419980.000
30	38313.920	84701.400	575525.000	3544640.000	*	**

*20 million
**102 million

APPENDIX C: PRESENT VALUE OF $1

Year	1%	2%	3%	4%	5%	6%	7%	8%	9%	10%	12%	14%	15%
1	.990	.980	.971	.962	.952	.943	.935	.926	.917	.909	.893	.877	.870
2	.980	.961	.943	.925	.907	.890	.873	.857	.842	.826	.797	.769	.756
3	.971	.942	.915	.889	.864	.840	.816	.794	.772	.751	.712	.675	.658
4	.961	.924	.889	.855	.823	.792	.763	.735	.708	.683	.636	.592	.572
5	.951	.906	.863	.822	.784	.747	.713	.681	.650	.621	.567	.519	.497
6	.942	.888	.838	.790	.746	.705	.666	.630	.596	.564	.507	.456	.432
7	.933	.871	.813	.760	.711	.665	.623	.583	.547	.513	.452	.400	.376
8	.923	.853	.789	.731	.677	.627	.582	.540	.502	.467	.404	.351	.327
9	.914	.837	.766	.703	.645	.592	.544	.500	.460	.424	.361	.308	.284
10	.905	.820	.744	.676	.614	.558	.508	.463	.422	.386	.322	.270	.247
11	.896	.804	.722	.650	.585	.527	.475	.429	.388	.350	.287	.237	.215
12	.887	.788	.701	.625	.557	.497	.444	.397	.356	.319	.257	.208	.187
13	.879	.773	.681	.601	.530	.469	.415	.368	.326	.290	.229	.182	.163
14	.870	.758	.661	.577	.505	.442	.388	.340	.299	.263	.205	.160	.141
15	.861	.743	.642	.555	.481	.417	.362	.315	.275	.239	.183	.140	.123
16	.853	.728	.623	.534	.458	.394	.339	.292	.252	.218	.163	.123	.107
17	.844	.714	.605	.513	.436	.371	.317	.270	.231	.198	.146	.108	.093
18	.836	.700	.587	.494	.416	.350	.296	.250	.212	.180	.130	.095	.081
19	.828	.686	.570	.475	.396	.331	.276	.232	.194	.164	.116	.083	.070
20	.820	.673	.554	.456	.377	.319	.258	.215	.178	.149	.104	.073	.061
25	.780	.610	.478	.375	.295	.233	.184	.146	.116	.092	.059	.038	.030
30	.742	.552	.412	.308	.231	.174	.131	.099	.075	.057	.033	.020	.015

Year	16%	18%	20%	24%	28%	32%	36%	40%	50%	60%	70%	80%	90%
1	.862	.847	.833	.806	.781	.758	.735	.714	.667	.625	.588	.556	.526
2	.743	.718	.694	.650	.610	.574	.541	.510	.444	.391	.346	.309	.277
3	.641	.609	.579	.524	.477	.435	.398	.364	.296	.244	.204	.171	.146
4	.552	.516	.482	.423	.373	.329	.292	.260	.198	.153	.120	.095	.077
5	.476	.437	.402	.341	.291	.250	.215	.186	.132	.095	.070	.053	.040
6	.410	.370	.335	.275	.227	.189	.158	.133	.088	.060	.041	.029	.021
7	.354	.314	.279	.222	.178	.143	.116	.095	.059	.037	.024	.016	.011
8	.305	.266	.233	.179	.139	.108	.085	.068	.039	.023	.014	.009	.006
9	.263	.226	.194	.144	.108	.082	.063	.048	.026	.015	.008	.005	.003
10	.227	.191	.162	.116	.085	.062	.046	.035	.017	.009	.005	.003	.002
11	.195	.162	.135	.094	.066	.047	.034	.025	.012	.006	.003	.002	.001
12	.168	.137	.112	.076	.052	.036	.025	.018	.008	.004	.002	.001	.001
13	.145	.116	.093	.061	.040	.027	.018	.013	.005	.002	.001	.001	.000
14	.125	.099	.078	.049	.032	.021	.014	.009	.003	.001	.001	.000	.000
15	.108	.084	.065	.040	.025	.016	.010	.006	.002	.001	.000	.000	.000
16	.093	.071	.054	.032	.019	.012	.007	.005	.002	.001	.000	.000	
17	.080	.060	.045	.026	.015	.009	.005	.003	.001	.000	.000		
18	.069	.051	.038	.021	.012	.007	.004	.002	.001	.000	.000		
19	.060	.043	.031	.017	.009	.005	.003	.002	.000	.000			
20	.051	.037	.026	.014	.007	.004	.002	.001	.000	.000			
25	.024	.016	.010	.005	.002	.001	.000	.000					
30	.012	.007	.004	.002	.001	.000	.000						

APPENDIX D: PRESENT VALUE OF AN ANNUITY OF $1

Year	1%	2%	3%	4%	5%	6%	7%	8%	9%	10%
1	0.990	0.980	0.971	0.962	0.952	0.943	0.935	0.926	0.917	0.909
2	1.970	1.942	1.913	1.886	1.859	1.833	1.808	1.783	1.759	1.736
3	2.941	2.884	2.829	2.775	2.723	2.673	2.624	2.577	2.531	2.487
4	3.902	3.808	3.717	3.630	3.546	3.465	3.387	3.312	3.240	3.170
5	4.853	4.713	4.580	4.452	4.329	4.212	4.100	3.993	3.890	3.791
6	5.795	5.601	5.417	5.242	5.076	4.917	4.766	4.623	4.486	4.355
7	6.728	6.472	6.230	6.002	5.786	5.582	5.389	5.206	5.033	4.868
8	7.652	7.325	7.020	6.733	6.463	6.210	6.971	5.747	5.535	5.335
9	8.566	8.162	7.786	7.435	7.108	6.802	6.515	6.247	5.985	5.759
10	9.471	8.983	8.530	8.111	7.722	7.360	7.024	6.710	6.418	6.145
11	10.368	9.787	9.253	8.760	8.306	7.887	7.499	7.139	6.805	6.495
12	11.255	10.575	9.954	9.385	8.863	8.384	7.943	7.536	7.161	6.814
13	12.134	11.348	10.635	9.986	9.394	8.853	8.358	7.904	7.487	7.103
14	13.004	12.106	11.296	10.563	9.899	9.295	8.745	8.244	7.786	7.367
15	13.865	12.849	11.938	11.118	10.380	9.712	9.108	8.559	8.060	7.606
16	14.718	13.578	12.561	11.652	10.838	10.106	9.447	8.851	8.312	7.824
17	15.562	14.292	13.168	12.166	11.274	10.477	9.763	9.122	8.544	8.022
18	16.398	14.992	13.754	12.659	11.690	10.828	10.059	9.372	8.756	8.201
19	17.226	15.678	14.324	13.134	12.085	11.158	10.336	9.604	8.950	8.365
20	18.046	16.351	14.877	13.590	12.462	11.470	10.594	9.818	9.128	8.514
25	22.023	19.523	17.413	15.622	14.094	12.783	11.654	10.675	9.823	9.077
30	25.808	22.397	19.600	17.292	15.373	13.765	12.409	11.258	10.274	9.427

Year	12%	14%	16%	18%	20%	24%	28%	32%	36%
1	0.893	0.877	0.862	0.847	0.833	0.806	0.781	0.758	0.735
2	1.690	1.647	1.605	1.566	1.528	1.457	1.392	1.332	1.276
3	2.402	2.322	2.246	2.174	2.106	1.981	1.868	1.766	1.674
4	3.037	2.914	2.798	2.690	2.589	2.404	2.241	2.096	1.966
5	3.605	3.433	3.274	3.127	2.991	2.745	2.532	2.345	2.181
6	4.111	3.889	3.685	3.498	3.326	3.020	2.759	2.534	2.339
7	4.564	4.288	4.039	3.812	3.605	3.242	2.937	2.678	2.455
8	4.968	4.639	4.344	4.078	3.837	3.421	3.076	2.786	2.540
9	5.328	4.946	4.607	4.303	4.031	3.566	3.184	2.868	2.603
10	5.650	5.216	4.833	4.494	4.193	3.682	3.269	2.930	2.650
11	5.988	5.453	5.029	4.656	4.327	3.776	3.335	2.978	2.683
12	6.194	5.660	5.197	4.793	4.439	3.851	3.387	3.013	2.708
13	6.424	5.842	5.342	4.910	4.533	3.912	3.427	3.040	2.727
14	6.628	6.002	5.468	5.008	4.611	3.962	3.459	3.061	2.740
15	6.811	6.142	5.575	5.092	4.675	4.001	3.483	3.076	2.750
16	6.974	6.265	5.669	5.162	4.730	4.033	3.503	3.088	2.758
17	7.120	5.373	5.749	4.222	4.775	4.059	3.518	3.097	2.763
18	7.250	6.467	5.818	5.273	4.812	4.080	3.529	3.104	2.767
19	7.366	6.550	5.877	5.316	4.844	4.097	3.539	3.109	2.770
20	7.469	6.623	5.929	5.353	4.870	4.110	3.546	3.113	2.772
25	7.843	6.873	6.097	5.467	4.948	4.147	3.564	3.122	2.776
30	8.055	7.003	6.177	5.517	4.979	4.160	3.569	3.124	2.778

APPENDIX E: AREAS UNDER THE NORMAL CURVE

Example

$$Z = \frac{X - \mu}{\sigma}$$

$P[Z>1] = .1587$

$P[Z>1.96] = .0250$

Normal Deviate Z	.00	.01	.02	.03	.04	.05	.06	.07	.08	.09
0.0	.5000	.4960	.4920	.4880	.4840	.4801	.4761	.4721	.4681	.4641
0.1	.4602	.4562	.4522	.4483	.4443	.4404	.4364	.4325	.4286	.4247
0.2	.4207	.4168	.4129	.4090	.4052	.4013	.3974	.3936	.3897	.3859
0.3	.3821	.3783	.3745	.3707	.3669	.3632	.3594	.3557	.3520	.3483
0.4	.3446	.3409	.3372	.3336	.3300	.3264	.3228	.3192	.3156	.3121
0.5	.3085	.3050	.3015	.2981	.2946	.2912	.2877	.2843	.2810	.2776
0.6	.2743	.2709	.2676	.2643	.2611	.2578	.2546	.2514	.2483	.2451
0.7	.2420	.2389	.2358	.2327	.2296	.2266	.2236	.2206	.2177	.2148
0.8	.2119	.2090	.2061	.2033	.2005	.1977	.1949	.1922	.1894	.1867
0.9	.1841	.1814	.1788	.1762	.1736	.1711	.1685	.1660	.1635	.1611
1.0	.1587	.1562	.1539	.1515	.1492	.1469	.1446	.1423	.1401	.1379
1.1	.1357	.1335	.1314	.1292	.1271	.1251	.1230	.1210	.1190	.1170
1.2	.1151	.1131	.1112	.1093	.1075	.1056	.1038	.1020	.1003	.0985
1.3	.0968	.0951	.0934	.0918	.0901	.0885	.0869	.0853	.0838	.0823
1.4	.0808	.0793	.0778	.0764	.0749	.0735	.0721	.0708	.0694	.0681
1.5	.0668	.0655	.0643	.0630	.0618	.0606	.0594	.0582	.0571	.0559
1.6	.0548	.0537	.0526	.0516	.0505	.0495	.0485	.0475	.0465	.0455
1.7	.0446	.0436	.0427	.0418	.0409	.0401	.0392	.0384	.0375	.0367
1.8	.0359	.0351	.0344	.0336	.0329	.0322	.0314	.0307	.0301	.0294
1.9	.0287	.0281	.0274	.0268	.0262	.0256	.0250	.0244	.0239	.0233
2.0	.0228	.0222	.0217	.0212	.0207	.0202	.0197	.0192	.0188	.0183
2.1	.0179	.0174	.0170	.0166	.0162	.0158	.0154	.0150	.0146	.0143
2.2	.0139	.0136	.0132	.0129	.0125	.0122	.0119	.0116	.0113	.0110
2.3	.0107	.0104	.0102	.0099	.0096	.0094	.0091	.0089	.0087	.0084
2.4	.0082	.0080	.0078	.0075	.0073	.0071	.0069	.0068	.0066	.0064
2.5	.0062	.0060	.0059	.0057	.0055	.0054	.0997	.0051	.0049	.0048
2.6	.0047	.0045	.0044	.0043	.0041	.0040	.0039	.0038	.0037	.0036
2.7	.0035	.0034	.0033	.0032	.0031	.0030	.0029	.0028	.0027	.0026
2.8	.0026	.0025	.0024	.0023	.0023	.0022	.0021	.0021	.0020	.0019
2.9	.0019	.0018	.0018	.0017	.0016	.0016	.0015	.0015	.0014	.0014
3.0	.0013	.0013	.0013	.0012	.0012	.0011	.0011	.0011	.0010	.0010

Source: "Areas Under the Normal Curve" in STATISTICS: AN INTRO-DUCTORY ANALYSIS, 2nd Edition by Taro Yamane. (Harper & Row, 1967). Reprinted by permission of the publishers.

INDEX